Arthur Mapletoft Curteis

History of the Roman Empire

From the death of Theodosius the Great to the coronation of Charles the Great.

Vol. 1

Arthur Mapletoft Curteis

History of the Roman Empire
From the death of Theodosius the Great to the coronation of Charles the Great. Vol. 1

ISBN/EAN: 9783337245658

Printed in Europe, USA, Canada, Australia, Japan

Cover: Foto ©ninafisch / pixelio.de

More available books at **www.hansebooks.com**

HISTORY

OF THE

ROMAN EMPIRE

FROM THE DEATH OF THEODOSIUS THE GREAT
TO THE CORONATION OF CHARLES
THE GREAT, A.D. 395–800

BY

ARTHUR M. CURTEIS, M.A.

LATE FELLOW OF TRINITY COLLEGE, OXFORD; ASSISTANT MASTER IN
SHERBORNE SCHOOL

WITH MAPS

PHILADELPHIA:
J. B. LIPPINCOTT & CO.
1875

PREFACE.

THIS book is the substance of a course of lectures, delivered to the two highest Forms in Sherborne School. It is meant to be a help towards bridging over the gulf between the two sections of history, which are popularly supposed to divide a little after the Christian era into "ancient" and "modern." Such a division, however, produces error and confusion, by obscuring the unity and continuity of history; the teaching of which loses half its value, if we forget that "Ancient" is the parent of "Mediæval," and therefore of "Modern" history, and that Imperial Rome is the centre and meeting-point of all history—"an Universal Empire in which all earlier history loses itself, and out of which all later history grew."[1] The position of Theodoric, Charles, or Frederick cannot be understood without reference to that earlier Empire of Theodosius, Constantine, and Trajan, of which the later was a direct consequence.

For this reason I hope also that the book may be

[1] Freeman's General Sketch, cap. i. p. 16.

used with advantage in the highest Forms in schools. The objection, indeed, is sometimes raised, that works of this kind are of little use, being too condensed to be interesting or to convey adequate information. The objection would be fatal if true. Their real utility, however, depends on two things—the way in which they are used, and the judgment with which a writer omits or condenses facts. It is clearly not necessary to lay equal stress on all parts of history alike, because not all great men are equally great, nor all important crises equally important. And it is one advantage of such a period as is embraced in this book, that it centres naturally, and without the sacrifice of any important point, round the lives of a few men, who from character or circumstances "made" the history of their times. It is a further advantage, that almost every page necessarily contains allusions which a competent lecturer may, if he will, make the text for illustration, comment, and amplification. As random examples of what is meant, p. 48 might suggest a lecture on the Aryan languages, and on the *kind* of proof which they afford as to the relationship of Aryan nations; pp. 137 *sqq.* might be illustrated by legends, similar to those there mentioned; while chap. ii. would afford scope for a fuller explanation of the history and government of the early Church. Used thus as a "text-book" to be indefinitely expanded, I believe that a

" hand-book " may be made the vehicle of instruction both accurate and wide.

My main authorities throughout have been Gibbon, and Milman's "Latin Christianity." The only original research to which I can lay claim is a frequent reference to Eginhard for the life of Charles the Great. To Mr Freeman's works I am largely indebted, while in chap. i. I have borrowed freely from M. de Coulange's "Cité Antique." Not only for that chapter, but for the majority of chapters, I cannot acknowledge too warmly the debt which I owe to the works of the late M. Amedeé Thierry.

Lastly, I owe to one friend special thanks for invaluable help and advice in every page of the book—my colleague, the Rev. O. W. Tancock.

A. M. Curteis.

Sherborne, *January* 1875.

CONTENTS.

Contents

CHAPTER III.

THE BARBARIANS ON THE FRONTIER. CENT. IV.

CHAPTER IV.

CHURCH AND STATE IN CONSTANTINOPLE, EUTROPIUS, AND CHRYSOSTOM.

CHAPTER V.

CHRYSOSTOM AND THE EMPRESS EUDOXIA.

CHAPTER VI.

ALARIC AND THE VISIGOTHS—A.D. 396-419.

CHAPTER VII.

GENSERIC AND THE VANDALS—A.D. 423-533.

CHAPTER VIII.

ATTILA AND THE HUNS—A.D. 435-453.

CHAPTER IX.

THE "CHANGE OF GOVERNMENT"—COMMONLY CALLED THE FALL OF THE WESTERN EMPIRE, A.D. 475–526.

CHAPTER X.

THE EMPEROR JUSTINIAN—A.D. 527–565.

CHAPTER XI.

THE EMPIRE IN RELATION TO THE BARBARIANS OF THE EAST—A.D. 450–650.

CHAPTER XII.

CHAPTER XIII.

CHAPTER XIV.

Contents

MAPS.

The Roman Empire.

CHAPTER I.

ADMINISTRATIVE AND LEGAL UNITY.

Death of Theodosius and Condition of Empire —THE YEAR A.D. 395—The year of the death of Theodosius the Great was important in the history of Rome. The Empire, which in 1,000 years had grown from the limits of a single city and a narrow territory to embrace under one government, one law, one religion, the whole civilised world, had fallen a prey to internal dissensions, and was to succumb ere long to enemies from without. The evils consequent on the incessant wars of the Republic, both foreign and civil, had wrought their effect. The middle class in Italy was almost destroyed, and its place filled by a vast slave population. Property had passed into a few hands. Conquest in the East had brought an influx of Oriental vice and luxury. The old Roman faith and morality were supplanted by mingled atheism and superstition. The gulf between rich and poor grew ever wider. Honour, morality, public spirit, decayed, until " the Empire," the irresponsible rule of a single man, had become the best hope of salvation for society, the only condition of impartial and just govern-

ment.   In fact, there had been for many generations two
opposite forces at work simultaneously : on the one hand,
and on the surface, the ever growing desire for equality
and unity; on the other hand, and beneath the surface,
the disintegration which follows from class hatred, from
decay of honour and political virtue, from immorality
and ignorance.   The disintegration was complete when at
the death of Theodosius the Empire fell asunder, and Milan
or Ravenna in the west, and Constantinople in the east,
became rival capitals of rival empires, never again united.

Influence of the Provinces.—The great Empire
had now completed the work, which beginning with the
foundation of the city took its final direction and received
its greatest impulse from Julius Cæsar.   Roman history
has many sides according to our point of view: revolu-
tions social and political; wars civil and foreign; its laws,
its great men; but Rome's place in universal history is
determined by the great result which she impressed on all
the nations brought within her influence—uniformity of
administration, law, and religion.   No doubt the process
was a slow one.   It needed 1,000 years to consolidate so
vast an Empire, and weld it into one homogeneous mass.
For 250 years Rome had withheld her rights of citizenship from her Italian subjects—rights only wrung from
her by defeat.   To the provinces, the confederate states,
the allied kings, the Roman Senate maintained a haughty
attitude, allowing them to groan beneath the rapacity
and tyranny of unscrupulous proconsuls, whom the tri-
bunals were too interested or too corrupt to convict.
But in their extremity they found allies.   The democratic
party in Rome, engaged in a desperate struggle with the
aristocrats, were glad to find allies in the provincials; the
provincials in their turn were ready enough to purchase
by alliance what they so much coveted, citizenship and

equality. And it was in the provinces that Julius Cæsar, the great leader of the democrats, found his staunchest supporters.

Policy of Julius Cæsar.—Of so many-sided a genius it is natural that men should form different estimates; it would be difficult to form an entirely just one. Beyond a doubt he was ambitious, immoral, and quite free from scruples. But if he had the ambition to be the first man in the state, he had also the foresight to see what a magnificent opportunity the errors of the aristocratical party had given him, and the genius to use it with success. Men act from mixed motives; and it would be as absurd to ascribe Cæsar's extraordinary career to motives of selfish ambition only, as to credit him with feelings of pure philanthropy. He had all the genius, rapidity of action, fertility of resource, and versatility of Napoleon, but he was a far greater man. It may have been cunning ambition, it may well have been some more honourable feeling, which prompted him from his entrance into public life to form and maintain friendly intercourse with the leading men and senates of various provinces—to procure the Roman franchise for Gállia Transpadana—to keep up a correspondence, even during his hottest campaigns, with all parts of the Empire—to spend money in repairing public buildings in Gaul and Spain, Asia and Greece. Whatever were his motives, he had his reward, and that without delay. The provincials, despised and ignored by the aristocracy of Italy, saw their opportunity in the impending struggle of parties, and when Cæsar crossed the Rubicon (B.C. 49), and committed himself to the contest with the Senate, it was with the open support of some, and the good wishes, expressed or understood, of all the Roman provinces. And, thus supported, in four years he was master of the Empire.

Reforms delayed by Cæsar's Murder—B.C. 44.—
The reorganisation of the body politic should naturally
now have commenced; it was a calamity for the world
that Cæsar fell a victim to political vengeance almost
before he had begun the work of reform. Some few
hints, however, are left us of his probable intentions. He
projected a codification of the laws—a geographical survey
of the Empire—a reform of the law courts—an increase of
the Senate to the number of 1,000, by the admission of
provincial notables, especially from Gaul and Spain—an
extension of the rights of citizenship (beyond the mere
accident of birth and locality) to all men of education,
intelligence, or wealth throughout the Empire, a principle
afterwards accepted and extended—and lastly, a large increase of colonies. Of these vast projects a part only
was even begun, but it is as easy to perceive the general
idea of their originator as to understand the rage of the
aristocratic party, whose most cherished privileges would
thus have been destroyed. Uniformity of rights and
privileges meant for them loss of power and dignity. The
death of Cæsar appeared their only means of safety; and
so the hand of the enthusiast Brutus was armed with the
assassin's dagger. But they had miscalculated the effect
of the blow. It simply threw the provinces into the
arms of Cæsar's adopted son, and rendered their own cause
and the cause of the Republic hopeless. It threw extraordinary powers into the hands of individual leaders, and
for one political purpose only—the unification of the
Empire on the ruins of the Republic.

Policy of Augustus, Tiberius, and Claudius.—
The policy of Julius was accepted by his successors more or
less entirely as a tradition of the Empire. Augustus, however, more cautious and less foreseeing, was content to consolidate and organise. In order to acquaint himself with

the needs of the provinces, he visited every one of them except Africa and Sardinia; he provided for their better government by their division into "imperial" and "senatorial" groups, reserving for his own supervision those which were from any cause especially exposed to danger, or especially important to the state, such as Transalpine Gaul or Egypt; he instituted a regular series of posts or couriers from one end of the Empire to the other; he rescued the provinces from one of their most bitter grievances, the corruption of the governors, by reducing them to salaried officials, who as government agents were in strict subservience to the home government, and forbidden to receive anything beyond the contributions allowed by the Senate or ordered by the Emperor. The successor of Augustus, the cruel and gloomy Tiberius, was popular out of Italy, and the first nine years of his reign were years of order and equitable government for the provinces. Tacitus, the best of authorities in such a case, assures us that the provinces were not harassed by new burdens, nor the old burdens made heavier by the avarice or cruelty of officials, while scourgings and confiscations were unknown; and Suetonius has preserved for us the *bon mot* of Tiberius, often repeated, that "the office of a good shepherd is to shear and not to flay his sheep." Claudius, himself a provincial and born at Lyons, always entertained a strong feeling of affection for the provinces, and especially for Gaul, the organisation of which he completed. It was, indeed, his firmness alone that, in the famous debate in the Senate which Tacitus records in the Annals (xi. 23), secured for the Gauls the coveted *jus honorum*. They had for some time enjoyed the *civitas*, and now claimed the completion of their privileges. In the arguments adduced in the Curia against the concession of their claims, we see the true spirit of the old Roman oligarchy.

"Could not Italy," it was urged, "find men enough to furnish her own Senate? At least she had done so in the good old days! And now a mass of aliens must be introduced to oust the poor nobles and senators of Latium—aliens, too, who but the other day had fought against Cæsar; and whose ancestors had even burnt Rome itself!" Tacitus has given us also the purport of Claudius' reply. He began by reminding his hearers that Rome owed even her origin and early fortunes, and many of her noblest families, to the principle of comprehension. "In the palmiest days of the Republic, Etruria, Lucania, all Italy, had sent members to the Senate. Nor was this all. The plebs had been admitted to share magistracies with the patricians, the Latins and other Italian nations with both. The peace of Italy had been assured from the day when the nations beyond the Padus had been admitted to the citizenship. Lastly," he asked, "why did Athens and Sparta, powerful as they were, perish, but for the fact that they kept their vanquished foes at arms' length, as though they were foreigners?" The demand of the Gauls was granted; but the savage indignation of the old aristocratical party, long pent up, broke out in innuendo and satire. "What else could one expect," says their mouthpiece, Seneca, "from one born in a province!"

Importance of the Provinces.—Yet in spite of the oligarchs the tide was now flowing strongly, and could not be stemmed. The provinces had made good their footing as integral parts of the Empire. The Senate (to which Tiberius had transferred the powers of the ancient "*comitia*," and which he transformed into a sort of immense privy council), the bar, the army, were all crowded with provincials. Rich men from the provinces flocked to Italy, and bought out the dissolute or impoverished representatives of old patrician families. Literary men opened schools. Nor was this all. With Galba the imperial secret was divulged, says Tacitus, that an emperor could be nominated elsewhere than at Rome; for Galba was made Emperor in Spain. And worse was yet to come, for even provincials, it seemed, might be emperors. Nerva was a Cretan by descent; Trajan and Hadrian were sons of Spanish colonists; Septimius Severus was an African, who never got rid of his Punic accent; Maximin, worst of all, was a barbarian. Every year the provinces grew in relative importance, and claimed more and more of the imperial attention. Hadrian spent no less than fifteen years of his long reign in visiting province after province, and by using the experience thus hardly won in improving the imperial administration, gained for himself the title of *locupletator orbis,* and the praise from Tacitus of having happily combined two things heretofore incompatible, power and liberty. Egypt alone seemed excluded from the privileges showered by Emperor after Emperor on the provinces. Egypt was the granary of Rome; and the necessities of Italy seemed to justify the exclusion of that province from the rights conceded to others. No admission to the Senate, no share even in Roman citizenship, was granted to Egyptians, except in the rarest cases, until Caracallus, the son of Septimius, relieved the province from this selfish interdict, and the unwonted sight was seen of an Egyptian sitting in the Roman Curia.

Edict of Caracallus—A.D. 212.—One thing now, and only one, remained to finish the important movement, which had been inevitable from the day when Rome's first province was annexed. In the year A.D. 212, an edict of Caracallus extended the rights of Roman citizenship to every free inhabitant of the Roman Empire. It is easy to assign motives, and historians, astonished that

this just and liberal edict should bear the name of one of
Rome's most worthless Emperors, have found its explanation in the fact that Augustus had levied a succession duty
of 5 per cent. on legacies and inheritances of all Roman
citizens, and that thus, by a stroke of the pen, the inci-
dence of the tax was universally widened, while the tax
itself was doubled.   Others have assigned the edict itself
to more probable originators, like Antoninus or Hadrian;
but this is quite unnecessary.   Even were the Emperor's
own motives purely mercenary, it would be idle to suspect
the motives of the great jurists of the day, who must
have had the arrangement, draughting, and application of
the Act; and no less idle to suppose that such an edict
would have been possible unless called for by the circumstances of the times.   Such Acts, indeed, recognise accomplished facts, and have nothing to do with producing
them.

Consequences of the Edict.—The consequences of
the edict were curious and far-reaching.   Henceforth the
old-fashioned distinctions—Roman, Latin, Federal, Ally,
Subject—all vanish.   There are but two words to express
the inhabitants of the world,—" Ingenuus," the Roman,
the Freeborn; and "Peregrinus," the Slave, the Barbarian.
Within the Empire the long struggle for equality was
finished.   In another way, however, its consequences
were disastrous to the Empire itself, while useful to the
world at large.   The glory of the name "Roman" became
less and less, as it was shared by greater numbers.   What
had once been a bond of union to a handful of men
among strangers, a badge of privilege, an object of ambition, a source of loyalty to the mother city, ceased to be
a distinction, or the cause of any great advantage, when
shared by all in common.   Rivalries had been forgotten,
local and narrow interests overlooked, as long as there

remained one coveted privilege enjoyed by some and denied to others ; but local interests gained fresh importance, and rivalries sprang up again, when the height of ambition was attained. Instead of one great centre of attraction there were henceforth many local centres.

Jealousy of East and West.—And now dangers were threatening the frontier on many quarters at once, on the Euphrates, the Danube, the Rhine. The second Persian Empire was just rising on the ruins of the Parthian (A.D. 226)—the Goths were on the Danube—Franks and Alemanni were menacing the West. And yet, at such a crisis it was that the jealousy of East and West made united action almost impossible,—a jealousy which, arising from diversity of language and ideas, and from contrariety of interests, had only lain dormant beneath the pressure of superior force, and now that from various causes the central power was weaker, began to gradually undermine the stability and unity of the Empire. Indeed, a tendency to division had shown itself many years before. Long since, on the death of Nero (A.D. 68), Spain, Africa, Gaul, and Syria had set up favourites of their own. In later days, when Commodus was murdered (A.D. 192), and the miserable Pertinax and Didius successively ascended and were hurled from the throne within six months, the choice of Emperor was contested by the legions of Britain, Pannonia, and Syria. This tendency in the outlying provinces to nominate Emperors of their own, and in the strong frontier armies to break loose from the central authority, increased as time went on, until in the middle of the third century, and under the feeble rule of Gallienus (A.D. 260–268), rival claimants of independent authority rose in many quarters at once (the so-called "Thirty Tyrants"), and only ten years later

(A.D. 270–275) Aurelian himself, every inch a soldier, had some difficulty in suppressing the attempt of Zenobia to erect an independent kingdom at Palmyra, and a similar attempt of Victoria and Tetricus in Gaul and Britain.

Diocletian—A.D. 300.—The difficulties, indeed, of the Roman government towards the close of the third century were not removed, but only changed. It was not now the persevering claims of provincials which had to be reconciled with the haughty exclusiveness of an ancient aristocracy. That was a thing of the past. What most embarrassed the governments of Probus and Diocletian was the vast extent of the Empire, coupled with the threatening attitude of the barbarians, and the independent mutinous spirit of the legions. Emperor after Emperor was murdered. Legion after legion revolted. To guard the frontiers, to anticipate dangers, to control the soldiers, to humour or repress powerful subordinates, and, meanwhile, to carry on the political administration of a huge empire, was a task too great for one man to fulfil. The problem was how to multiply and extend the direct action of the central power without destroying the hardly-won unity of the Empire. An attempt to solve it was made by Diocletian (A.D. 284). He conceived the idea of an undivided Empire governed by two Emperors,—one in the East, the other in the West,—governing in concert, on the same principles, and by the same laws. Frequent interviews were to insure their unanimity. Even so, however, there remained the danger of either or both the Emperors falling, as before, under the influence of some prætorian prefect or court favourite, and the yet greater danger of an unsettled succession. Accordingly, the governing power was again doubled. To each " Augustus " was attached a " Cæsar," a subordinate colleague ; and these, in their turn, were to rise to the highest rank, and thus supply an undisputed and uninterrupted succession of Emperors. The Augusti, while exercising a joint supervision of the whole Empire, had each a separate jurisdiction. Thus, Diocletian ruled the East, with Nicomedia (in Bithynia) for his capital ; Maximilian, Italy and Africa, with Milan for his capital. Of the two Cæsars, Galerius was intrusted with Illyricum and the Danube, Constantius Chlorus with Gaul, Spain, and Britain. The Empire was practically ruled by four Emperors, to resist whose power, so long as they were unanimous, might well seem hopeless. The imperial dignity was further fenced round by a largely increased number of functionaries and officials, forming, as it were, a barrier against undue familiarity ; and for the first time was introduced into common use the ominous title of "Dominus" (Sire). In fact, everything was done to elevate, isolate, consecrate as much as possible the person of the Emperor, as though it had become too cheap in popular estimation. It is curious to reflect how public opinion must have changed in 300 years. Augustus, undisputed master of the world, with all the reins of government gathered in his hands, was content with the reality of power, and careless of its parade and show, studiously avoiding ostentation, and living only as the first of Roman gentlemen. Diocletian and his successors surrounded themselves with Oriental magnificence, to dazzle men's eyes and enthral their imaginations, and so paved the way for the minute ceremonial and slavish reverence for title and rank which afterwards distinguished the Byzantine Court.

Diocletian's Failure.—On the other hand, while the court and Emperor were thus hedged round with external respect, and government agents and officials indefinitely multiplied throughout the provinces, the influence of the Senate was sapped and ultimately destroyed, not only because it ceased to be consulted, but also by the removal of the court from Rome. Rome herself was discontented at the loss of prestige; while Italy, hitherto privileged by exemption from certain taxes, and especially the land-tax, was for the first time, and to the great satisfaction of the provinces, surveyed and assessed with a view to its payment. For the new imperial system was expensive. The number of salaried officials—that is, of persons with-drawn from industrial pursuits—was largely increased; the industrial classes themselves had been decimated generations before by civil war, and were now compara-tively a mere handful; slave labour had been substituted for free; prices had accordingly risen, and money was scarce.

The effect of the reforms introduced by Diocletian was not precisely what he had contemplated. Their principle, indeed, the principle of duality in unity, was recognised up to the downfall of the Western Empire, and even later, and was more thoroughly carried out by his greatest successor Constantine, than by Diocletian himself. The main evil, however, which they were intended to correct they did in truth aggravate. As long as the four rulers of the Em-pire were unanimous, and each subordinated his private interests to an imperial policy and the common weal, disruption was impossible, and the mutual jealousies of East and West were repressed by sheer force. But when the interests and ambition of one Augustus conflicted with those of the other, when Cæsar intrigued against Cæsar, and the Empire was again desolated by civil wars, the old jealousy broke out with redoubled violence; while in each quarter of the Empire there was now an armed force, and a great military chief able to asser this independence. Constantine's vigour and force of cha-racter, it is true, once again held together the discordant mass (A.D. 306–337), but it was only for a few years.

On his death anarchy again ensued; reunion became more and more impossible; and in A.D. 364, Valentinian divided the Empire with his brother Valens,—a division which meant no longer the joint rule of an undivided Empire, but two Emperors ruling two Empires, never again united.

Constantine—A.D. 330.—The name of Constantine will be remembered mainly for two reasons—his recognition of Christianity, and his foundation of a new capital. The same motives which actuated Diocletian in abandoning Rome deterred Constantine from returning to it; and he had another besides. Not only was he equally alive with Diocletian to the special dangers of the time, which he strove to avert by an extension of Diocletian's policy, but he was also a Christian; and a Christian Emperor committed to a policy of despotic absolutism could hardly find a congenial or suitable capital in Pagan Rome, where a Senate was still sitting, and the traditions at least of liberty and equality were still alive. Constantine, however, victorious in many a pitched battle over formidable rivals, was not one to acquiesce quietly in the dismemberment of the Empire. He clung to the imperial tradition of its unity, and for him, therefore, Nicomedia and Milan were as impossible capitals as Rome. In the final struggle with Licinius (A.D. 323), he had seen and noted the unrivalled position of Byzantium, the home for centuries of a Greek colony. Standing, like Rome herself, on seven hills, and midway as it were between Europe and Asia, it possessed a magnificent harbour of seven miles in length, the so-called " Golden Horn," a temperate climate, a fertile soil; and the approach on the land side was of narrow extent, and easily defensible. Here in less than seven years arose the glorious city, whose successful resistance to all attacks for 1 100 years is in itself a proof of its founder's wisdom. Constantinople (so the new capital was named), the abode of the Emperor and his court, the seat of government, the headquarters of Christianity, was soon filled with a dense population, drawn thither from all quarters of the Empire by one motive or another, and was solemnly inaugurated as the capital of the Empire on May 11th, 330. In less than a century the new Rome had surpassed the old both in wealth and numbers.

Changes in the Constitution.—Nor was Constantine content with a mere change of capital. The numbers of the "bureaucracy," or government officials, were continually increased; military and civil functions were for the first time separated; a new order of nobility was introduced; the term "patrician" ceased to be an hereditary, and became a purely personal distinction; agents were employed in hundreds as "king's messengers," to convey despatches, who too soon became also informers to headquarters; lastly, to diminish the possibility of revolt, the number of men in a legion was reduced from 6,000 to about 1,500, while the actual numbers of the army itself were increased. Each legion had been a *corps d'armée*, and was now reduced to the position of a regiment, or at most of a brigade. There were six prætorian prefects with administrative functions only (the prefects of Rome, and Constantinople, of the East, Illyricum, Italy, and Gaul), and two masters-general of cavalry and infantry, responsible for the military arrangements of the Empire. This organisation of ranks and honours was carried from the highest down to the very lowest classes of society, even the working-classes in city and country being arranged in guilds and corporations, with similarity of occupation as their basis. Thus, from the Emperor on the throne to the serf on the farm, there was a settled gradation of ranks, the object of which was to secure to the Empire stability and peace, and to the Emperor respect.

Modification of Roman Law.—The administrative unity thus completed had been accompanied, almost *pari passu*, by a remarkable modification of Roman law, calculated to meet the needs of a vast empire. The contrast between the haughty exclusiveness of the patrician aristocracy of the Republic, and the humane and just comprehensiveness of the Empire, is not more striking than that between the stern and almost brutal law of early Rome and the equitable maxims and philosophical principles of the later imperial jurists. Roman law, indeed, was only one instance of the rigid spirit pervading all Aryan law. "In ancient law," says Mr Maine, "we are met by the *family* as the unit of society, in modern by the *individual*." Now the constituting principle of the family, according to primitive Aryan ideas (see chap. iii.), was neither blood-relationship nor natural affection, but family worship,—the worship in earliest times not of various gods representing the forces of nature, much less of one God (a much later development), but of the dead. The due worship of the departed members of the family was the primary duty of its living members, and to secure this was the object of ancient law. And this is the key to the otherwise unintelligible severity of Roman law. The priest of the family was the father, invested, therefore, with all the stringent privileges of *patria potestas*. Hence the importance of the male, of the son, who in his turn was to become the family priest, and the utter unimportance of the female, who as daughter only assisted at her father's worship, as wife at her husband's. Apart from father or husband, she had no existence in the eye of the law; and marriage, performed with certain definite religious ceremonies (*confarreatio*), was in fact her initiation into a new religion, the worship of the ancestors of her husband. She passed thereby into her husband's power (*manus*), and became his "daughter." Of course, as time went on and ideas developed, civil marriage (by *usus*, a year's cohabitation, or *coemptio*, purchase) became common enough; but *confarreatio* was the original and formal celebration of Roman marriage. Hence arose the distinction between *agnati* and *cognati*,—between those members of the family who traced their connection exclusively through males, whether by blood or adoption, and those who drew their descent from the same original parents, whether through males or females. Hence, again, the importance of the family property, of the house and hearth where its gods were worshipped. Alienation was entirely forbidden by ancient law, and not allowed even by the twelve tables, except on certain conditions and with express formalities; for the property of the family, like the relations of its members, depended altogether on its worship. As the son, in the eye of the law, was all-important and the daughter nothing, the son inherited and the daughter did not; his sons likewise inherited, but her sons, being only *cognati* to her own family, had no such power; even a stranger adopted as son by a paterfamilias inherited, while the emancipated son, cut off as it were from the family, did not; wills were unknown, for the father was but a temporary representative during life of a corporation that never died, the family, and was not allowed to interfere with property in which he had only a life interest. Hence, lastly, the severity of the law of debt. On the other hand, the *patria potestas* of the paterfamilias, clung to at Rome long after it had really become an anachronism, gave him absolute rights *within* the family short of the above conditions. He could acknowledge a child, repudiate a wife, marry or disinherit a son at pleasure. The wife's dowry and the son's labour belonged to him of right. Within the walls of his house he was sole judge, and could in certain cases even condemn to death without appeal. Long after the worship of ancestors had ceased, long after the "family" had expanded into the "gens" or "clan," and the gens into the "curia," and the "curia" into the "tribe," and the "tribe" into the "city," these ancient prerogatives were still enjoyed by the paterfamilias.

Roman Law gradually Softened.—The reason of this harshness, it may be, lies in the fact that the *social* customs and institutions of the Roman Republic were identical with those of the great Aryan family prior to its disruption, while their *political* institutions were totally different, being of far later growth under quite other conditions of life. Now, " social," no less than "political," relations modify, at the same time that they are regulated by law. We should expect, therefore, what actually happened, that when Rome came in contact with other nations beyond her frontiers, Roman law was profoundly modified. A comparative study of alien laws and customs gave rise to a new term, *jus gentium*, expressive of the general point in which they were observed to agree ; while by a further induction the Roman lawyers strove to arrive at the abstract principles of justice, *jus naturale*, underlying them all, with a view to the modification of their own barbarous civil law. These principles were gradually embodied in the "edicts" of the prætors, the " rules" which they published annually on their entrance into office ; and by slow degrees tended to banish the study of the Twelve Tables even from the schools, where they had formed part of the usual course. But in this, as in the wider field of political right, there were two parties, and a struggle between the con-

servatives and the reformers. The new views mainly
affected such questions as the position of slaves, the marriage and dowries of women, wills, wardship, disinherit-
ance, titles to property, debt,—questions on which the
civil law was most obviously at variance with natural
justice. And the general tendency was always towards a
relaxation of strictness.

**Responsa Prudentum and the Edictum Per-
petuum.**—It remained for the Empire to *organise* these
new principles of law, as it had organised the political
administration. Since the Emperors concentrated in their
own hands every old republican office, amongst others
the *tribunitia potestas*, they became, therefore, in their
own persons a court of final appeal. Part of the onerous
duty they delegated to the prætorian præfect, in part
they were assisted by a commission of lawyers, whose
opinions (*responsa prudentum*) were supposed to emanate
from the Emperor himself, and to guide the decisions of
judges. Thus by a legal fiction the Emperor was the
interpreter of the law. Moreover, when Tiberius transferred to the Senate the legislative and other powers
of the comitia, *senatus consulta*, being discussed and
passed beneath the Emperor's eyes, were in fact his
work, and before long imperial " decrees" and "rescripts"
were published as *ipso facto* laws. It is clear, however,
that such a system had no method, and that the *edicta
prætorum* and the *responsa prudentum* must have been
innumerable, and always increasing, shifting, and sometimes contradictory. With the view, therefore, of reducing chaos to order, the Emperor Hadrian published
the *edictum perpetuum*. Taking the edict published by
the great lawyer, Salvius Julianus, during his year of
office, he made it the standard of legal decisions for Rome
and Italy,—a rule to which subsequent prætors were

bound to conform, save in new and exceptional cases. Marcus Aurelius extended its application to the provinces, under the name of *Edictum provinciale*. More and more henceforward the civil law and the *jus gentium* tended to agree, until at last Christianity introduced a principle which human law could not, the brotherhood of all men, and so fundamentally changed their relations, at least in theory. Little by little the *patria potestas* was deprived of its absolute character, until under Justinian it meant no more than the *moral* authority belonging to the head of the family. Marriage with religious ceremonies became confined to the *pontifices;* the wife's dowry became inalienable without her consent, and afterwards inalienable altogether; the distinction ceased between *agnati* and *cognati*, and with it the necessity for adoption ; in the case of property natural relationship began to occupy a larger and larger place, and the law of succession became gradually regulated on simple principles of greater or less "proximity." These few instances will serve to illustrate how law became gradually synonymous with equity.

Summary.—Thus at the death of the Emperor Theodosius (A.D. 395), we have before us the spectacle of a vast Empire, troubled indeed by internal jealousies, and weakened by causes past remedy, yet presenting on the surface, at least, an appearance of unity,—governed in the same way and on the same principles from end to end, in Asia as in Italy, in Africa as in Gaul, and subject throughout to the same laws.

CHAPTER II.

THE CHRISTIAN CHURCH IN THE FIRST FOUR CENTURIES.

The Church recognised by Constantine.—Little has been said as yet of one of the most important forces at work within the Empire—the Christian Church. In three centuries the small body of first believers in Christ, a mere handful in numbers, having all things in common, had grown into a vast and organised Church, wealthy and powerful, whose bishops took equal rank with the military and civil officers of State, and which counted followers in every province of the Empire. Indeed, at the time of its recognition by Constantine, Christianity was already an established society, with its own officers, its own revenues, its own code of laws; and after Constantine's conversion Christians stepped at once into prominence and influence. Thousands of the best and most upright men in the Em pire, previously ignored or persecuted by the State, were thus restored to civil and political life; and of course the State benefited accordingly.

This chapter will narrate the fortunes of the Church to the end of the fourth century, and touch upon the means whereby she won her way to recognition, equality, supremacy, and the special difficulties with which she had to contend

Christians confounded with Jews.—Perhaps the most remarkable thing in the rise of Christianity is the silence and obscurity in which it worked its way, and the scanty records that remain to us of its progress. We gather, indeed, from the Acts of the Apostles and the Epistles, that the work of "organisation" had begun before S. Paul's death, and that the number of believers increased continuously; we know that as they became more numerous the Christians were confounded with the Jews in common estimation, and thus suffered persecution (not only from them but) in common with them. Yet up to the persecution under Nero (A.D. 64) they attracted so little attention at Rome by their numbers or religious observances, that S. Paul was detained for two years (A.D. 61–63) as a mere political prisoner in what was called *Custodia militaris*, and then probably set at liberty, while contemporary writers—like Lucan and the elder Pliny, Persius and Juvenal—make no mention of them. Even the persecution just named, consequent on the great fire of Rome, and set on foot (if we may believe Tacitus) by Nero himself, very probably arose from Christians being confounded with Jews in the eyes of the people, or from the Jews accusing them to screen themselves. One thing is certain, that the Christians in Rome suffered dreadful tortures at this time, while before they had enjoyed complete toleration; and it is not improbable that the persecution itself first opened the eyes of the Roman government and people to the existence of the Christian Church, among them but not of them, while it made subsequent persecutions seem natural and defensible. Amidst all the pomp and bustle of the great capital, a Roman would hardly stop to distinguish in his own mind Jew from Christian, or either of them from the votaries of other Eastern religions who were always flocking to Rome.

But when the existence of this new sect, and its aggressive, uncompromising temper were once fairly realised, it is evident that the average Roman was much perplexed by the attitude of the Christians, by their obstinate firmness, coupled with their innocence of vice or crime. This is clear from Pliny's letter of inquiry to the Emperor Trajan regarding his treatment of them in his province of Bithynia. He does not understand, nor apparently much care to understand their views and hopes; yet he admits their singular purity, honesty, and simplicity, while stating that acknowledgment of their faith met with capital punishment at his hands. And the Emperor expresses approval of this policy, merely warning Pliny not to allow search to be made for the offenders, nor to accept anonymous information.

Christians Disliked and Persecuted.—There was, in fact, more than one reason why a Roman should feel suspicion and jealousy towards Jews and Christians alike. Both announced their confident hope in a "Deliverer" soon to come. Both held aloof, almost with horror, from the social life and customs and religious practices of the people around them. If the former seemed the more dangerous, because still a nation, still capable of sudden and dangerous rebellion, the latter were not less obstinate in their nonconformity, while they had apparently less reason for it. They were a sect or (even worse) a "secret society," whose objects were imperfectly understood, and therefore all the more hateful to a despotic government. To a soldier and disciplinarian like Trajan, Christianity seemed little better than treason. On the other hand, men's minds were being deeply stirred by vague rumours, now of an expected return of some pretended Nero from the East, now of intrigues in Parthia, now of fires and earthquakes and eruptions, all tending to rouse and inflame fanaticism. Of this latent dislike and suspicion, easily fanned into active hatred, the Christians became the objects. And they did not shrink from the ordeal, more and more terrible as time went on. Bishops and leading men like Ignatius and Polycarp even courted a death which they least deserved. It may well have been, moreover, that the dislike felt in the highest as well as the lowest circles towards the Christians, when once attention had been drawn to their existence, was aggravated by the mutual jealousy of East and West. For Christianity was of the East, its language, organisation, Scriptures, and liturgy, being all alike Greek—that is, to a Roman of those days, foreign. If we attempt to estimate the converging force of all these prejudices—of the dislike felt by soldiers and statesmen, and the hatred of the fanatic, licentious, and ignorant—we shall be surprised that Christianity survived the storm at all.

Effects of Persecution on the Church.—But the blood of martyrs is the seed of the Church. The persecutions in the reigns of Nero and Trajan may have been local, and traceable to accidental and temporary causes; not so the subsequent persecutions under Aurelius, Septimius, Decius, and Diocletian. That which to Trajan had been merely a breach of state discipline, and punishable accordingly, seemed to his successors a far more serious crime, in proportion as to neglect and insult the national gods at a moment of increasing disaster was worse than merely declining State duties in a time of comparative peace and tranquillity. Now began, also, the publication of those "Apologies" for Christianity which served to show at once that Christians were too numerous to be any longer overlooked, while they were too few or too true to their principles to offer resistance to persecution. The reign of the great and good Aurelius, so terrible to the

Christians, was marked by the appearance of many such
·works. It is scarcely wonderful to find, on the other hand,
that men and women quailed sometimes before the storm,
and that a practice began to arise which, intended as a
means of escape, eventually proved a stimulus to persecution. No longer overlooked with contemptuous indifference,
but exposed to the hatred of the mob, the jealousy of the
authorities, the coldness and perhaps treachery of friends
and relations, what wonder if weak brethren here and
there yielded to temptation, and stooped to *purchase* from
the magistrate his connivance in their secret profession of
Christianity? The evil grew. Not individuals only, but
whole churches raised funds for buying off their members
from molestation, while the funds themselves only served
to stimulate the cupidity of informers and officials, and
so to aggravate the sufferings threatened or inflicted. A
further abuse followed. The magistrates received powers
to issue an order that so and so, mentioned by name,
should do sacrifice to the gods, and thus prove that he was
not a Christian. It became gradually a common practice
for such a person to give notice, through a friend, that he
was in reality a Christian, and therefore could not sacrifice,
but was ready to pay a fine to be excused. On this he
received a *libellus* or certificate of his having duly offered
the required sacrifice, and being accordingly exempt from
the penalty of the law. The acting of this practical lie was
sharply denounced by Cyprian, Bishop of Carthage (about
A.D. 250), as a sin. But the custom was in fact only a
symptom of what is harshly called the "degeneracy" of
the Catholic Church, that is, of the effects consequent on
its increase of numbers, and unavoidably increased connection with the non-Christian world. It was no longer
unusual for Christians to resort to heathen courts of
justice, to be servants in heathen households, to contract

marriage with heathens, to frequent heathen theatres and spectacles, and to defend the practice by appeals to Scripture. Such an intermingling invariably results in a certain relaxation of original strictness, and in the growth of abuses.

The Decian Persecution—A.D. 248.—The "accidental tempest," as Gibbon calls it, of the persecution under Septimius (about A.D. 200) was followed by an almost complete lull of thirty-eight years. But the short reign of Decius brought such suffering on the Church as made previous years since the times of Domitian and Nero seem all like years of peace. Like Aurelius, this Emperor was called upon to face new and unexpected dangers on the frontiers from the Goths; and like Aurelius, anxious to restore the power and unity of the empire, and perplexed as to the causes of its growing weakness, he seemed to perceive them in the obstinate nonconformity of the Christians. Instruments were found only too readily to act upon the imperial ideas. For the Christian theory and practice were too high not to excite dislike, which soon passed into active hatred and violence. The test of sacrifice to the gods was, by a special edict, ordered to be applied at once to all suspected persons. Numbers were consigned to prisons and to mines. Multitudes fled from their homes to the mountain or the desert, only to fall victims to starvation or wild beasts. Antioch, Alexandria, Carthage, and not cities only, but even villages, suffered from this inquisition. Rome for the first time saw her bishop suffer martyrdom (Fabianus, A.D. 249); Cyprian escaped from Carthage for a while, but was beheaded eight years afterwards, the first martyr among African bishops. Origen of Alexandria was tortured at Cæsarea, and died of injuries then received. But in churches, as in individuals, times of trouble are often less dangerous to virtue than times of peace and prosperity, and the Decian persecution purified while it tested the Christian Church.

Fifty Years' Peace.—And now, once again, for more than fifty years, there was comparative rest for Christians. Either their relative importance had so far increased, or the world at large had become so familiar with their name and customs, that they were permitted to avow their faith openly, to.conduct their elections publicly, to fill offices, to build churches. We are, in fact, approaching the time when the State was no longer able to withhold recognition from a body, which counted its adherents by thousands in every province of the empire. Even in the reign of Decius (A.D. 250) the Roman Church itself had a bishop, forty-six presbyters, who were the parish priests of Rome, seven deacons, and ten "suburbicarian" or suffragan bishops of adjacent towns, like Ostia or Tibur, who met in Synod at Rome. By the end of the fourth century the bishops of the empire numbered 1,800,—1,000 in the Eastern provinces, and 800 in the Western, who were elected by the inferior clergy, the nobles, and people of the diocese, and the election ratified by the bishops of the province. That the doctrines of Christianity should find favour with women and slaves was not, perhaps, astonishing, considering the position they occupied in the world. We find them even penetrating, not now for the first time, to the interior of the palace, and the wife and daughter of the Emperor Diocletian, and many of his principal officers, embraced the tenets and protected the faith of Christianity. The first eighteen years' of Diocletian's reign, indeed, were years of perfect toleration, for the Emperor was a man of great breadth of view, and of a generally humane disposition. But its close was disfigured by a fierce persecution, the order for which was wrung from him rather than voluntarily issued. There is no question that for nearly 200 years the influence of Christian ideas had been secretly working an effect beyond the limits of the Church in reawakening belief, not perhaps in polytheism, but in natural religion. And this reaction operated in two ways. While it inclined the more virtuous and thoughtful to view the Christians with tolerance, it influenced the religious fanaticism of the ignorant, and supplied a ready mine of violence, when violence was needed. At times this fanatical spirit was exasperated beyond bounds, by the knowledge that not only was the number of converts to Christianity daily increasing, but the area from which they were drawn was daily widening—that not only the poor but the rich, not only the ignorant but the educated, not only the slave but the high born lady, were falling within the fatal influence of the new religion, and alienating the gods by their apostacy. And this helps to explain the curious fact that, while on the whole, from Trajan onwards, the Christians enjoyed longer and larger intervals of toleration and peace, the persecutions when they arose were more and more searching and terrible.

The Diocletian Persecution—A.D. 303.—The persecution of the year 303 seems to have differed somewhat from others in its origin, as well as in its character. Diocletian's colleagues, Maximian and Galerius, entertained a strong dislike towards Christianity—a dislike deepened and strengthened by the discovery, that the army also was tainted with these dangerous notions. No thorough-going soldier, indeed, could possibly overlook such conduct as that of Marcellus, the centurion, who, at a public festival, being called upon to sacrifice to the gods, threw away belt and arms, and insignia of office, and exclaimed aloud that he would obey none but Jesus Christ, the eternal King, and that he renounced for ever the use of human weapons. He was tried, condemned, and beheaded for mutiny and desertion. This was martial law, however, not religious persecution ; but this and other like incidents appear to have sunk deeply into the mind of Galerius, as being symptoms of prevalent principles, dangerous to public safety. Accordingly, after the Persian war, when Galerius spent the winter of the year 302 with Diocletian at Nicomedia, he used, and used successfully, his utmost efforts to induce the Emperor to assent to a fresh trial, whether this *imperium in imperio*, with its own taxes, and officers, and code of laws, could not finally be extirpated. The opening act of the drama was the destruction, on February 23, 303, of the principal church in Nicomedia by the imperial troops. On the next day an imperial edict was published, ordering that all churches throughout the Empire should be demolished, that those who held secret assemblies for religious purposes should be punished with death, that all sacred books and writings should be publicly burnt, and the property of the Church confiscated. Freeborn Christians were debarred from honours or employment, Christian slaves from all hope of emancipation. . Scarcely, however, was the edict posted in Nicomedia when it was torn down by the hand of a Christian, who paid the penalty of his life. He was arrested and roasted to death over a slow fire. Diocletian's alarm at the approbation expressed at the act was further increased by his palace being discovered to be on fire twice within fifteen days—a deed, of course, attributed to Christian malice. Accordingly, his scruples were silenced, and the bloody work of persecution began. Some opposition and slight disturbances in the execution of this edict increased his indignation, and led to the publication of further and severer edicts, directing the arrest of all ecclesiastics, and the

employment of any severity to reclaim Christians from
their rebellion against the gods, and their treason to the
Empire. Even inmates of the palace and high officials
were compelled to abjure Christianity, or were put to death.
The Bishop of Nicomedia was beheaded. Many Christians were burnt alive, many thrown into the sea with
stones round their necks. From the capital the persecution spread into the provinces, where they were assailed
by the united forces of the government, the pagan priesthood, the mob, and the philosophers. Gaul alone in a
measure escaped, thanks to the humanity, or (if we may
believe Eusebius) the Christian sympathies of Constantius Chlorus. It is the worst evil of religious, perhaps of
all persecution, that in order to succeed it must have recourse to always increasing severities, and be prepared
to go all lengths, even to extermination. There is only
one alternative, the acknowledgment of failure. Hence,
in the present case, edict succeeded edict, each more
barbarous than the preceding, as Christian courage and
heroism rose higher. The illness and abdication of Diocletian even aggravated the evil. ' For Galerius in the
East was more implacable than Diocletian in his hatred
of Christianity; and Maxentius in the West, driven to
stand on the defensive against the rising ambition of the
young Constantine, purchased the support of his pagan
subjects by persecution of the Christians, whom they detested. It is no wonder that throughout the Empire the
churches began to turn their eyes with hope towards the
West and Gaul, for the enemies of Christianity were the
enemies of Constantine. His mother Helena, they may
well have remembered, was a Christian, and his father,
Constantine, had at least not wholly yielded to the inhuman policy of Diocletian and Galerius. To him, therefore, they naturally began to look as a possible protector.

Toleration under Galerius and Constantine.—
Meanwhile persecution, which had thinned the numbers
and fallen heavily on the leading members of the Christian body, had not dimmed the faith, nor blunted the
devotion of the mass of believers. And now they were
about to enjoy a well-deserved triumph. Galerius, in the
18th year of his reign, was attacked, like Herod the Great
and Philip II. of Spain, by a loathsome and agonising
disease. From his dying bed he published an edict,
acknowledging the failure of the severities he had advised
against the Christians, permitting the free exercise of
their religion, and finally imploring their prayers for their
suffering Emperor. The news, of course, spread rapidly.
Prison doors were thrown open. Mines gave back to life
and light their labourers. Churches were repaired, and,
ere long, filled with throngs of thankful worshippers. The
reaction was complete, when the victorious Constantine
avowed himself a Christian, and by the famous edict of
Milan (A.D. 313) gave *to Christians, as well as to all others,*
free toleration to follow whatever religion they pleased.
All buildings and churches previously confiscated were
restored, the Emperor himself giving large sums of money
to build new and rebuild old or ruined churches. He
even attempted to adjust disputes within the Church, was
present at synods, and presided at the first œcumenical
council at Nicæa (A.D. 325). The triumph of Christianity
was still further assured by the rise of the new capital
(A.D. 330), which, if not distinctly Christian, certainly was
not pagan. As yet, no doubt, and almost to the end of
the century, the two religions stood side by side, pagan
temples side by side with Christian churches ; yet the
great influence of Christianity can scarcely be doubted,
when we know that the amphitheatre of Constantinople
was never from its foundation disgraced by the bloody

spectacle of gladiators, and that to accommodate the number of Christian worshippers the Basilicæ, or "Halls of Justice," in many towns were consecrated to their use.

Christianity the dominant State Religion— ABOUT A.D. 380.—One attempt, and only one, was made to galvanise the dying paganism into renewed life by the Emperor Julian (A.D. 361–3); but its ill success served to show how deeply the roots of Christianity were planted, and that paganism was practically dead. Perhaps no happier event could have befallen the world than Julian's death in the heart of Persia, apparently so unfortunate and ill-timed. Had he lived to persecute it would have been at the peril of his fame, and success could hardly have been obtained except by civil war. This, happily, was not to be. In the reign of Theodosius (A.D. 379–395) Christianity became the recognised State religion, and it is hardly surprising that in the hour of victory the aggressive side of the now dominant religion hitherto repressed by force began to show itself, and the heathen party in the Empire to feel the heavy hand of government as the Christians had felt it before. Almost the first act of Theodosius was an edict commanding universal obedience to the Catholic faith; his last edict went far towards exterminating paganism, by insisting on the destruction of temples and idols, the alienation of temple revenues, the cessation of priestly privileges, and by proclaiming the ancient worship a treasonable and capital crime. Thus the unity of the Empire, which (as we have seen) had been gradually attained by uniformity of government and law, was further secured by uniformity of religion. And this unity, was not only in the judgment of early Christian writers but in reality, a primary condition as well as the most efficacious means of spreading Christianity. When Gaul, and African, and Italian, and

Egyptian were all members of one great political body, governed by the same laws, using the same language for legal and political purposes, moved by the same ideas, then, and not till then, was it possible to include nations so many and diverse within a common church.

Influence of Christianity on the Empire?—But the question may possibly here be asked, "What influence did Christianity exercise on the Empire? Did not the religion which converted it to a purer faith and uniform worship, thereby infuse also some vigour into the decaying body?" For at first sight it seems strange that an Empire thus consolidated should have fallen so easy a prey to enemies from without as it afterwards did. In truth, however, there were, and for centuries had been, evils lying at the root of society, which were inveterate from long standing, and had eaten away the very pith and marrow of Roman probity and manliness—evils which even Christianity could only cope with in individuals, and some of which lay entirely out of its province to correct. There were even some, by contact with which Christian purity and simplicity were seriously impaired.

Moral Evils deep-seated when Christianity was introduced.—The lustre of an unbroken series of foreign conquests for 130 years (B.C. 266–133) dazzled men's eyes, and blinded them to the evils which were silently accumulating at home. To later generations, the period after the fall of Carthage seemed the golden age of Rome; in reality (as has been well said) it was the "calm before a storm." The tide of luxury and immorality which set in from Greece and the East was beginning to sap and undermine the old discipline and administrative justice for which Rome had once been famous. Not only had war destroyed the flower of the population of Italy, but war taxes had raised prices, and impoverished the already thinned middle classes to such a degree that they were either driven into the towns, or gladly sold their properties and worked as tenants and labourers for the capitalists who had bought them out. Prisóners of war supplied slaves in abundance—those "living chattels" who could be bought like cattle, and when no longer serviceable, be sent off to the slave-market. And the number of slaves was always increasing, because slave labour was thought to be cheap, while the number of free farmers was always diminishing. In fifty years (between B.C. 252 and 204) the Roman citizens capable of bearing arms sank from 298,000 to 214,000; while Gibbon estimates, though the estimate is open to question, that in the early days of the empire the slaves numbered as many as the free citizens and provincials put together. Still, if it be true that the long wars with Carthage ruined and decimated the population, it is also true that the Roman capitalists had their share in reducing the vigour and numbers of the Italians, by substituting slave labour for free. *Latifundia perdidere Italiam.* And slave labour not only reduces the slave to the level of a beast, but demoralises the society which employs it. Slave labour attaches discredit to free labour, and so raises a false standard of honour in the community, making idleness respectable. Slavery is the fruitful parent of vice, and directly fosters the more selfish and brutal side of the slave-owner's character. Meanwhile there was rising in Rome itself, and probably in other large places also, that "city rabble," whose cry was, *panem et circenses*, to pacify whom the government deranged the commerce of Italy, by importing and selling wheat below cost price, and to gain whose support candidates for office half ruined themselves by extravagant gladiatorial shows. The country was left to the occupation of hordes of slaves and of the *villicus,* or resident steward.. The cities were filled with absentee landlords,—rich men, able and willing to purchase luxury, pleasure, office,—and with a mob of artisans, tradesmen, and bankrupt farmers eager to sell their vote and influence. What room was there here for the ancient Roman virtues? Religion languished more and more; education was neg lected; liberty and independence ceased to be anything more than names. The conflict was impending which is always inevitable when the middle classes vanish,—the conflict between those who have and those who want, be tween rich and poor. If we remember, further, that there was now an instrument ready to the hand of any man who knew how to use it, in the shape of a standing army, which the military reforms of Marius had converted into a "professional machine," we shall scarcely wonder that the political virtues vanished amid factions, violence, intrigue, and riot, and that riot before long passed into open civil war, which desolated Italy for nearly 100 years. The result was "the Empire." Speak as one will of the evils of despotism (and it is hardly possible to speak too strongly), the Empire certainly did secure to Italy and the world blessings which at that period could hardly have been obtained otherwise. Exhausted by internecine struggles, the Roman world longed for one thing, and that one thing was peace. Peace and unity were secured to it, at least for a while, by the Empire.

Effect of Christian Morality.—And now into this vast mass of wealth and oppression on the one hand, of degradation and misery on the other,—with its outside pomp and grandeur, and the festering sore of slavery and corruption within,—was silently introduced a little germ, destined by-and-by to grow and overspread the earth. A little band of despised Jews, disciples of One who had died the death of a slave, " undertook (we may say almost in the words of Tacitus) to convert an Empire, and did convert it." The victory was a slow one, as men measure time, for it took 300 years to gain ; and it was gained by the strange weapons of purity, charity, and moral courage. It speaks well, however, for human nature that the mere spectacle of these virtues in men who shrank from the unutterable depravities around them, and were not ashamed to help the poor and sick, nor afraid to face even death rather than do what they thought wrong, should have had so great an attraction. Doubtless to the wretched the good news of a happier life hereafter was enough in itself to arrest attention, just as the new doctrine of the equal rights and brotherhood of all men appealed irresistibly to women and slaves ; but the mere proclamation of future happiness or of natural equality will gain no credence of itself, unless credit attach to him who proclaims them. It is a question of moral influence. And it is to the honour of the Christian Church that, in a world demoralised by sensuality, idleness, and violence, the first apostles and preachers could insist, and insist successfully, on the sanctity of marriage, the duty of labour, the wisdom of self-restraint ; and that by these means they should have gathered in converts from north and south, and east and west, until all the Roman world was (at least nominally) Christian.

Excellent Organisation of the Christian Church. —But these means were not all. A society which is to grow and show signs of vigorous life must have *organisation* as well as principles ; and it remains now to sketch the organisation of the early Church, which enabled it, in the first place, to have a corporate existence of its own ; and, secondly, to wage war against the evil of the world. The earliest Christian communities were founded by the apostles, in whose absence from time to time they were ruled by presbyters or bishops (for the terms were at first convertible), and below the presbyters were deacons. So it was in the churches of Ephesus and Philippi. At a very early period, however (the apostles and first teachers being practically missionaries, and so always moving from place to place), we find in the several churches a single bishop or overseer (ἐπίσκοπος), holding a position superior to that of the presbyter bishops. It matters little how the custom arose; it certainly existed. And originally popular election, in the widest sense, was the rule for that and other offices. There was at first no essential distinction between clergy and laity; all alike were members of the same congregation. But it is easy to see how rapidly a line of demarcation might arise between the more eminent, zealous, or religious members, and the rank and file. They were ordained to their office to teach as well as rule; they admitted new members to the body by the initiatory rite of baptism; they presided in the administration of the Lord's supper. It would have been strange had men in such a position *not* become a sacred order; equally strange, in that case, had not the reverence of their fellow-Christians and their own *esprit de corps* insensibly increased the distance between them and those to whom they ministered. Thus gradually, from mere force of circumstances, the presbyters became a priestly caste, bishops became pontiffs, and the foundations were laid of a long series of ecclesiastical usurpations, which have ever since obscured and troubled Christianity. When once this natural reverence began to assert itself towards the natural leaders of the society, there was no limit practically to the lengths to which such reverence might lead men. Further, the more the churches grew in numbers and influence, the more difficult and necessary became the duties of their rulers. Men began to be Christians, not only, as at first, from conviction, but from selfish interest, from love of novelty, or because their parents were Christians. Admission and expulsion, therefore, from the Christian body became a very responsible duty. In such a body, moreover, dissensions, perhaps sects, would arise, needing firmness and authority to repress. Nothing could be more natural than that the Christians of the second and third centuries should regard their bishops and presbyters with almost exaggerated reverence, and that the gulf between clergy and laity, rulers and ruled, became impassable. It is quite in accordance with this that the mode of election began to change. A bishopric was a prize, an object of ambition ; some members of each church, at least, would be open to pressure or bribery ; the right of election, therefore, was gradually withdrawn from congregations and presbyters, and replaced by nomination at the hands of the Emperor. Again, congregations became united into dioceses, especially in cities, and the dignity of bishop at once rose in proportion. Thus in Rome, at the beginning of the fourth century, there were more than forty churches in subordination to the Bishop of Rome. Or, again, dioceses were united into a province, under one metropolitan, with suffragan bishops beneath him. Or, lastly, provinces were united under a single bishop, called Patriarch, standing but little below the level of the Emperor himself. The difference between the wealth, rank, and influence of the patriarch of Antioch or Alexandria in the fourth century, and the comparative obscurity of a bishop of the first century, will serve as a measure of the way in which the hierarchy of the Church had developed, and of the extended ideas which had arisen in the interval as to its sanctity and separateness. Contemporaneously with the rise of metropolitan bishops, synods began to be convened, at first in the East, and of bishops only; afterwards, throughout

Christendom of the whole body of clergy. They met once or twice a year, and the metropolitan presided. Lastly, there were general councils, meetings of bishops and clergy from all parts of Christendom,—instrumental beyond anything else in defining the creed and maintaining the unity of the Church. The first general council, recognised as œcumenical, was that of Nicæa, in A.D. 325, in which the Emperor Constantine presided. It will enable us to realise the ever increasing power of the clergy, if we reflect on the position of a heretic or schismatic who dared to stand aloof. As in the Empire, so in the Church, a rebel was one who had no place of refuge where the strong arm of authority could not reach him. And exactly in proportion as the triumphs of orthodoxy over heterodoxy increased, and uniformity of discipline and doctrine grew more rigid with each triumph, so it became less and less possible to dissent with impunity. Submission or excommunication were the only alternatives. A caste or order, wielding such powers as these, challenged no longer mere respect and reverence as being the most pious or intelligent members of a congregation, but would claim submission and implicit obedience as of right, which it had ample power to enforce. The use of such absolute power, indeed, was perhaps a possibility rather than a fact in the early centuries of the Church's history; but the feelings of both clergy and laity increasingly tended in that direction from the moment when first the two orders were separated. And these feelings were further increased by the pomp, wealth, and dignity which the recognition of Christianity conferred on the officials of the Church, not less than by the charitable uses to which they devoted their wealth, and the undoubted austerity and purity of their lives. Not that the celibacy of the clergy was as yet insisted on, nor was any regulation on the subject enforced during the first three centuries. But it was (so to speak) "in the air," and was little by little defended, recommended, urged, and at last, in the teeth of opposition and urgent remonstrance, peremptorily commanded. And the feeling on this subject worked undoubtedly for good as well as for evil. If, on the one hand, the enforced celibacy of the clergy led to evasions, secret marriages, and other customs often denounced after the middle of the third century, on the other hand it cut a priest free from the distractions of domestic life ; it gave him liberty to devote himself and his time unfettered to the cause of God (such was the beautiful ideal!); it secured him a vantage ground in dealing with the most pressing evil of imperial times, the facility of divorce, and the consequent low tone on moral questions.

Christianity the State Church.—The various powers of the priesthood were vastly enhanced when the civil power allied itself to the ecclesiastical, and Church and State were one. Heresy became a crime, and by Theodosius was declared a capital offence, punishable by the civil power ; but, as has been well said, "the Christian hierarchy bought the privilege of persecution at the price of Christian independence." Bishops became officers of State as well as Church; but unlike civil offices, theirs were gained, for the most part, not by favour and intrigue, but by ability and activity, and could be discharged without fear. Moreover, the Church possessed within herself a principle of liberty, which gradually reacted on the Empire. She professed to be, and was, independent of any authority upon earth. Indeed, it is difficult to realise without an effort, the profound effect which such a sight as Athanasius confronting Constantine, or Ambrose rebuking Theodosius, must have had on minds blinded by the passive submission of generations to the possibility of successful resistance. It cannot but have increased the respect already inspired by the undoubted virtues and sacred character of the clergy. And in the West this effect was still further increased when the court and government migrated to Milan or Constantinople. The Bishop and clergy of Rome, eclipsed before by the splendour and consequence of the civil officers around them, and having been (as it had happened) men for the most part of little mark, rose suddenly to the rank of great functionaries. The bishop became " the first Christian in the first city of the world ;" and as the elections to bishoprics and ecclesiastical offices had become matters of State ; so the election to the Roman bishopric, the greatest see of the West, became the most important State business of the West. In the hands of men like Innocent and Leo in the fifth century, and Gregory in the sixth, this grand power was utilised to advance the supremacy of the See of Rome over Western Christendom. It may be conceded that the effect on the Church herself was not wholly good ; that as fashion or indifference, or timidity, brought in crowds of converts from the palace or the street, human passions and lower motives—ambition, jealousy, tyranny—began to influence the ever growing body, and that the simple moral standard of the earlier Church was insensibly lowered, and in a measure replaced by quite another standard, orthodoxy. Neither, however, was it wholly bad. For the general tone of society was raised. Christian virtues were at least made possible to all, and a new and noble career thrown open to those who would adopt it. Nor, indeed, is it probable that without this complete and vigorous organisation the Christian religion could have stood its ground during the succeeding times of disaster and violence—when it often happened that the

Christian bishop stood firmly at his post while the Roman officials fled, and when the clergy alone seemed undaunted by the surging barbarism around them.

Lastly, it will aid us to realise the vast benefits which the Christian Church conferred upon the Roman Empire, if we attempt to imagine what that Empire would have been without it—rotten with immorality, and debased by slavery, overrun by swarms of barbarians, and with no influence at hand, ubiquitous and powerful, to check brutality, to soften cruelty, to assimilate conflicting races, to maintain religion, to save civilisation.   That and nothing less is the debt of gratitude which Europe owes to the early Church.

CHAPTER III

THE BARBARIANS ON THE FRONTIER.
CENT. IV.

Romans and Barbarians from the same Stock.
—Around the mighty Empire, united and consolidated by
the efforts of 400 years, and it might have seemed invul-
nerable, lay, north and east, a vast swarm of barbarous
nations, whom pressure from behind was gradually thrust-
ing up to and over the frontiers. It would have seemed
an insult to have told Aurelius or Decius that the barbarians, against whom they were defending the Empire,
were kinsmen of their own, sprung from the same ancestors. And yet it would have been strictly true. The
greater part of the inhabitants of the Roman Empire, and
nearly all the barbarians who invaded that Empire, from
the Persians in the south-east to Saxons in the north-
west, were, in fact, without knowing it, scions of the same
stock. They nearly all belonged to the Aryan family.

Who were the Aryans ?—We have, it is true, no
historical proof as to when, or even where the original
Aryans lived before their dispersion from the earliest
home of the race ; for they lived before history (even on
rocks and monuments) was written, and they appear to
have led a nomad life, in which all desire or power to
write history is unknown. Yet the comparative study of

languages tends to the conclusion, that in prehistoric times there must have been such a people, and that their probable home was in Central Asia, to the east and north of the Caspian Sea. The evidence of language shows that this people must have been the progenitors of Hindoos, and Persians, and Greeks, and Italians, and Germans; the joint evidence of language, law, and traditional customs shows that even in primeval times, before they began their wanderings southward and westward, they were at least partly civilised, and knew how to build, and plough, and grind corn—that they had family life, and something like government and religious ideas. The name itself is a Sanskrit word, meaning " noble," " of good family;" it appears in the inscriptions of Darius Hystaspis, who styles himself an Aryan, as well as in the modern name of Persia, Irán.   It can even be traced with some probability westward, in the track of the Aryan migrations, though with decreasing frequency, so far as Thrace, the old name of which is said to have been Arya, and the Vistula, where was a German tribe called Arii. The theory is that, as this people grew and multiplied, a migration became necessary, and that successive *waves* or swarms of population moved southwards and westwards, relieving the pressure on their brethren whom they left be-hind ; and that in the course of generations they conquered or peopled Southern and Western Asia and Europe—con-quered if it was already occupied, peopled if it was empty.

Semitic and Turanian Races.—There were other races also, with whom at various times and in different places they came in contact, Semitic and Turanian, and with whom here and there they combined. The former comprised Phœnicians, Hebrews, and Arabs; the latter all those scattered peoples, both in Europe and Asia, which were neither Aryan nor Semitic, such as Basques, Finns,

Lapps, Huns, Turks, and the like.   In Europe, they were
driven by the Aryans into the remoter corners.   In Asia,
they encircled them with a vast though widely-scattered
ring of populations, which constantly encroached on their
grazing and hunting grounds, and in the end drove them
headlong upon the Roman Empire.

Aryan Migrations—Kelts—Teutons—Slaves.—
The Aryan migrations began before the beginnings of history, and appear to have taken a twofold direction, southward and westward.   Thus separated from the first, and
gradually changed in appearance and customs by the influence of climate and mixture with other races, the two
great branches diverged so far as to lose almost all vestige
of relationship.   The southern portion were the forefathers of the Hindoos and Persians, and occupied little
by little Hindostan and all the country lying between
India and the Euphrates; while the western branch
gradually moved into Europe by way of Southern Russia,
or the Black Sea, wave after wave, tribe after tribe, until
in the course of perhaps centuries the whole Continent
was occupied by them and their descendants.   The first
wave of Aryan emigrants which broke over Europe, and
swept before them certain non-Aryan tribes already settled
there, was the Kelts.   Of this there can be little doubt;
for Gaul and Britain, and parts of Spain and Italy, were
inhabited by Kelts when authentic history begins; and
the records of history describe the way in which they invaded and conquered, or were themselves conquered,
absorbed, or pushed westwards by later Aryan tribes.
Just as the Kelts pushed on the non-Aryan tribes in front
of them, so the second Aryan wave of Teutons—the forefathers of Germans, and English, and Scandinavians—
pressed in turn upon the Kelts and drove them westwards; so that partly from this cause, partly from having

been absorbed in and transformed by the Roman Empire, pure Kelts and the Keltic tongue are now found only in Brittany and parts of Great Britain. And, further, as the Aryan Kelts had pushed the non-Aryan Basques into a corner of Spain and Gaul, so the Aryan Teutons in Scandinavia found a non-Aryan population in their way, the Finns and Lapps, whom they gradually dispossessed and drove to the north. The last wave of Aryans which moved westwards from Asia was the Slaves and Lithuanians, who occupied the east and north-east of Europe,—the most numerous and hitherto least important of all the intruding peoples.

Relations between Empire and Barbarians— Cent. I.–IV.—The history of these Aryan nations is the history of Europe, and its most important section is the history of Rome. For all previous empires were merely preludes to the Roman; almost all later kingdoms were outgrowths from it. And of this marvellous history there is, perhaps, no epoch of deeper interest than that in which the elder Aryan population, the civilised Christian Empire, was for the first time brought face to face with the younger and less civilised peoples of its own family, and forced to fight for bare existence. All along the frontier of the Rhine and Danube, in the fourth century, lay tribe after tribe of Aryan wanderers, eager to ravage the fertile lands and pillage the rich inhabitants of Greece, and Italy, and Gaul; while on the Euphrates another Aryan people, the Persians, had defeated the old enemies of Rome, the Turanian Parthians, and founded an empire destined to last for 400 years (A.D. 226). Already the pressure in the far north-east of Slaves and Turanians, Huns and Alans, had driven in Ostrogoths upon Visigoths, and Gepidæ upon Quadi and Marcomanni. Already urged by that pressure, and nothing loth, the Daci had in

Domitian's reign (A.D. 81), burst across the Danube and ravaged Mœsia. The Marcomanni and Quadi, in Aurelius's reign, had desolated Rhœtia and Noricum (A.D. 167). The new Persian dynasty of the Sassanidæ had signalised its victory over the Parthians (A.D. 226) by aggressions upon Rome, and a defeat of Alex. Severus (A.D. 232). The short reign of Decius (A.D. 249–251) had been one long struggle against Goths, on the Danube and in Mœsia, with varying success; while Valerian (A.D. 253–260), whose armies were scarcely able to make head against inroads of Franks in Gaul and Spain, and Alemanni even in Italy, and Goths in Asia Minor, was himself defeated and taken prisoner by Sapor the Persian, in a battle near Edessa. Within fifteen years (A.D. 268–284) formidable invasions of Goths, Alemanni, Alani, Franks, and Sarmatians, in Mœsia, Italy, Asia Minor, Gaul, and Illyricum, bore witness to the growing weakness of the Empire, and the military energy of the barbarians. The immediate danger was arrested, though only for a time, by the abilities of Claudius (A.D. 268), Aurelian (A.D. 270), and Probus (A.D. 276); while the internal reforms of Diocletian and Constantine helped to secure for the Empire a new, if a short lease of life. From the time of Diocletian (A.D. 285) to the death of Theodosius (A.D. 395), Rome preserved her frontiers and her unity intact.

Tribes lying on Roman Frontiers.—The order of facts in the history of the barbarian invasions of the Empire depends so much on the position of the barbarians themselves upon the frontiers, that it will be well to describe exactly their relative situations along the Danube and Rhine at the end of the fourth century. Beginning from the Euxine, and running the eye along the line of the above rivers, there will be seen a bewildering succession of unfamiliar names, from which, however, seven stand out as of prominent importance, viz., Goths, Vandals, Burgundians, Franks, Saxons, Lombards, and Huns. The first six belong to the Teutonic branch of the Aryan family; the seventh to the Ugrian or Finnish branch of the Turanian; and as the condition of the Gothic and Vandal tribes at the time above mentioned depended in a great measure on the power of the Huns, it will be well to begin with the Hunnish Empire, and give a brief sketch of its rise and history.

Huns.—The vast plain of Europe lying between the Ural Mountains and the Volga, the Danube, the Rhine, and the Baltic,—the scene of the great movements of the fourth and fifth centuries,—was unequally divided between tribes of Teutonic and tribes of Finnish descent, between Aryans and Turanians. Foremost among the latter was the confederation of the Huns. It had been seated since the second century on the Volga and the slopes of the Ural, and probably comprised Turkish races in the East, Finnish races in the West, and, dominating all, a great Mongol tribe. In physiognomy, customs, and character, they differed wholly (according to contemporary writers) from the Aryans of the West. They lived by theft, by hunting, by the produce of their flocks. In ferocity they surpassed any barbarians of whom Roman soldiers had had experience, while to the civilised eye their ugliness was revolting. Of the habits of civilised life they were utterly ignorant, even of the use of fire for cooking, and of covered huts. Their days were spent almost wholly on horseback. Their chief weapon of offence was bone-tipped arrows. Religion, or form of worship, it is said, was unknown. Such is the account of Ammianus Marcellinus, written about A.D. 375; and making all allowances for the passionate language of hatred and fear, it is clear they were a very terrible foe

to face, with nothing to lose by defeat but their lives'
and everything to gain by success. But contact with
more civilised tribes modified their customs, if not their
characters, and they quickly learned to build villages and
live in huts, and adopt some of the habits of civilised life.
The empire of the confederation gradually spread.   In
A.D. 374 the Huns fell on the Alani, Turanians like themselves, and destroyed or absorbed them. The next victims
were the Goths of Ermanaric's Empire. The Ostrogoths
were absorbed into the ranks of the victors, the Gepidæ
pushed north, the Visigoths west and south; and by the
end of the century the confederates had established a vast
empire reaching from the Volga to the Theiss, and from
the Black Sea nearly to the Baltic,—an empire before
which weaker tribes were forced in upon the territories of
the Roman Empire, and in the minds of whose leaders
was presently developed the ambitious idea of sharing the
world with Rome. We shall see hereafter. how in Attila
this idea grew into a dream of universal dominion.

The Teutonic Races.—The tribes that suffered from
the pressure of the Hunnish confederation were of a different and more civilised type. The sketch of the Germans
given by Tacitus was written with a purpose, and is
therefore not entirely trustworthy; but their salient characteristics described by him and attested by other writers,
are both remarkable and credible. Independent, chaste,
faithful, warlike, hospitable, yet fierce and often cruel,
the Teutons of those days were not very unlike the
Teutons of these. They were marked by blue eyes, light
hair, and large frames. In the day of battle, squadrons
and battalions fought side by side, drawn from the same
families and clan. They showed a deep reverence for
women (being almost the only barbarians content with
one wife), and a genuine if somewhat mystical religious

feeling. Their government was popular, for while on minor matters the chiefs deliberated alone, the whole tribe debated in a body questions of greater moment. Slaves were treated with far more consideration than in the civilised Empire, and to strike or bind them was as rare as it was thought dishonourable.

The Goths.—The first nation that suffered from the encroachments of the Huns was the Goths, of all the Teutonic tribes the largest and most important. In the earliest historic times their home appears to have been Scandinavia and the shores of the Baltic, which they probably abandoned in consequence of intestine struggles. From the shores of the Baltic to the shores of the Euxine they gradually made their way through the midst of the Slaves, as far as the valley of the Dnieper, the direction of their wanderings being probably determined by the position and relative strength of other tribes. At any rate they settled on the Dnieper, the Ostrogoths to the east, the Visigoths to the west, and the Gepidæ to the north; and there they waxed in power and numbers until their Empire reached almost to the Baltic, and under Ermanaric included nearly all South Russia, Lithuania, Courland, Poland, and part of Germany. But the Empire had been won by force of arms, and was held together by no tie but force. So when the Huns were invited by the Roxolani, a tribe subject to the Ostrogoths, to come and help them, and the invitation, was accepted, the Gothic Empire fell to pieces at once. After a few fruitless struggles, the Ostrogoths submitted, and were incorporated for a while in the Hunnish Confederation, while the Visigoths fled before the storm to take refuge behind the Pruth. Even here, however, they did not feel safe. The pagan minority went off under Athanaric into the Carpathian Mountains, while at the suggestion of Bishop Ulfilas, who had converted a large part of the nation, the Christian majority resolved to place the Danube between themselves and their dreaded foes, and to offer their services to the Roman Emperor. The offer was made and refused, unless they would consent to adopt certain definite views regarding the second person in the Trinity, which owed their origin to Arius, a Presbyter of Alexandria (about A.D. 320), and were widely held in the Eastern part of the Empire. Time pressed. The lives of men and the honour of women were at stake. The concession, it might be thought, was a small one. So Ulfilas yielded; and the Visigothic nation, now become Arian, crossed the river with arms in their hands. They crossed as friends. But the treachery, licentiousness, and avarice of the Roman officials charged with the duty of receiving and settling them, infuriated the only half-civilised barbarians, who took a fearful revenge. Falling suddenly on the defenceless province of Mœsia, and ravaging far and near, they defeated and slew the Emperor Valens in a pitched battle at Adrianople (A.D. 378), and overran the whole country between the Euxine, Ægean, and Adriatic for nearly a year. Indeed the defeat was more fatal to the Empire than Cannæ had been to the Republic. The loss from the latter, both of men and prestige, was speedily repaired: while after Adrianople the Empire was never again wholly freed from barbarians. Theodosius, it is true, by mingled firmness and diplomacy, succeeded in confining the Visigoths within definite limits, *but it was south of the Danube;* and after his death, a very few years of the feeble rule of his sons left Alaric, or men like Alaric, practically masters of the Empire.

The Vandals.—From the Goths we pass to the Vandals, divided also into two nations, the Vandali proper and the Vandali Silingi, though apparently never wholly separated, as were the Ostrogoths and Visigoths. Their name in history has suffered a strange misfortune, having become a synonym for all that is barbarous and destructive: whereas in reality they are said to have been among the noblest and least ferocious of the barbarians, given to commerce and agriculture, until in their case, as in that of the Goths, the perfidy of the Roman government exasperated and called out the fiercer elements of the barbarian character. Their earliest settlement in Europe was apparently between the rivers Elbe and Vistula; from whence they were dislodged by the Lombards about the Christian era. By the year A.D. 150 they had wandered as far south as Bohemia, and probably formed part of the great confederation which for thirteen years taxed the energy and resources of Aurelius to resist (A.D. 167–180). In the reign of Probus they were on the Danube (A.D. 276–282) and the Theiss, but coming in contact with the Visigoths, and being defeated by them, begged and received permission from Constantine to settle in Pannonia. There they remained for seventy years, and were converted to Christianity, not moving thence until famine compelled them, like so many others, to join the great westward migration of 406 into Gaul.

The Burgundians were like the Vandals in their aptness for civilised and commercial life; unlike them in that they wandered but comparatively a little way from their earliest home. About the middle of the fourth century they were seated on both sides of the Elbe; at the end of it on the Main. In A.D. 406 they joined in the migration of the Vandals into Gaul, where they found a permanent home on the banks of the Rhone and Saône, and about the middle of the century embraced with eager zeal the religion of the Romans, whose God alone seemed able to save them from the terrible Huns.

The Franks belonged to the Low Dutch branch of the Teutonic races, as it is called—that is, the branch which occupied the Lowlands of Germany between the Rhine and the shores of the Baltic. They were in reality a confederation of eight tribes, the Chauci, Sicambri, Attuarii, Bructeri, Chamavi, Catti, Salii, and Cherusci, who appear to have taken the name of Franci or "Freemen" about the middle of the third century, and to have possessed the greater part of Westphalia, Hanover, and the Netherlands. Many of these tribes had fought bravely against Drusus (B.C. 12–9), and Germanicus (A.D. 15, 16); and the Confederation had maintained a long struggle against the Roman Empire in the times of Valerian (A.D. 256), Probus (A.D. 277), and Julian (A.D. 356–9). At the end of the fourth and beginning of the fifth century they began that movement towards the west and south, which was the first step in the formation of their afterwards mighty Empire.

The Saxons, low Dutch like their neighbours the Franks, occupied for centuries the country lying between the Ems and the Oder, forming the Eastern frontier of the Frankish kingdom. Their name still survives in the kingdom of the German Empire called Saxony, a very different district, it must be remembered, from the Saxonia of Roman and Frank times. They were divided into three tribes, Ostphalians, Westphalians, and Angarians. Lying as they did along the shores of two seas, and in a barren country of forests, moors, and morasses, but intersected by large rivers falling into those seas, it is not surprising that they were a seafaring rather than an agricultural or pastoral people. No shore was safe from their depredations. In the reign of Valentinian (A.D. 371), the maritime provinces of Gaul suffered grievously from their attacks; and scarcely a century later the withdrawal of the Roman forces in Britain enabled them to find another and larger outlet for their surplus population, and in company with Angles and other cognate tribes to lay the first foundations of what was afterwards the kingdom of England.

The Lombards.—To the East of Franks and Saxons lay a tribe, the Langobardi or Lombards, whom Tacitus speaks of as scanty in numbers, but of extraordinary valour. Certainly their influence on the course of history was out of all proportion to their importance among the German tribes. When first we hear of them about the time of Augustus, it was as with so many other Teutonic tribes in the district between the Elbe and the Oder, and probably, therefore, allied with or subject to the Saxons. They gradually moved or were driven southwards, until at the end of the fourth century they were in the centre of Europe, and at the beginning of the sixth on the Danube, preparatory to their descent some fifty years later into Italy.

There were, of course, other tribes and confederations, many and various, lying between the Volga, the Danube, the Rhine, and the Baltic, at the end of the fourth century, besides the seven thus briefly described. But few if any were mixed up with Roman history in so special a way as these: none produced more remarkable men, or affected so largely the subsequent course of events: none left such marked traces of their influence in Italy, Spain, France, and England.

Summary of First Three Chapters.—Briefly to sum up the contents of the first three chapters, we see two vast groups of Aryan populations on either side of the Danube and the Rhine gradually approach, touch, and at last clash with one another along the whole line of those rivers. One group had probably been settled in its first home before a part of the other even began its wanderings.   One was now civilised and Christian; the other semi-civilised or barbarous, and for the most part pagan.   One group was bound together in the equalising grasp of a centralised despotism; the other shifting and mobile as the waves of the sea, or the sand of the shore, with no bond of cohesion beyond occasionally common interests and similar customs.   At the moment when this history begins, they had already touched, and at points the frontier had been passed by the barbarians.   The crisis was approaching.   And for all men of foresight, who could appreciate the danger, it must have been an anxious question whether the Empire, with its vast frontier line, would be able, in spite of centralised power, administrative unity, and disciplined armies, to make head against the dimly looming swarms of warriors from behind the Danube, whose numbers seemed to increase with every year.   Nor were they more than vaguely conscious of the fatal weakness within the Empire, which made the battle, as far as they were concerned, a lost one before it began.

N
A
V
O
E
N
T
S
R
R. Dniester
Danu
(Ister
Pon

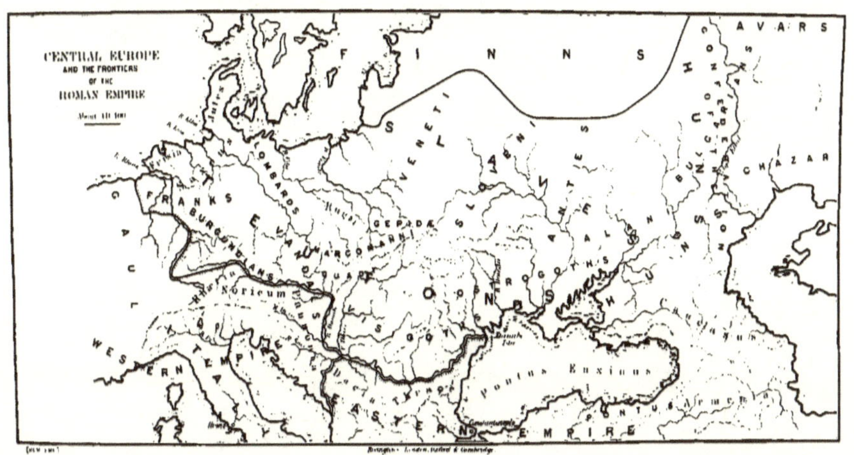

CENTRAL EUROPE
AND THE FRONTIERS
OF THE
ROMAN EMPIRE
About AD 500
FINNS
AVARS
CHAZAR
VENETI
SLOVENES
ANTES
GEPIDÆ
LOMBARDS
MARCOMANNI
QUADI
FRANKS
BURGUNDIANS
GAUL
Noricum
WESTERN EMPIRE
OSTROGOTHS
HUNS
ALANS
BULGARS
Danube
Pontus Euxinus
EASTERN EMPIRE
Caucasus
Pontus Armen

CHURCH AND STATE IN CONSTANTINOPLE, EUTROPIUS, AND CHRYSOSTOM.

Death of Theodosius—A.D. 395.—The Emperor Theodosius the Great died on January 17, 395. On his death-bed he dictated a will, proclaiming a general amnesty, and entrusting the care of his sons, Arcadius and Honorius, to Stilicho the Vandal, who had married his niece Serena. Thus passed away the last great Cæsar, too soon for the happiness of the world. After his death the Western Empire went through a series of misfortunes, till it fell wholly into barbarian hands; while the fate of the East, if less tragic, was hardly less sad. The successors of Theodosius at Constantinople were, with few exceptions, mere cyphers in the hands of wives or favourites; and their history is little but the barren record of intrigues, by which those favourites won or lost their power. Of this state of things the first ten years of Arcadius' reign are an excellent instance; when the greedy ambition of a Rufinus or a Eutropius, and the imperiousness of a Eudoxia threw an empire into confusion, and when, not for the first or last time, the dauntless self-sacrifice of a priest, such as Chrysostom, was the one ray of light in the surrounding darkness.

Sons of Theodosius.—The gap which was left in

the political world by the death of Theodosius might well
have seemed irreparable. A man of energy and experience was replaced by two feeble and ignorant boys,
unworthy sons of a noble father. Arcadius, the elder,
who inherited the Eastern Empire, was only eighteen ;
Honorius was but eleven. The elder was weakly in body
and in mind—a character both dull and timid, which had
been spoiled by the flatteries of a court. The younger,
more attractive, yet capricious and uncertain, was fiercely
jealous of the elder brother, to whom he had been subordinated from infancy, and for whose slights he longed
to take vengeance. Each was ruled by a will stronger
than his own ; Honorius by Stilicho, Arcadius by Rufinus
the Gaul ; and the hostility of the Ministers aggravated
the jealousy of the Emperors. The two men were
singularly unlike. Both were intelligent and well educated ; but Stilicho possessed the best qualities of the
soldier, Rufinus the worst vices of the diplomatist. Each
was ambitious, but, in a different way ; Rufinus aimed at
power for his own advancement, Stilicho merged his personal interests in devotion to the State. Though a Vandal by birth, he was a Roman at heart, and valued the
historic glories of his adopted country far more deeply
than did the degenerate Italians, who despised him. He
had the rare merit of justice, which won for him the dislike of many, the respect of a few. Rufinus, on the other
hand, possessed graces which Stilicho lacked. His wit and
good taste, his versatility and complaisance ensured him
a welcome in all societies, even in the highest ; but at the
core he was selfish, insincere, and unscrupulous. Such an
one, moreover, makes enemies of men, whom in his up-
ward course he outstrips, offends, or ruins ; and when
Rufinus, blinded by ambition, sought to marry his daughter to Arcadius, and to become himself an Emperor's

colleague, these enemies combined to ruin him. By a stratagem of Eutropius, to which he was himself a party, the Emperor was married to Eudoxia the Frank; and Rufinus was murdered at the very feet of Arcadius during a military review.

Rise of Eutropius.—The ringleader of these enemies was Eutropius, the Chamberlain, who stepped into his fallen rival's place, and for four years disputed with the Empress the direction of the Emperor and the Empire. He was the son of slave parents, and born in Armenia. He was himself more than once sold as a slave; and being turned out of doors by an elegant and capricious mistress, because he was no longer young, was saved from starvation by a kind-hearted officer, who enrolled him among the slaves of the palace. There his intelligence and apparent piety soon attracted observation, especially that of Theodosius, who ere long attached him to his own person, and often sent him on confidential embassies. Thus the slave's fortune was made. But previous hardships had spoiled his temper and ruined his character. He was greedy, cunning, bitter; and hated the world that had ill used him. For one person, and one only, had he any tenderness in his heart, and that was his sister.

Allies of Eutropius.—It is a curious illustration of the difference of sentiment between East and West, that the custom of having effeminate slaves about the household, which was regarded with horror in Italy, was thought proper and fashionable in Constantinople. Hence the rise of Eutropius to be the Emperor's Chamberlain and confidante was viewed with disgust in Rome, but in the East thought worth only a jest or a passing smile. Nor was this all. Not only was the eunuch's high position looked on as an amusing freak of fortune, rather than a portent, but when he became the minister of Arcadius, and his rival Rufinus was dead, then in every household throughout the East there were numerous members who felt a sort of pride in Eutropius' elevation, and were eager to become agents or spies in his interest. Woe to the master who during those four years dared in his slave's presence to hint dissatisfaction with the course of affairs. It was at once reported at headquarters. In the palace, indeed, the chamberlain was wise enough to dissemble, and to gild as far as possible the imperial fetters, though his power was none the less absolute. Little by little Arcadius was isolated from his court, his officers, and even his wife, until his thoughts and daily life, and very pleasures were dictated by Eutropius. But the eunuch was not satisfied with supremacy. He knew that he, too, must have enemies, and that if he would be secure he must be feared—must have, in short, the means at hand for striking a rapid and decisive blow. His enemies, therefore, must not be able to escape him, either by flight or by taking sanctuary in a church; and this reason it was which led to the famous law of A.D. 397, which caused so much sensation among the clergy.

Right of Asylum—A.D. 397.—The right of asylum, of taking shelter in a sanctuary from the pursuit of justice, was a pagan custom, which in the latter days of the Republic had fallen into discredit, owing to its abuse; but with Christianity it once more revived. Christian churches succeeded to Pagan temples as places of refuge for criminals, with the difference, that the superior sanctity attaching to the Christian clergy made the asylum more secure than it had been before, while the abuses were as great as ever. Debtors, bankrupts, criminals of all kinds fled for once in their lives to the interior of a church to evade justice, and so escaped. In September, however, an imperial decree was issued, inspired by Eutropius, which practically, though not verbally, withdrew the right, especially from debtors and " State criminals ;" and State criminals were defined to be those who conspired, not only against the Emperor and his family, but also against his ministers and officers, including, of course, Eutropius. The punishment was death, confiscation of property, and outlawry of children. Well might the great man think himself secure with such a weapon in his hands ; and the irony of fortune was complete, when three years later he sought and found safety for a while in that very right of asylum which his own law had denied to others !

Chrysostom : Life at Antioch—A.D. 397-8.—The next year (A.D. 398) brought upon the scene another actor whose public life was a perpetual conflict with both Eutropius and the Empress. This was John of Antioch, the Golden-Mouthed (Chrysostom), afterwards archbishop of Constantinople. He was at this time fifty years old. Though a Christian born, he had been a favourite pupil of the Pagan Libanius, and was so distinguished for his impetuous flow of ideas and language, that his teacher looked to him as a possible successor. But the passion of asceticism had arisen in his, as in so many hearts, and led him to court solitude, first in his home, then in a convent, then in the desert ; and to practise such fasting and watching as permanently injured his health. From the desert he returned suddenly to Antioch, for he was almost too conscious of his own powers, and was ordained deacon and priest. Like, yet far greater than, Savonarola at Florence, he became a distinct "power" in the state. He drew the wealthy and the educated to listen to him, no less than the poor and the ignorant,—the sinner no less than the saint. And among these casual hearers, as it happened, had been Eutropius.

Death of Nectarius—A.D. 397.—On September 17, 397, Nectarius died, who for sixteen years had been archbishop of Constantinople.   A fierce struggle at once arose as to his successor, for the archbishopric was a post of growing importance, involving great influence in matters of both church and state.   The election was in the hands of the people and clergy of the city, and of the " Honorati," who had filled high offices of state, and the electors were canvassed and unblushingly bribed by the various candidates and their friends.   The clergy were anxious to secure the prize for one of themselves ; but there was an influence at work, which bade fair to overpower all resistance, and to seat an outsider on the archiepiscopal throne. It happened that a number of foreign bishops were assembled at Constantinople, when Nectarius died.   It happened also, that Theophilus, patriarch of Alexandria, was one of them ; and being anxious, for purposes of his own, to forward the promotion of a certain Isidore, presbyter of Alexandria, he secured the interest of a majority of the bishops, who claimed to direct or control the electors in their choice.   Isidore was suspected of being in possession of a highly compromising letter of Theophilus, which he had written in duplicate during the struggle between the Christian Theodosius and the Pagan Maximus (A.D. 394), and given to Isidore to deliver to whichever of the two might be victorious.   Theodosius was victor, and Isidore handed him one of the letters of congratulation ; the other, he said, had been stolen from him, though he was suspected of having reserved it for his own use in the future.   Hence the anxiety of Theophilus to shut his mouth by a golden bribe ; while such an appointment would, at the same time, present himself in the light of patron of the see of Constantinople, and therefore superior to its archbishop ; for Theophilus was as ambitious as he was unscrupulous, and not more unscrupulous than he was learned and able. Learning, however, with him was only a means towards gratifying ambition,—ability a means of evading dangers or realising wishes.

Eutropius appoints Chrysostom.—But amid all the turmoil of canvassing, one part of the electors, the people, became weary of the struggle, and resolved that the nomination should be left unreservedly to the Emperor. Of course, it was Eutropius who made it. He remembered the wonderful preacher whom he had once heard at Antioch, and determined that he was the man to be appointed. It was no easy task, however. Once already he had declined a bishopric ; and even if *his* scruples were overcome, would Antioch consent to part with him or Constantinople to receive him? Secrecy and rapidity were alike essential to success. Orders were accordingly sent to the Count of the East, resident at Antioch, to secure and despatch Chrysostom at once under safe guard to the capital. The order was obeyed. Chrysostom was invited by the Count to a conference outside the city,— was then seized, and committed to a military escort without a word of explanation, and finally arrived at Constantinople more like a criminal for trial than an archbishop designate. His arrival was like the springing of a mine beneath the feet of the bishops and clergy, while the people applauded the unexpected choice. The bishops, indeed, protested against this interference with freedom of election, while Theophilus even refused to ordain Chrysostom. But a whisper from Eutropius led him to see matters in a different light, and the episcopal opposition could be safely disregarded. Chrysostom was ordained by Theophilus, and enthroned as archbishop on February 2, A.D. 398.

Character of Chrysostom.—But the character of

the archbishop was not such as to be an element of peace in the heated political atmosphere of the capital. With all his knowledge and genius, his simplicity and unselfishness, his eloquence and energy, Chrysostom was imperious and somewhat impracticable,—more apt to drive than to persuade men to what he himself thought right. His tenderness for the poor was almost exaggerated into intolerance of the rich. In such a position as his, it was not wise to reverse all at once the hospitable customs of his predecessor, or to cut down as much as possible the expenditure of his household; and certainly it was not prudent to isolate himself (even at meals) from all society. Not only did he thereby lose some opportunity of influence for good over the upper classes, but, in attempting to force his clergy to conform to his example, forfeited much of their loyalty and attachment to himself. His efforts at reform were at once despotic and premature. Nor was he sparing of the frivolities of the court, against which he protested, at first privately and in writing, then openly and in public. What wonder if courtiers, ladies, clergy, and the less strict and honourable of all classes, ere long combined against the self-opinionated churchman, who wished, as it seemed, to set everybody right, and to reverse all that had been usual under the beloved Nectarius.

Hatred of Eutropius—A.D. 399.—If Chrysostom was disliked, he was also respected. But towards Eutropius there was no feeling, save mingled hatred and contempt; and in A.D. 399 a variety of circumstances united against the minister all his isolated enemies, and gave them the opportunity of striking a blow. He had been so unwise as to restrict still further the right of asylum; a step which arrayed against him all the clergy, with Chrysostom at their head. His enemies were overjoyed at the good fortune, which gave them so firm and powerful an ally; still more so, when the Empress, with a woman's rapid insight, threw her weight into the scale, made overtures of alliance to the archbishop, and gave proofs of her sincerity by an excessive though short-lived devotion. Eutropius, however, was blind to his danger, and even assumed the consulship,—a usurpation which seemed only ludicrous to the East, but sent a thrill of indignation throughout the West. It seemed a revolting sacrilege, that a eunuch and a slave should hold the oldest and grandest historic office of the Roman world.

Quarrel between Eutropius and the Empress. —One act of supreme insolence sealed his fate. Conscious at last of the tide of opposition and hatred rising around him, he lost the equanimity which had characterised him. Being aware of the Empress' intrigues with Chrysostom, and meeting her one day accidentally in the palace, he ventured to upbraid her with ingratitude, and to threaten, that he who had raised her to the throne could also banish her from it. The barbarian spirit rose within her. Motioning Eutropius aside, she rushed to her apartments, caught up her two little daughters in her arms, and hastened to the Emperor's presence. For some minutes indignation choked her utterance, while the children, frightened by their mother's emotion, filled the palace with cries and sobs. At last she mastered her passion sufficiently to make the terrified Arcadius understand what had happened, and the outrage she, his Empress, had suffered at the hands of a slave! Even the Emperor was roused by such an insult. Eutropius was immediately summoned to his presence, and before he had time to defend himself, or even realise the state of affairs, heard himself condemned to disgrace and degradation. He was stripped of all his offices, his property was confiscated, and he was bidden to leave the palace at once. Eutropius did not deceive him-

self as to the extent of the catastrophe. He knew that
this was ruin. He passed rapidly through the halls and
chambers where only an hour before his smile had meant
fortune, and his frown destruction, and leaving the palace
by a private door hastened to the great church, not far
distant, pursued, at Eudoxia's orders, by some soldiers and
palace servants. At the door he stooped, and seizing a
handful of dust placed it on his head, as a sign of mourn-
ing, then rapidly strode on to the sanctuary, lifted the
veil separating it from the body of the church, and falling
on his knees clasped suppliantly one of the pillars sup-
porting the altar, and there awaited the archbishop's
coming. Outside the sanctuary, meanwhile, surged to and
fro an ever-increasing crowd, while the tramp of soldiers'
feet and the clash of arms was heard, and presently loud
cries for the archbishop. But Chrysostom was already
on the spot, prepared to vindicate the right which he
had supported even against this very Eutropius, that
the sanctity of the Church was sufficient protection for
the very greatest criminal. Seizing him by the hand, he
led the trembling minister to the sacristy, and concealed
him there for the moment among the sacred vessels, and
then returned to confront the troops, who were threatening to intrude into the holy place. "Bishop," they cried,
as Chrysostom appeared, "Eutropius is concealed here,
and we have orders to seize him. Deliver him up." But
the man before them was not so easily daunted. He forbade them to violate the sanctity of the place ; he bared
his chest when they ventured to threaten, and dared them
to do their worst ; he demanded to be led to the Emperor's
presence. Great was the amazement in the streets, when
Chrysostom was seen escorted by a guard of soldiers
towards the palace,—hardly less great than the exultation
in the amphitheatre, where, at the news of the minister's

downfall, the whole audience rose to their feet as one man and demanded the head of Eutropius.

Interference of Chrysostom. —The firmness of Chrysostom triumphed over the vacillation of Arcadius. For the moment, at least, he assented to the archbishop's demand, that the sanctity of the church should be respected, and the criminal, however guilty, be spared; and even the soldiers were persuaded, though not without difficulty, to obey orders and leave the wretched Eutropius where he was. Thus a slight respite was gained; the claims of the Church were for a while conceded; and it was the very man who would have refused those claims who owed his personal safety to their assertion.

His famous Sermon.—The next day was Sunday. From daybreak the church was filled with eager throngs, anxious to hear what the archbishop would say on the all absorbing topic. Every class of society, all shades of feeling were there represented; but there was one feeling shared by all alike, a sincere hatred of Eutropius, and an overpowering curiosity to see how it would all end. And again, we are reminded of Savonarola, when we think of Chrysostom mounting the pulpit of the great church on that Sunday to address the vast multitude below, and to teach them the meaning of what they saw. Both alike were animated with the idea, that in *their* day and through *their* means, God's cause was triumphing over the powers of earth. Both alike thought they could see the finger of God working by them in the events of which they were a part. All was hushed as the preacher motioned with his hand for silence. It was the perfect hush of high-wrought expectation. But he did not at once break the silence. An impression yet more profound was in store for that expectant crowd. He would appeal to eye no less than to ear.   A thrill of deep emotion passed through the vast congregation when the curtain of the sanctuary was suddenly drawn back, and Eutropius was seen clinging to the altar, pale and trembling.   Then the archbishop turned to his hearers.   "Vanity of vanities," he cried, "all is vanity!   Where now are the splendours and banquets, the acclamations of the streets, the flatteries of the amphitheatre?   Where are the false friends, the swarms of parasites?   Gone—gone for ever!"   Presently, turning to Eutropius, "Did I not tell thee," he continued, "that riches had wings? thou wouldest not believe!—that friends were false? thou wouldest not believe!   Thou didst persecute the Church, and the Church opens her arms to receive thee!"   Then he went on to speak of the contrast between the past and the present, and of all the horrors of death which were agonising the wretched man's heart; and, as the climax of his sermon, touched on that which to him was the central point of interest, the glory to the Church of protecting so great a criminal, so bitter a foe.   Last of all, he invited his audience to accompany him to the palace, and to join him in imploring pardon for Eutropius.   But in this he overshot the mark, and mistook his own power over a susceptible but vindictive and passionate audience.   The chamberlain had been too overbearing, unscrupulous, and selfish in his day of greatness to awaken any active sympathy in his fall.

Condemnation of Eutropius.—Eutropius remained in sanctuary for some days, and then suddenly disappeared.   It was presently known that he had left the church under a promise of his life being spared, if he would go quietly on board ship and allow himself to be conveyed to Cyprus; and, meanwhile, a commission of inquiry was named, under the presidency of the prætorian prefect, Aurelian, before which evidence was laid to show that the minister had been guilty of high treason, especially in using imperial insignia during his consulate. The legal punishment was death. At first, however, Arcadius felt genuine scruples as to authorising the execution of such a sentence, in face of the promise which alone had drawn Eutropius from his refuge. But his council were urgent that the promise only extended to Constantinople itself, not to other parts of the Empire; while Eudoxia pressed eagerly for the punishment of death, feeling that as long as Eutropius lived her power was not assured, over either the Empire or her husband. Overpowered by this joint pressure Arcadius yielded. An imperial decree was shortly published, deposing Eutropius from all his dignities, confiscating his property to the treasury, and ordering the demolition of all the statues of him in every town and village. Finally, a vessel was sent to Cyprus to bring him home for punishment. He was brought to Chalcedon and there beheaded.

Sequel of his Downfall.—Arcadius, however, had only exchanged one tyrant for another—the acute and supple man of the world for an imperious and hot-headed woman. Eudoxia was now mistress of the situation, surrounded with favourites both male and female, seeing with their eyes and hearing with their ears. It was not long before her pride and self-will brought her into conflict with Chrysostom, and occasioned that famous struggle which involved the whole East in confusion, and during which the archbishop was twice exiled and twice condemned, St Sophia was reduced to ashes, and Constantinople was half destroyed. It remains to trace the history of this conflict between the Empress and the archbishop in the next chapter.

CHAPTER V

CHRYSOSTOM AND THE EMPRESS EUDOXIA.

Difficulties of Chrysostom. — After the fall of Eutropius the Eastern Empire was ruled by a woman. Arcadius—less than thirty, yet prematurely old—was too timid and too indolent to resist Eudoxia's superior force of character; and she far too imperious and ambitious to be content with anything short of absolute power. There was, perhaps, only one human being whom the Emperor feared not less than he feared the Empress, and that was the archbishop. Not only was he sincerely afraid of embroiling himself with the Church generally, but Chrysostom was the recognised patron of the poor and the lower classes, and on the few occasions on which he had visited the palace it had been almost without exception to prefer complaint against the injustice or corruptions of the court, and to threaten ecclesiastical censures; and on each occasion Arcadius had been forced to yield. The Empress soon discerned in this bold and eloquent priest a rival, whose influence might be fatal to her own; and selfish ambition led her ere long to become the centre of a vast intrigue, whose object was Chrysostom's destruction. There was no lack of willing allies, for there were few classes, save the very poor, whose susceptibilities he did not succeed in offending. Fashionable ladies, pagans, monks, even priests

and deaconesses were arrayed against him from one cause
or another ; and as he was peculiar in his habits, impetuous, and terribly in earnest, there were plenty of
stories, ill-natured or amusing, for the world at large to
spread and discuss, which were carefully told and doubtless improved in the telling to court circles.　Three great
ladies in particular were, beside the Empress, his sworn
enemies,—Marsa, Castricia, and Eugraphia,—for he was
merciless to their special foibles.　In his passionate tenderness for the poor he could hardly find words of scorn
strong enough to express his contempt for the luxuries
and follies of the rich, and, whether in the drawing-room
or the pulpit, did not mince matters.　He almost condescended to personalities.　That wealthy ladies of middle
age should take the lead in society, not by alms and simplicity of life, but by flirtations and intrigues, by rouge
and false hair, and by setting outrageous fashions, seemed
to him scandalous ; and when he mounted the *ambo*
and fixed his eyes on the ladies' gallery running round the
nave, and inveighed against the indelicate dresses and
ordinary fashions of high society, it is intelligible that the
allusions were relished by the crowd below, and gave great
offence to those whom he all but named.　Nor were the
mendicant monks, who thronged the streets of the capital,
and degraded the service of religion by grotesque cos-
tumes and unworthy buffooneries, less hostile to Chrysostom.　He had tried to suppress their convents, or to
compel the monks to labour and to adopt a more seden-
tary life.　He had tried, but failed.　And as the attempt
exasperated, so the failure encouraged them in their hostility.　The pagan party, meanwhile, watched the struggle
with curiosity.　Though indifferent to Eudoxia, yet they
disliked the narrowmindedness, as they thought it, of
Chrysostom, and naturally sympathised with the less

formal and precise views of the court and the fashionable world.

Chrysostom unpopular with the Clergy.—Nor was the archbishop less unpopular among the ministers of the Church itself. From the first he had set his face like a flint against the luxury, greed, and avarice of the clergy, and thus raised up a host of enemies among those by whom he was daily surrounded. And indeed there were vices prevalent among them calling for the sharpest reform. It was not with Chrysostom as with those prelates of a later age, who fought a long and arduous battle against the marriage of the clergy, and by sheer exercise of despotic power won a victory over human weakness. He had, indeed, like them, to face an inveterate custom of long standing, in defence of which all sorts of feelings were enlisted against him ; but it was a custom, which, though innocent in its origin and capable of innocent use, was also open to terrible abuse. It had become the practice within comparatively recent times for the clergy to introduce into their houses a "beloved sister" (ἀγαπητή), to be an associate in all good works, and to live with them. But too often in this world "noblest things find vilest using ;" and what was in theory a beautiful and innocent fashion, suited to a society whose tone should be too lofty for human passion and weakness, degenerated in practice into a mere excuse for idleness, worldliness, and sensuality. Marriage, indeed, was a recognised and honourable estate, which had its safeguards as well as temptations; but the relation just described had temptations without safeguards. If nothing worse, the priest certainly could not give that undivided attention to clerical duties, which his celibacy implied that he would. His moral tone was gradually lowered. He would be tempted (it is Chrysostom's own accusation) to waste time and energy in tittle-tattle and shopping. He would become enslaved to petty interests, or need money to support his household, and feel it no shame to lay hands on Church funds to which he had access, or on legacies or alms for the poor. Finally, too often, even before he suspected danger, he would be surprised by passion and tempted to live in open sin. It was clearly a dangerous custom. Yet Chrysostom's attack upon it raised against him a host of enemies, whose interests were bound up in defeating the projected reform.

Unpopular with the Rich.—Nor was Chrysostom's tenderness for the poor a source of popularity, except among the poor themselves. He held those peculiar views with regard to the duties and responsibilities attaching to wealth, which were not more popular with the wealthy then than they are now. He was " tribune of the people " almost as much as "priest." If he was pained by the sufferings of the poor, he was not less shocked at the inequalities of society. In his eyes the selfishness and cowardice of the rich was only equalled by the marvellous goodness and unselfishness of the poor. It was poverty which had inspired Elijah with courage to rebuke Ahab, John the Baptist to rebuke Herod, and, as every one might infer, Chrysostom to rebuke Eudoxia and her luxurious court.

Even his private habits and most innocent practices were sneered at and misrepresented by his enemies. The asceticism of his earlier years had produced a permanent weakness of digestion, which prevented his entering into society ; he was often ill and dared not touch wine ; yet because he always dined alone, for there was hardly anything which he could eat with impunity, and refused all invitations, even to the palace, he was accused of indulging in solitary orgies. No man was more charitable than Chrysostom ; yet his immense charities did not save him from the accusation of stinginess or avarice, because his life was so simple. He founded hospitals for the sick; he urged the wealthy to contribute to them; he even desired that every house should have its vacant room, in which to shelter the poor and homeless. "Christ is at your doors," he says in one of his sermons; "open to Him. You ought to give Him your best chamber, but He only asks for the least corner. Place Him where you will, in the attic with your servants, in the cellar, in the stable with your horses. Only take Him in." And yet the rancour of his enemies accused him of avarice and gluttony!

The Friends of Chrysostom.—But it was also a matter of course that a man of so elevated a character, of such courage and strength of will, should attach to himself devoted friends. And the devotion of his friends compensated in some degree for the general atmosphere of dislike and suspicion in which he lived. There were some few, indeed, like Serapion, the Egyptian, whose devotion to him (or, perhaps, to themselves) was greater than their discretion, and who, by flattery and adroit persuasion, fostered the weaker side—the imperiousness and obstinacy of the archbishop's character. But there were others, the salt of the earth, women as well as men, who clung to him faithfully through evil and good report, and were the great consolation of his life.

Chrysostom, indeed, was a man to make both friends and enemies; but his friends loved him "with a love stronger than death." He has been compared to a "day in spring-time, bright and rainy, and glittering through its rain,"—a man with faults, indeed (and who has not faults?), yet of "noble earnestness and singleness of purpose"—"a bright, cheerful, gentle soul . . . . with a vigour, elasticity, and sunniness of mind all his own."[1]

[1] *cf.* Newman's "Historical Sketches." "Last Years of St. Chrysostom.'

Intrigues against Chrysostom—A.D. 401.—The war between Eudoxia and Chrysostom, which ended in his banishment and death, began in the year A.D. 401. An appeal had been made to him in the previous year, while a synod of twenty-seven Asiatic bishops was sitting, under his presidency, at Constantinople, to investigate certain charges publicly made against one of the bishops present, Antoninus of Ephesus. The archbishop was at first unwilling to interfere ; but the charges were precise and grave, and yielding at last to the pressure of popular indignation, he called on the accuser, a certain Bishop Eusebius, to present his proofs before a council to be convened for the purpose. Meanwhile Antoninus died, and Ephesus at once became a prey to the bribery, intrigues, and violence of competing candidates for the bishopric. In the universal confusion there seemed to the better disposed part of the population only one means of escape from the evils around them, an appeal to Chrysostom. Accordingly a letter was dispatched, entreating his presence. On January 9, A.D. 401, he started from Constantinople for Ephesus, leaving Severianus, Bishop of Gabala, to discharge the duties of bishop during his absence. Now this man was a type of a class especially prevalent at this time,—an adventurer, ambitious and vain, and open to corruption. He had a good presence, a real gift of eloquence, a large knowledge of Scripture. He affected a deep admiration for Chrysostom, but in heart was jealous of his fame, and like many other Asiatics, was eager to share in the glory and the more substantial advantages, which this eloquence had won for him. Here was an ally worth winning indeed by the enemies of Chrysostom at court ; and a little judicious flattery soon won him. His sermons were pronounced by a fashionable audience superior to Chrysostom's, and the Empress even went so far as to transgress ordinary custom, and, instead of waiting for the archbishop's return, to hasten the baptism of her lately born son, afterwards Theodosius II., and had the ceremony performed by Severianus. But it was no mere ceremony; the administration of the rite (according to Eastern ideas) conferred on a priest a kind of spiritual paternity, and bound him to the newly baptized by a bond that lasted through life. And thus Severianus was no longer a mere foreign bishop accidentally sojourning in Constantinople, but a prelate attached to the court and the Empress by a very special tie. For the same reason, also, he was an enemy of Chrysostom.

There was yet another ally whom the court party gained during the archbishop's absence, and by means even more dubious. Acacius, Bishop of Berœa, a man far advanced in years and respected wherever he was known, had been a firm friend of Chrysostom's, and being in Constantinople on business, was invited to stay at the episcopal palace. The old man had the failing of many old men, and looked forward with some complacency to the comforts and luxuries he would find there; but he reckoned without his host. The archbishop's asceticism applied to his friends no less than himself. Simplicity of life was the rule for all alike within the palace; and Acacius, already piqued by what he thought his friend's want of courtesy towards an old man, was easily roused to irritation, and then dislike, and then hostility, by a dexterous insinuation from the court that such treatment was not only discourtesy, but studied insult.

Troubles with the Arians.—Chrysostom returned only to discover the defection of his supposed friends, and to find that his difficulties were increased. Not only did his own impetuosity of temper betray him into sarcastic remarks, the drift of which was obvious, about Jezebel and her friends, but he quarrelled with Severianus, and was then forced into an open, if hollow, reconciliation. A further unlucky circumstance about this time tended to increase the prevalent feeling—so fatal when it exists, and so difficult to eradicate—that Chrysostom was a stubborn and maladroit person, whose presence always meant failure if not strife. During the reign of the orthodox Theodosius, the Arians had not been permitted to have churches within the walls of Constantinople. They had protested, but in vain. Under the more feeble Arcadius, however, and relying on the "barbarian" influence then so strongly felt throughout the East, the Arians hoped to regain at least toleration. At first they ventured only to assemble in small bodies on Sundays and feast days, under the various porticoes and in the streets, and so to go to their churches. Thus gradually arose formal "processions," unrecognised rather than unobserved. But while Chrysostom was absent in Asia, Severianus had winked at their growing boldness, until the weekly procession had developed into something like a weekly challenge to their antagonists, with chants and litanies sung as they marched, and had too often degenerated into mere provocation and insult. Immediately on his return the archbishop called upon the civil powers to stop the scandal, and when nothing was done, proceeded to organise a counter-demonstration of the faithful, with more orthodox litanies and chants. In effect this was a direct invitation to riot, if not bloodshed. When the angry controversialists met in the streets, and a struggle ensued, and a servant of the Empress was killed and many wounded, and Arcadius threatened to fine the præfect heavily if such a scene occurred again, it was perhaps not just, but it certainly was not strange, that the odium fell upon Chrysostom. To him, probably more than to any man, the whole thing was a grief and a shame; yet he had to suffer for the evil passions of others and for his own mistake.

The "Tall Brothers" of the Nitrian Desert.—It might have seemed ill fortune enough to have succeeded in arousing the enmity of so many and such diverse enemies at once as the Arian heretics, the heathen party, the foreign bishops in Constantinople, the monks, and the world of fashion and high life. But beyond this Chrysostom became presently entangled in the fortunes of the so-called "Tall Brothers" of Nitria, and again exposed to the intrigues of his old enemy Theophilus. These four brothers, named respectively Ammonius, Dioscorus, Euthymius, and Eusebius, were anchorites of great repute for sanctity and learning, living in the desert of Nitria, between the Nile and the Libyan mountains. For a long time they had been the glory of the patriarchate of Alexandria; the eldest had accompanied Athanasius on his exile to Rome and the West; and Theophilus, ever alive to his own interests, had for a while carefully cultivated their acquaintance, and even tried to ordain three of them in succession bishops. But they steadily refused, much to his chagrin, and at last an obscure quarrel, originating in the avarice of Theophilus and the probity of the "brothers," turned the one-sided friendship into bitter hostility. The patriarch accused the "brothers" of the heresy of Origenism, of denying the "personality" of God. They might, indeed, have been well content to be confounded with a Jerome or an Epiphanius in the anathemas of a Theophilus; but a yet graver quarrel ensued, fraught with yet graver consequences. The enmity of Theophilus could not be satisfied without revenge. In an interview between them and himself relative to the pardon of a certain Isidore, who had offended the patriarch, he pretended to have been in-

sulted, threw them into prison, sent them in chains to
Nitria, excommunicated them, and finally, ordered the
various convents, with which they were connected, to
destroy at once all their books that were in any way
tainted with heresy. Spies were surreptitiously introduced into the monasteries to watch whether the order
was obeyed ; and when obedience was delayed, a pre-
concerted petition was got up and presented to Theophilus, praying him to take action in the matter. This
was all that was wanted. The præfect was requested
to lend some troops for the occasion, at whose head
marched the patriarch in person, like a general to battle.
The expedition was timed to reach the scene of action in
the darkness of night, and then ensued what to our ears
sounds almost incredible, a veritable night attack on the
unsuspecting convents, which, under pretence of a search
for heretical books, were forcibly entered, pillaged, and
in some cases even burnt to the ground. The monks fled
in all directions, and with them the " brothers," on whose
capture Theophilus was most intent. The rendezvous
was to be the borders of Egypt and Syria. But among
300 who had escaped, age, fatigue, and misery wrought sad
havoc. Only eighty reached the rendezvous safely, whence
after some deliberation they resolved, on the advice of
Isidore and the " brothers," to repair to Constantinople
and lay their appeal before the Emperor and Chrysostom,
never doubting to obtain justice from the former, and
from the latter protection. Out of eighty only fifty
reached Constantinople. The archbishop at once interested himself in their case, and satisfied himself of
their orthodoxy. He promised to call a speedy council,
or to obtain their pardon from the patriarch, meanwhile
advising them to keep clear of the Emperor, and not bring
an ecclesiastical matter before a civil judge. As for him-

self he could not, he said, receive them under his own roof or at his table while still under excommunication, but they might lodge in the cloisters of the church. The great alarm of Chrysostom, in fact, was that the unsophisticated monks, in their indignation or impatience, would carry their matter straight to the Emperor, and that then the unedifying sight would be seen of the second bishop in the East placed on his trial before a lay judge. To prevent this it was that he wrote a letter to Theophilus, conjuring him to pardon the fugitives as a favour to himself. But Theophilus was a good hater, and the advocacy of Chrysostom was to him a sufficient reason for continuing his persecution. He returned a curt answer to the archbishop's letter, bidding him practically mind his own business, and shortly afterwards sent an embassy, consisting of a bishop and four abbots, to request the Emperor to banish from Constantinople certain fugitive monks, condemned and excommunicated for rebellion, heresy, and magic. The last word was an artful addition to a false accusation. Magic was "high treason," and regarded with horror, as implying evil intentions towards the head of the state. It was a crime to be investigated by a special commission, and punishable with banishment or death. To represent these poor monks as a band of magicians, therefore, was a master-stroke of policy, and was certain to arouse against them popular indignation, the suspicion of the Emperor, and the hostility of all time-servers. The charge was false indeed, and known to be false ; but that made no difference. The Patriarch of Alexandria was too great a man in Constantinople for his words to be slighted ; for Alexandria fed Constantinople, and a large part of the population of the capital were Egyptians, engaged in the corn trade—that is, spiritual subjects and political dependants of the patriarch. To offend the patriarch therefore was no light matter. The "brothers," indignant at the false charges brought against them, and the scorn to which they were subjected, and finding no help in Chrysostom, who recoiled from exposing a brother bishop to a civil court, resolved at last to appeal to Arcadius. The enemies of Chrysostom exulted, and strained every nerve to widen the breach, and encourage the exiles to throw themselves on the mercy of the Emperor, and even more of the Empress. In short, the "brothers" became the fashion, and were run after by all the great people of Constantinople. Presently a meeting was arranged, apparently accidental, between them and the Empress at a church in the suburbs, at which, while imploring their prayers and blessing, she promised to use all efforts to obtain the convocation of a synod and the arraignment of their enemy ; nor had many days passed before a synod was convoked, and Theophilus summoned to appear.

Intrigues of Theophilus.—The strategy of Theophilus to escape the danger was admirable. Two points seemed clear to him,—first, that Chrysostom was probably at the bottom of the matter; and, secondly, that it would be well to secure an ally for the impending battle. If possible, therefore, a counterblow must be aimed at Chrysostom. An ally he secured in Epiphanius, Bishop of Salamis. Epiphanius was a man whom the patriarch had attacked years before as a heretic. He was now more than eighty years of age, and with advancing years had lost something of the generous earnestness of earlier days, while a long pre-eminence in the Church as a doctrinal authority had somewhat impaired the balance of his own judgment, and his respect for the judgment of others. He was within a little of being a tyrant, and had all the air of infallibility. On such a vain and simple nature the patriarch knew well how to play. First, he professed sorrow at ever having been misled into Origenism, and expressed gratitude to his friend through whom he had seen his errors. Next, he suggested that the real question at issue in the coming council would be the truth or error of Origen's views, and urged him, therefore, in concert with his suffragans in Cyprus, to draw up a statement of the orthodox doctrine thereon, and forward a copy to the archbishop, who, as a friend of the "brothers," was presumably a partner in their false notions. Could the idea fail to occur to the mind of Epiphanius, so dexterously insinuated, that the glory might be before him of converting Chrysostom, as it appeared he had converted Theophilus, and that he might be able once again to guide, perhaps preside over the decisions of a great council! And yet the poor old man was only a cat's-paw. Chrysostom returned a cold answer to Epiphanius' statements of doctrine, and the old man was irritated. His authority was questioned, and he resolved to go to Constantinople and recall the archbishop to his duty. But when he arrived, he was so ill-advised as to make peace impossible, first, by ordaining off-hand a deacon of whom he knew nothing, and that in another man's diocese; and, secondly, by refusing to reside in the palace unless the archbishop would excommunicate the "brothers" and interdict the writings of Origen. But Chrysostom steadily refused to anticipate the decision of the pending council, and so the enmity between them was aggravated. It was not, however, for long. The excitement of the actual conflict, and an interview with the "brothers," in which he discovered that he had in ignorance been wronging them, determined the aged bishop to abandon a strife to which he was no longer equal, and to turn his back on the capital. He hastened to set sail, but it was only to die on the voyage homewards.

Council of the Oak—A D. 403.—Meantime Theophilus was on his way to the capital, and was met at Chalcedon by twenty-eight bishops from various parts of the East summoned to attend the council in July (A.D. 403). The Emperor assigned a palace in Pera for his use, and the patriarch lost no time after his arrival in conciliating or securing the goodwill of the court ladies by presents of silks and scents. The lower orders were not so easily won; and indeed so great was the agitation among Chrysostom's friends, the artisans and labouring classes, that it was deemed hardly safe to hold the council in the city, and a suburb of Chalcedon, on the opposite side of the Bosporus, was fixed upon. Hence the name of the "Council of the Oak." There were eighty bishops present at the time in Constantinople, but no more than forty-five were ever present at the council, the residue remaining with Chrysostom on the other side. The Patriarch of Alexandria presided.

The first witness summoned was Chrysostom's archdeacon, an official who, presiding over the external administration of the diocese, was supposed to be specially behind the scenes. This man owed Chrysostom a grudge, and now trumped up a series of charges against him, which were only serious from the position of the man who made them. The accusations comprised personal violence, insult, violation of the canons, theft, immorality; and a citation was presently served on the archbishop from the council summoning him to appear before them. It ran as follows :—"The Holy Synod assembled at the Oak to John. We have received a schedule of accusation against thee, denouncing thee as guilty of an infinity of crimes. We require thee to appear here before us, and bring with thee the priests Serapion and Tigrius, for we have need of them." To this curt and insolent letter, omitting even

the archbishop's title, two answers were at once returned:
one from the bishops of Chrysostom's party, warning
Theophilus not to interfere in another man's province;
the other from Chrysostom himself, protesting against
their place of meeting (which by every rule should have
been the city of Constantinople), but nevertheless agreeing
to appear before them, provided that his personal enemies
—the Patriarch Theophilus, Acacius of Beræa, Antiochus
of Ptolemais, and Severianus of Gabala—were not present.
Hereupon the *soi-disant* council despatched two priests of
the church of Constantinople to cite the archbishop once
more by word of mouth. " Why delayest thou?" they
said; "the council expects thee, and thou hast to clear
thyself, if thou canst, of the crimes alleged against thee."
It was a studied insult to cite an archbishop thus by the
mouth of two of his own clergy, and Chrysostom felt it
to be such. He immediately returned a verbal answer
by three of his own bishops, protesting against such a
step. But the council was already in a ferment after the
receipt of his first reply; and when the three emissaries
appeared and delivered their message, an extraordinary
scene ensued. The reverend fathers rose from their seats
and condescended, some to menaces and insults, some
even to violence. One unfortunate ambassador received
a severe blow; another had his clothes torn to ribbons;
while the third, yet more unhappy, was graced with the
chain originally intended for the archbishop's neck, had
he been rash enough to appear, was dragged out of the
church, thrown into a boat, and committed to the more
tender mercies of winds and waves. Twice again was
Chrysostom summoned to appear before the council;
and twice he returned the same answer as before. At
last, foiled in his efforts to entice the archbishop over
the water, and so to secure his person, Theophilus re-

solved if possible to enlist the Emperor's feelings in the struggle.

Condemnation of Chrysostom.—With this idea, an addition was made to the previous charges, to the effect that the archbishop had publicly insulted the Empress in his sermons, comparing her to Jezebel and Herodias. At its twelfth sitting the council proceeded to judgment, in the absence of the accused. Forty-five bishops were present and voted. Chrysostom was condemned to deposition from the archbishopric, of which immediate notice was sent to the metropolitan clergy; and a full report (*relatio*) of the acts of the council and the grounds of condemnation was dispatched to the Emperors Arcadius and Honorius. The execution of the sentence was left to the civil power.

Sermon against the Empress.—Three days passed, and Chrysostom was still in occupation of his church and palace, notwithstanding that the Imperial assent had been given to the sentence. All was confusion and indecision in Constantinople. Ever and anon an Imperial officer appeared at the palace, requiring the archbishop to prepare to go. The order was always disregarded, and the officer retired. Meanwhile Arcadius shrank from using force; for vast crowds of people voluntarily mounted guard night and day round the palace; force would have been resisted and blood shed. The universal cry was for "a general council"—a larger synod to try the cause again. A single rash act brought matters to a crisis. Severianus of Gabala, two days after the condemnation, was bold enough to cross the water, enter a church, and deliver an address on recent events, commenting severely on Chrysostom's pride. The audience rose upon him in such fury that he had difficulty in escaping. Nor was the archbishop himself less angry, believing the attack to have been really imagined and directed by the Empress Eudoxia; and his anger found relief in a famous sermon which sealed his fate. After describing the storms and waves which threatened to engulf him, he bade his hearers not be discouraged, for that Christ would never forsake His Church. "And do you know, my brethren," he continued, "why it is they seek my destruction? It is because I have no rich hangings, no grand dinners, no open house. . . . Herodias, too, is here; and Herodias dances, and demands the head of John! My brethren, it is a time for tears; for everything is tending to *dishonour* (ἀδοξία). Money alone gives honour and glory. Yet hear what David says, 'If riches increase, set not your hearts upon them.' And who was David? Was he not a man raised to a king's throne—but," again almost naming Eudoxia (εὐδοξία), "he never showed himself the slave of a woman! O woe, woe to women, who close their ears to the warnings of Heaven, and, drunk not with wine but with avarice and hate, besiege their husbands with evil counsels."

Deportation of Chrysostom to Chalcedon.— There was a woman in the palace hard by whose husband was her very slave, and whose character belied her name, a second Herodias to a second John, to whose ears these harsh words were carried at once. And at once the blow fell. The next day an Imperial officer of high grade presented himself, and ordered the archbishop, in the Emperor's name, to quit the town immediately. And this time there was no hesitation. A vessel was ready, and in case of need a military force at hand. To spare needless bloodshed Chrysostom acquiesced. Leaving the cloisters by a private door, he lay concealed with a guard until nightfall, and was then conducted by retired streets to the harbour and placed on board a vessel, which instantly weighed anchor. The Propontis was crossed, and their prisoner landed not far from Chalcedon, while they returned. But this was to be within grasp of his enemies. It was still night, and the exile hired a boat, put out to sea again, and coasting southward to the Gulf of Astacus, landed near the little town of Prænetus, where a friend of his had a villa, and there concealed himself.

Riot and Earthquake in Constantinople.—That was a sad night for Constantinople. Half alarmed, half indignant, vast crowds flocked to the churches when these events became known; and when the churches were filled, formed meetings in the streets and colonnades. But there was no violence, only a hushed and foreboding despondency. And the next day was yet sadder. Theophilus, flushed with triumph, crossed from Chalcedon, recommended the various priests, his friends, to take possession of their respective churches, and himself essayed to force an entrance into the archiepiscopal basilica. But force was met with force. A veritable battle ensued. Presently, to make the matter yet worse, soldiers appeared on the scene. Blood was freely shed. Churches were piled with dead bodies—were barricaded, besieged, and stormed like fortresses. And as the excitement rose higher, and bloodshed whetted the thirst for blood, the massacre became indiscriminate, innocent victims were cut down in the streets, and even monks were slain and their convents sacked. A day of horror was followed by a night of terror; for Constantinople was shaken from end to end by a shock of earthquake, and even the Imperial sleep disturbed. In an agony of fright at this manifest display of the wrath of Heaven, Eudoxia besought her husband to recall the archbishop, and with her own hand wrote him a letter repudiating all share in his banishment.

Chrysostom Recalled.—Before daybreak a hurried envoy was dispatched, and then a second, and yet a third, to deliver this letter, and to urge Chrysostom to return at once, and save the city from destruction. He returned, and his progress was one scene of triumph and rejoicing. Despite his own wishes, the exultant people compelled him to repair to his own church without delay, and with violent though loving hands lifted him to the pulpit and implored him to address and bless them. To his adversaries there remained only flight or concealment. Indeed the council broke up the same day without finishing its business. Theophilus set out for Alexandria, Severianus for Gabala; and an Imperial decree, at the instance of Chrysostom, was signed and issued for a new council.

Statues of the Empress.—But fear is not as lasting as pride or hate, and with its causes the Empress' fear passed away. Not so her dislike to her old enemy, which, ere two months had passed, circumstances fanned again into a furious flame of hostility and persecution. Whether suggested by her own pride or the servility of her courtiers, an idea presented itself to the mind of the Empress as foolish as it was unprecedented. She succeeded in inducing Arcadius to allow statues of herself to be set up in the empire and " adored," as were those of the Emperor. To the West this seemed simply monstrous, and even to the East strange, and rather ridiculous. The Emperors were incarnations, so to say, of the great Roman people, and as such, in a sense, divine; but Empresses—what were they beyond being wives and mothers of Emperors? Eudoxia, however, insisted; and Arcadius gave way. Above all, she set store by a silver statue of herself, erected on a porphyry column, and placed in the centre of the Forum, where, with the church of St Sophia on one hand, and the senate-house on the other, the palace beyond, and the busiest street of Constantinople at her feet, she might seem, as it were, to dominate palace, church,

and city, and even to inspire the wisdom of the senate.
The statue was inaugurated with rejoicings worthy of
the occasion, which lasted for several days. But the
austere soul of Chrysostom was disgusted with the scenes
that went on just outside his church, and with the inter-
ruptions of services and sermons caused by the music and
shouting. He complained to the prefect. But the prefect was too wise a man of the world to offend an Empress needlessly, and referred the archbishop to Eudoxia.
Next day the noise and interruption was even greater,
and Chrysostom deeming it, perhaps not unnaturally, a
bravado and provocation, not only of the prefect, but of
the higher powers, ascended the pulpit, and once more, as
so often before, inveighed against all who took part in or
countenanced such doings. His personal allusions were
soon the talk of the town, and duly reported to Eudoxia,
who hastened to the palace and demanded from the Emperor " vengeance " on her enemy; and the Emperor,
deeply offended, declared that it was time to put an end
to such factious insults ! Once more, then, the court became the centre of intrigues directed against the archbishop's peace and life; once more his old enemies appeared upon the scene, and insidious suggestions were
heard to the effect that the council which Chrysostom so
earnestly desired might, perhaps, by good management
turn out to his ruin. Indeed, all efforts were now
directed to this end, that the council should be held in
Constantinople, that is, under the eye and influence of
the court, and that it should not rescind, but repeat and
confirm the decisions of the Council of the Oak. Arcadius, meanwhile, refused to hold any intercourse with the
archbishop, or even to communicate at his church (as was
the immemorial custom) on Christmas day (A.D. 403).

Council of Constantinople—A.D. 404.—The council assembled in January A.D. 404, and as before, fell at once into two parties; and its difficulties began at once. How could it reconsider the decisions of a former council without going into details? How go into details when many of the accusers and witnesses were dead, or far away? Worst of all, how face the eloquent indignation of Chrysostom, who would have to be heard? Were these not reasons for temporising and delay? At this juncture an Egyptian bishop, and we know in whose spirit he spoke, suggested a preliminary question—was it in their power, or indeed in that of any ecclesiastical tribunal, to try the archbishop's case at all? By virtue of ecclesiastical law, he was no longer either bishop or priest; and the speaker proceeded to quote two canons passed at a council held at Antioch in A.D. 341, under the presidency of the Emperor Constantius, of which the former declared that a bishop deposed by a council, and taking upon himself to resume his functions without reversal of sentence, or without being reinstated by his judges, should be *ipso facto* excommunicate; the latter, that a bishop or priest thus excommunicate, and continuing to excite trouble in the Church, should be dealt with by the secular power. If, therefore, the canons of Antioch applied to this case, it would seem that the archbishop, who had been deposed by the Council of the Oak, and had resumed his position without their authority, was excommunicate thereby, and not in a position to appeal to another council, being practically out of the Church. Chrysostom, however, was as well acquainted with Church history as his enemies, and succeeded in placing them in a disagreeable dilemma. The Council of Antioch was a council of Arians, presided over by an Arian Emperor, and its object was the deposition of the orthodox Athanasius; its canons, therefore, were Arian and heretical.

With what grace, then, could an orthodox council appeal to the canons of a heterodox council, if they cared to preserve their orthodoxy ? And further, whether orthodox or heterodox, the canons quoted did not apply to his case, for he had not been deposed by a genuine council, but by a packed meeting of his private enemies, who had condemned him unheard, and not even conveyed to him their own sentence of deposition. The question thus raised by Chrysostom as to the orthodoxy of the Council of Antioch became at once the general topic of conversation in public and private circles, and was hotly discussed without much effect. At length a committee of twelve was nominated—six from each side—to discuss the question in the Emperor's presence,—a struggle in which the spokesman on the archbishop's side gained a ready victory by inviting his opponents to declare their faith to be that of the council whose canons they relied on. They shrank from declaring themselves heretics, and so the discussion ended.

Chrysostom forbidden to Leave the Palace.—Meanwhile a straw began to show which way the tide was turning—the fashionable world began to desert the archbishop's sermons ; and he felt it acutely, and touched on it severely more than once. Nay more, Easter was approaching with its grand series of services and ceremonies, and more than 3,000 catechumens were awaiting their baptism at the archbishop's hands on Easter Eve. The Emperor chose this solemn time to forbid his entering the church, and ordered him to confine himself to the palace adjoining. Chrysostom obeyed, but it was with a heavy heart, and with painful uncertainty as to whether it was his duty to obey. Further reflection convinced him it was not ; and he resolved at last to brave consequences, and to perform in person the duties which were rightly his.

His Disobedience.—On the morning of Easter Eve the archbishop left his involuntary prison and proceeded to St. Sophia. The officers in charge of him had strict orders to use no violence; so that, baffled by his firmness, and unable to persuade where they could not prevent, they had nothing to do but to hasten to the palace and report to the Emperor what was happening. Arcadius was both irritated and alarmed, and at the same time at a loss what to do, for he shrank from using force at such a season. But his counsellors, especially the Bishops Antiochus and Acacius, were at no loss. Careless of consequences, they took on their own heads the responsibility of his condemnation before the council, and urged Arcadius to act at once. And so the flood-gates of violence and riot were once more thrown open. The services at St. Sophia had begun, the catechumens were succeeding each other in order at the font, when a noise was heard at the doors, and a body of troops, sword in hand, marched into the Basilica. The archbishop first was seized and dragged off. The soldiers then divided, and, so to say, swept the church. Men, women, children, were struck, knocked down, and even wounded, and the sanctuary itself desecrated. The frightened crowds fled, and reassembled to conclude their service in the Baths of Constantius. But there, too, after a short delay, they were followed and ejected with more bloodshed and greater violence. Even some few, who still persevered and tried to finish in the country what they had begun in the city, were tracked, plundered, beaten, and dispersed. And then began a more odious persecution still. House after house was visited by police in search of " Joannites," as Chrysostom's followers were named; and the prisons were filled to overflowing with clergy and laity, whose only crime was fidelity and love.

The Council Ratifies his Condemnation.—The council in the meantime, whose existence had been almost overlooked during the last few days, concluded its business, and, as everybody had foreseen, bowed to the sinister influences all around, and signified its ratification of the acts of the Council of the Oak. "John had been deposed, and having thereupon resumed his functions without license, was *ipso facto* excommunicate. Let the civil power therefore now act." In accordance with this recommendation Chrysostom was kept a close prisoner in his palace, from Easter to Whitsuntide, preparatory to sterner measures.

Chrysostom Appeals to the West.—Despairing of any further justice from his brethren in the East, he used the interval in composing and dispatching his famous "Appeal to the West," and specially to the three great bishops of Italy,—Innocent of Rome, Venerius of Milan, and Chromatius of Aquileia. It detailed the disorders of the Church in the East, and described the fearful scenes in St. Sophia, concluding with an earnest request that his cause might be fairly tried before an Œcumenical Council. Four bishops and two deacons were the bearers of these letters, who would also be able to attest as eye-witnesses the truth of what was stated. Innocent was profoundly impressed, though his immediate reply was calm and dignified. He ordered a solemn fast throughout the Roman Church, and prayers to be offered for the restoration of peace and unity to the East. At the same time he wrote two letters—one to Theophilus, announcing his intention of summoning a general council; the other to Chrysostom, sympathising with and consoling him under his afflictions. More than this, he used his great influence with Honorius to induce him to espouse Chrysostom's cause with his brother Arcadius.

Second Exile of Chrysostom—A.D. 404.—But events were marching rapidly at Constantinople. Two attempts were made to assassinate the archbishop, and barely failed. The population was growing more and more excited; his enemies more and more earnest to induce Arcadius to act. Again they undertook to bear the whole responsibility of his deposition. Thus urged, and perhaps eager to buy a little peace at any price, the Emperor yielded.

Riot and Burning of St Sophia.—On the 20th of June A.D. 404, early in the morning, strong detachments of soldiers took up positions round the church and the archbishop's palace, and about mid-day an Imperial officer presented himself before Chrysostom, and delivered a letter ordering his immediate departure. Fearing the result of delay or refusal, the archbishop took a hasty farewell of the bishops and deaconesses, and leaving the church by the eastern door, while the crowd was expecting him at the western, surrendered himself to the soldiers there posted. The people, however, became suspicious. Some ran to the harbour, where they saw the vessel containing Chrysostom and his few companions already crossing the Bosporus. Others penetrated into the church, which, however, they found already occupied by troops. Blows followed, and cries were heard; while those outside, thinking some harm was being done to the archbishop, attacked the closed doors and forced their way in. The soldiers at once used their weapons; oaths and shouts filled the air, mingled with the groans of wounded and dying. Presently a fearful storm burst over the city, with an awful darkness that added to the confusion; and while men's minds were thus overwrought, and as though the anger of Heaven were to be yet more clearly manifested, the church itself on a sudden was discovered to be in flames, which soon mastered the whole building, and, fanned by the gale, swept across the Forum, enveloped and destroyed the senate-house, and even threatened the Imperial palace. Such were the omens which accompanied the final departure of the archbishop from Constantinople.

Chrysostom Conveyed to Cucusus.—He and his companions—two bishops, named Eulysius and Cyracius, and certain priests of his own church—had been landed at Chalcedon, and ignorant alike of their own destination and of what had happened in Constantinople, were proceeding sadly towards Nicæa, escorted by Prætorian guards, when they were overtaken by a small body of cavalry soldiers, the officer of which had orders to bring back the archbishop's companions on a charge of complicity in the burning of St. Sophia. Then, for the first time, the little party learned to their dismay all that had taken place; and then, for the first time, torn from his friends, Chrysostom was left alone. And so he set off into exile. His destination, he discovered at last, was Cucusus, a place lying on the military road from Constantinople to Mesopotamia, and about 120 miles north of Antioch. The three years which he spent there (A.D. 404–407) were the most glorious, perhaps the happiest of his life. In exile, his faults were forgotten, his virtues remembered, and he himself had no fears for the future. He kept up a close connection with his own church of Constantinople and his many friends within it, and maintained a correspondence with many and distant provinces.

Removal to Pityus.—But there were dangers to be faced even there from marauding Isaurians, and hardships to be undergone from the severities of the climate,—dangers and hardships which his enemies at home, it seems, hoped might end his hateful life. But whensuch was not the case, and he lived on through three weary winters, his enemies petitioned the Emperor, and obtained a "rescript" ordering his immediate removal to Pityus. This was a town lying at the remotest frontier of the Roman Empire, on the shore of the Euxine and at the foot of the Caucasus, once a large and flourishing place, but at that time ruined by the gradual westward advance of the barbarians, with a surrounding nomad population, and peopled almost solely by a garrison as barbarous as they. Probably all alike were pagans. In this wild place it was hoped he might die, and at the least his eloquent tongue would be silent. But he was not destined ever to reach it. The two soldiers responsible for his safe conduct took the road from Cucusus northwards, which would lead through Sebaste to Neo-Cæsarea, and so to the coast; and for three months they toiled on, through rain and sunshine, careless of his sufferings, anxious only to be rid of their burden.

Death at Comana in Pontus—Sept. 14, 407.— They reached Comana in Pontus, and there fatigue, exposure, and illness relieved them of their wearisome task, for Chrysostom died on September 14. "When he got to the shrine of the martyr Basiliscus," says Palladius, his biographer, "he asked for white vestments suitable to the tenor of his past life, and taking off his clothes of travel, he clad himself in them from head to foot, being still fasting, and then gave away his old ones to those about him. Then, having communicated in the symbols of the Lord, he said his customary words, 'Glory be to God for all things,' and having concluded with his last Amen, he stretched forth those feet of his which had been so beautiful in their running, whether to convey salvation to the penitent or reproof to the hardened in sin. . . . . And being gathered to his fathers, and shaking off this mortal dust, he passed to Christ."

CHAPTER VI.

ALARIC AND THE VISIGOTHS—A D. 396-419.

State of Italy—A.D. 400.—The foremost man in the Western Empire at the beginning of the fifth century was Stilicho the Vandal. Able and experienced—barbarian by birth and Roman in feeling—he was better able, perhaps, than any man to understand the needs of Italy, and to enforce the discipline and forbearance which was so necessary for peace. His very name was a terror to evil-doers, and for a while a guarantee against invasion. His position was further strengthened by his own marriage to Serena, the niece of Theodosius, and by the marriage of his daughter Maria to Honorius. But the difficulties of government were such as might have taxed the wisdom and energy of even a Constantine or an Augustus. In all the Roman world, West and East alike, there was the same decay of political principles and public spirit; but Italy and the West presented special difficulties of their own besides. If there were still pagans and heretics in the East, they were a small and powerless minority; while the paganism of Italy, and specially of Rome, where every street and almost every building were memorials of an antiquity wholly pagan, was a distinct power and influence of which every statesman must take account, and a centre round which heretics and Jews, and all the discontented members of a large and divided society might rally. It was this party which had revolted against Theodosius in A.D. 394, and so nearly defeated him in the battle of Sept. 6, at the foot of the Julian Alps; it was still hostile to his family. It was at the same time a *coalition* of much that was noble and much that was base, of noble senators and aristocratic philosophers, with fanatics, scoffing unbelievers and plotting conspirators, who had one common watch-word indeed, "religious liberty," but whose real interests were so diverse that their power was limited to simple opposition. To them, as to so many "coalitions," success would have been fatal. Fronting them stood the great and united Catholic party, headed by the court and the bishops—a party conscious of its strength, intolerant of opposition, and disposed to tyrannise in the hour of victory. Between them, and identified with neither, was the Regent of the West, armed with the amnesty which on his deathbed Theodosius had charged him to publish, and both able and willing to enforce it. Nevertheless the peace thus enforced was felt to be nothing but an armed neutrality, and perhaps was only maintained in consequence of the disquieting rumours which reached Italy from the north-east; for the Visigoths were moving, and no one knew precisely where the storm might burst. It was indeed nothing but the precautions taken by Stilicho, in the summer of the year A.D. 400, in raising levies and strengthening fortifications in the north of Italy, especially Brescia, Aquileia, and Ravenna, that saved the country from the horrors which it suffered eight years later. For in the autumn Alaric did actually cross the Alps, but finding everything ready for resistance, returned to Illyricum whence he came.

Alaric the Visigoth.—The questions at once occur, Who was Alaric? How did he come to be in Illyricum?

and in what capacity was he there? The Visigoths, as we have seen (chap. iii.), driven before the advancing Huns, had been compelled to cross the Danube, and after winning a great victory and defeating a Roman Emperor (A.D. 378), had been settled by Theodosius in Mœsia. The ascendancy of his character won their loyalty; and when he left Constantinople in A.D. 394 to engage the insurgent forces of Arbogastes in Italy, a large body of their best soldiers joined his army. Among them was a young chieftain of the family from whom the Visigoths always chose their kings, hitherto unknown to fame, named Alaric, but afterwards not the least famous of those barbarians whom contact with Rome and Romans transformed into civilised men. He was still young; yet he had seen and taken part in all the tragic events of the twenty previous years—in the flight before the Huns, in the passage of the Danube, in the battle of Adrianople, in the ravaging of Thrace and Macedonia. It would have been strange had his eyes not been opened to the disorganisation of the Empire, and the secret of its weakness; or to the chance of success for an active and able adventurer. Political hatred threw in his way the opportunity which otherwise he might long have waited for. It was a question of property in provinces.

Province of Eastern Illyricum.—Up to the reign of Theodosius Greece and Macedonia had been part of the western half of the Empire, as though annexed to Italy, under the name of Eastern Illyricum, separated from Western Illyricum, which lay between it and Italy, by the river Drinus, a tributary of the Save. It was an unnatural arrangement; for between Greece and Italy there was community neither of language nor feeling, while the language and literature of Greece had been adopted throughout the East. Identity of interest, there-

fore, seemed to mark this Illyricum as naturally a province of the East.   Moreover, when the Emperor Gratian
summoned Theodosius from Spain to retrieve the disaster
of Adrianople, he had handed over to his special charge
this very province then overrun with victorious Goths,
in common with the eastern half of the Empire, of
which he named him Emperor.   It was, doubtless, meant
as a temporary arrangement to meet a temporary danger ;
but by his will Theodosius, in dividing the Empire between his sons, assigned Eastern Illyricum (Epirus, Macedonia, Thessaly, and Achaia) to the share of Arcadius,
and thus completed its severance from the West.   The
assignment was hailed with equal annoyance in Italy and
exultation at Constantinople, and increased the already
bitter feeling existing between the Imperial brothers and
their ministers, Stilicho and Rufinus.   There even seemed
reason to fear that Honorius or his ministers might try to
regain by force a province whose loss they so much resented.   Accordingly, Rufinus kept urging Arcadius to
take military possession of the province at once, and so
anticipate the danger.   But this was easier said than
done.   A large part of the army of the East was in the
hands of Stilicho.   Hence the repeated despatches addressed by Arcadius to Honorius, claiming the return of
these troops.   Hence the agitation of both Arcadius and
Rufinus when Stilicho declared his intention of handing
them over to Arcadius *in person*.   Hence the means
which they adopted to secure the troops, but to keep
Stilicho at a distance, and the vengeance which the latter
took on Rufinus by the hands of Gainas the Goth.   But
before all this actually happened, Rufinus had bethought
him of possible allies in the Visigoths of Mœsia, and
opened communications with Alaric for that purpose,
meanwhile sending on two agents of his own to replace

the governors of Achaia and Thessaly. Alaric was only too eager to seize the opportunity for action. Without delay, and massing together his own people, and some Hunnish and Sarmatian allies from the north of the Danube, he burst through the pass of Succi in Mount Hæmus, and descended into Thrace, his advanced guard even appearing before the walls of Constantinople. The whole province and capital were panic-stricken, and asked in terror what it could mean. It is hard to realise that it was only a piece of cunning diplomacy, intended to secure the influence and personal safety of Rufinus. Yet so it was. Alaric was to approach the capital in warlike guise, and Rufinus to have the credit of persuading or bribing him to turn away from it. The protection of Rufinus would thus seem essential to the safety of Arcadius.

Alaric in Illyricum.—All turned out as arranged; and when Rufinus suggested that the Visigoths should retire, not to Mœsia, but to Eastern Illyricum, and occupy that, it was, of course, with the idea of placing a strong barrier between himself and Stilicho, and it mattered little to him that they treated the province as a conquered land, and fell to pillaging.

Stilicho prepares to Attack.—The news created a profound impression in Italy. Not only was a province which the Italians looked upon as by rights their own oppressed by barbarians, but it was a province actually touching their frontier. Another step and Alaric would be in Italy! But Stilicho was alive, not only to this danger, but to the fact that Alaric in this case was a puppet in the hands of Rufinus. His resolution, therefore, was soon taken, to carry the war into the enemy's country, to drive Alaric out of Greece, and confine him once more to Mœsia, and then to settle matters with Rufinus in person at Constantinople. No time was to be lost.   Although it was winter, Stilicho crossed the Alps, descended the Rhine to its mouth, inspected the garrisons, and withdrew such troops from Gaul, and even from Britain, as he thought might safely be spared.   Bitterly was their loss regretted a few years later when Picts and Scots descended upon Britain, and Vandals, and Burgundians, and Goths swept through Gaul; but for the moment, when he returned with a powerful army at his back, all Italy was exultant, and the troops of West and East, so lately enemies, fraternised in common devotion to Stilicho.

Alaric, meantime, was overrunning Northern Greece and levying requisitions.   From Macedonia, which was exhausted, he had repaired to Thessaly, and there Stilicho came up with him (A.D. 396).   But while the two armies lay confronting each other a letter reached Stilicho from Arcadius, calling upon him to abandon Illyricum, to leave Alaric alone, and to send the money and troops belonging to Arcadius at once to Constantinople.   Stilicho, unwilling to injure a son of Theodosius, detached Gainas with the soldiers and the money for Arcadius, and by his means revenged himself on Rufinus.

Weakened, however, by the withdrawal of a large part of his army, Stilicho for the moment was unable to cope with Alaric, who, breaking up from his intrenched camp, marched at leisure through Thermopylæ and Phocis into Attica.   At Athens the magistrates were politic enough to disarm his hostility by submission, to humour his superstitious fears of offending their goddess, to flatter his vanity by splendid entertainments.   And thus Athens, her temples, and works of art escaped the pillage which, we are told, the Christian monks urged upon Alaric.

Alaric and Stilicho in Peloponnesus.—Eleusis was not so fortunate.   Town and temple alike were sacked. The Isthmus was passed with the connivance of Gerontius, the governor of Achaia nominated by Rufinus; Corinth was in ashes; and Alaric was in full march upon Argos and Sparta, when Stilicho, who had returned to Italy after the break-up of his army to collect reinforcements, was despatched by Honorius once more at the urgent demand of the Corinthians, and landed in the Peloponnesus. He was too late to save Corinth; but overtook Alaric in the valley of the Eurotas, defeated him in a pitched battle, and succeeded eventually in surrounding the Goths in Mount Erymanthus, north of Olympia and Pisa. But Pisa proved the Capua of Stilicho and his army. The generals feasted and amused themselves; the soldiers deserted; so that Alaric found no difficulty in breaking through their lines, and making his escape by way of Corinth and the Isthmus. Meanwhile, in pursuance of what was now traditional policy, Eutropius had offered Alaric the post of "Master-General of Eastern Illyricum," on condition of his ceasing hostilities and retiring at once to Epirus. Thus armed with full powers, no sooner did Alaric find himself on the north side of the Isthmus than he issued orders as master-general of the province to Stilicho to evacuate it, and Stilicho, baffled, was forced to acquiesce. But it was a fatal blow to his reputation. All hope now of reaching Constantinople, and making himself regent of the two Empires, was at an end. Alaric had gained the right of bidding Stilicho evacuate Peloponnesus; and Stilicho, if he refused, would be a "rebel." He embarked with precipitation, and landed in Italy. But it was a step which exposed him to both ridicule and direct attack. In the East he was laughed at; in the West he was accused of "treason." And there can be no doubt that Alaric's success did reveal to the barbarians the extent of their own power.

Revolt of Gildo Suppressed.—And now Eutropius, who had thus cleverly set up a barrier between Italy and Constantinople, between Stilicho and himself, was not only dreaming of launching these same Goths upon Italy, but also of further troubling that unhappy country by involving her in war with Africa—his object still being, like that of Rufinus, to keep Stilicho so far occupied at home, that he should have no time to interfere at Constantinople.   Gildo the Moor, Count of Africa, was secretly encouraged by Eutropius to transfer the allegiance of the province of Africa from the Western to the Eastern Empire.   Gildo (with ulterior designs of transferring Africa to himself) assented, seized the corn fleet about to sail for Italy, and threatened to destroy Carthage if he were attacked.   Rome was at once a prey to terror and indignation, and Stilicho's energy taxed to the utmost.   But the danger was met without much difficulty; Africa was recovered; Gildo was captured, and destroyed himself in prison; and the influence of Stilicho in Italy was increased rather than weakened by the tact and activity which he showed in meeting the emergency.

Threatened Invasion of Italy.—Nevertheless there were clearly dangers threatening in the immediate future greater than any yet faced.   Alaric was watching his opportunity to descend upon Italy, and Eutropius urging him to do so.   The province of Illyricum was nearly exhausted by constant requisitions; while the political troubles consequent on the fall of Eutropius (A.D. 399) left the court of Constantinople neither time nor will to trouble itself about the Visigoths.   Alaric meanwhile was as restless as a wild beast in a cage, a prey to opposite feelings.   The grandeur of Stilicho exasperated him.   Why was it Stilicho rather than himself!   At one time he was possessed with the idea of falling upon Italy, violating the eternal city, and making himself an awful name by some terrible deed. At another, the majesty of Rome subdued him, and he yearned to be a Roman, the foremost of Romans! But beneath all moods there was the same agitation and excitement—an agitation which spread wherever he went, and in the barbarian world was like fire in stubble. Disquieting rumours filled the air, and Stilicho was thoroughly alarmed. Urgent orders were sent to Gaul for reinforcements, the walls of Rome were repaired, and the fortifications of Ravenna prepared to shelter the Emperor and his court in case of need. Perhaps the worst sign of all was the attitude of the Italian population. Courage and patriotism seemed to have vanished. The calm despair of the Christians was not so spiritless as the abject terror of the superstitious, who saw signs and portents everywhere, or as the craven selfishness of the well-to-do, who withdrew in crowds, anxious only to be quit of Italy! Even Honorius was only deterred by the personal influence of Stilicho from placing the Alps between himself and Alaric, and from inaugurating a new capital at Arles or Lyons. In the meantime (spring of A.D. 402) disturbances had already broken out among the barbarian levies in Rhœtia, fomented by Alaric; and the war there languished during the summer; for Alaric was on the alert, and Stilicho, whose presence alone could have finished the matter, was afraid to leave Milan and the Emperor undefended while he crossed the Alps. At last he had no longer any choice. Leaving Milan strongly garrisoned, he hastened across the Alps, pacified the province by his mere name and presence, and returned by forced marches to Italy with strong reinforcements, hoping to arrive before Alaric had time to hear of his absence. Alaric had spies in plenty; and no sooner was he informed of Stilicho's departure, than he passed the Julian Alps—passed by the towns of Venetia and Upper Italy, and made a rapid dash upon Milan.   His hope was to capture Honorius.   But rapid as were his movements, Stilicho was yet faster.   The Visigoths had not yet crossed the Adda, when he descended the southern slopes of the Alps under the cover of night, and in the thousand watch-fires that gleamed like stars across the plain below him, read the story of Alaric's advance and Honorius's danger. Pushing on with a small escort, he dashed through the river under a shower of darts from the enemy's sentinels (which in the darkness happily missed their aim), and by morning light was under the walls of Milan.   Claudian, his friend and panegyrist, describes the cries of triumph which welcomed him, and the joy at the sight of the well-known grey head; for the city was now safe.   Alaric retreated with as much speed as he had come, not halting till he reached Venetia; while Stilicho provided, as best he could, for the immediate protection of Italy by conveying the Emperor to the shelter of the impregnable morasses of Ravenna, and by covering the roads to Rome. But it was impossible for the Visigoths to remain in Venetia, where the towns were shut against them, and the country inundated.   Retreat or advance they must—retreat to Illyricum, or advance where fortune led them !

Battle of Pollentia—A.D. 403.—In spite of opposition and warning, Alaric resolved to advance—moved by the conviction (if we may believe Claudian)[1] that he was

---

[1] Non somnia nobis
   Nec volucres, sed clara palam vox edita luco est :
 " Rumpe omnes, Alarice, moras : hoc impiger anno
   Alpibus Italiæ ruptis penetrabis ad Urbem."

De Bel. Get. v. 544.

destined to see Rome. He professed to have heard a voice bidding him march without delay. Breaking up from Venetia he moved westward, avoiding Milan, and followed at a short distance by Stilicho. He entered Liguria, crossed the Po, and at last halted at Pollentia, about twenty-five miles south-west of Turin, whence he could march either east or west—on Rome if victorious in the coming battle, on Gaul if defeated. On April 5th, 403, the two armies faced one another, Alaric's flanks and rear being protected by a forest, which then lined the banks of the river Tanarus, and by a little stream strangely named "Urbis,"[2] while Stilicho lay between him and Gaul. The next day was Easter Sunday; and, as though by mutual consent, a suspension of arms seemed to be agreed upon between the leaders, when on a sudden the silence was broken by shouts and cries, and fighting was seen to have begun. In Stilicho's army was a contingent of Goths, led by a pagan named Saül; and it appears that, moved either by contempt for their Christian scruples, or a desire to take vengeance on his renegade Christian countrymen, or a fear of losing so favourable an opportunity of attack, Saül had fallen suddenly on the Visigoths in his front, reckless of consequences. The battle once begun soon became general, and raged along the whole line. It was, however, very nearly lost by Stilicho at the outset. For the leader of a contingent of Alani, whose fidelity was mistrusted by Stilicho, resenting the doubt, put himself at the head of his men, and led them in a desperate charge, regardless of orders, on the very centre of the Visigoths. A furious *melée* ensued, from which but few escaped, their leader having barely strength sufficient to present himself before Stilicho, and drop dead at his feet. It was very magnificent,

[2] Pervenit ad fluvium (miri cognominis) Urbem.—*Ib. ib.* 555.

but it was not "war." For Stilicho had the utmost difficulty in restoring the balance of his line, and in rally-
ing the fugitives from the charge. But the union of
skill and obstinate courage at last won the day, and when
the Roman centre succeeded in reaching the waggons,
containing the wives, children, and booty of the Goths,
the day was practically won; and Alaric retreated along
the Tanarus towards Asta, leaving in the conqueror's
hands his wife and children,—treasures of gold, and
vases and statues, the spoil of Greece, with a crowd
of Italian and Greek prisoners, who were thus restored
to liberty. Too wise to drive his enemy to despair,
Stilicho pursued, but offered terms. Alaric agreed to evacuate Italy, but there was fierce disappointment in his
heart, and the pangs of wounded pride, for he had been
defeated by the man of whom in all the world he was
most jealous. Above all, he writhed at the thought of
returning in this guise to Illyricum. He would make
one more throw for victory, and so, despite agreements,
he seized Verona as he passed eastward, and prepared to
hold it desperately. But famine and discontent obliged
him to give it up, and at last (after some further fruitless
struggles) to cross the Alps once more, and to abandon
Italy for a while.

Inroad of Radagaisus—A.D. 405.—It was but a
brief respite, however, that was thus won from danger.
And the next enemy that threatened Italy was not an
Alaric, but worse. Alaric was at least a Christian and
semi-civilised. Radagaisus was a pagan, and utter barbarian. Whatever may have been the cause—whether
exhaustion of their own lands, or more probably pressure
from the Huns in the north-east—there suddenly appeared
in A.D. 405, and surged over into Italy, a huge wave (so to
call it) of men, women, and children, mostly Vandals,

numbering at the lowest estimate 200,000 fighting men, and led by a Goth, whose name was borrowed from a Slavonic deity, Radegast, the god of war and hospitality. At the same time, another division of the same army passed along the valley of the Danube, crossed the Rhine, and precipitated itself upon Gaul. For this sudden inroad Stilicho was wholly unprepared, and was forced to take shelter behind the fortifications of Pavia, and watch for an opportunity of attack. Radagaisus meanwhile had crossed the Po and the Apennines, and was making straight for Rome, whose inhabitants he had vowed to sacrifice to his gods; and Rome trembled for her safety. But once more Stilicho was equal to the emergency. It is needless to dwell upon the skill with which he intercepted the vast mass of human beings on their descent from the hills, and succeeded in enclosing them with an intrenched camp near Florence, till half their number had fallen by famine and pestilence, and the residue who surrendered were sold as slaves. It is more curious to remark, though it is no isolated case in history, that this victory of courage, patience, and skill was claimed by the Christians as a manifest interposition of God himself, and as designed to confound their pagan countrymen at Rome! And as a matter of fact it became the occasion of an outburst of fanaticism on both sides and of religious hatred, which involved even Stilicho himself. Moderation is always a virtue more praised than valued; and Stilicho's moderation as a political, and toleration as a religious ruler, exposed him to bitter attacks from both Christians and pagans. So unsparing, persistent, and ingenious, however, were the charges brought against him or insinuated, that it is difficult to believe he did not partly deserve them, until we realise the despicable character of the people whom it was his ill-fortune to have to rule, and who seemed long ago to have lost all courage and self-respect.   His son Eucherius was accused of being a pagan; he himself of an intention of placing that son on the throne of the childless Honorius.   His enemies forgot, apparently, that the two charges were in reality destructive of each other, and that if Eucherius were a pagan, Christian opposition would prevent his being Emperor. Nevertheless, the charges were made, and served to alarm alike the court and the Christians.   Nor was this all. The "semi-barbarian" (as Jerome calls Stilicho) was accused of "treason," in having denuded Gaul of her soldiers on purpose to expose her to the fury of Alani, Suevi, and Vandals, and to be better able in the general confusion to seize the Empire.   And not only was political and religious feeling thus dexterously irritated by Stilicho's enemies, but the old jealousy between Romans and non-Romans, between Italians and barbarians, burst out afresh, and even threatened to issue in bloodshed, and Stilicho was accused of a partiality of which he had shown himself incapable, and of showing favour only to barbarians; and, worse still, barbarians who were Arians and heretics !   Such were the flimsy accusations in which the jealousy of some, the ingratitude of others, and the fatal fanaticism of all alike found expression.   All they needed was a spokesman and leader; and of course they found one.

Olympius.—Among the officers of the palace was a man named Olympius, who owed his fortune to Stilicho— a man whose ambition was veiled by simplicity of life, and his incapacity by exceeding godliness.   He was the trusted agent of bishops and Emperor, and became the mainspring of the growing conspiracy against Stilicho.   And at this moment it was that the latter inadvertently gave a handle to his enemies which they were not slow to use.

He had been struck by the tenacity and boldness shown by Alaric in the late campaign; and, appalled by the perils of the Empire, he resolved, with Honorius' consent, to enlist Alaric as an ally rather than to meet him as a foe, and either to entrust him with the reconquest of Gaul, or to recover Illyricum by making him governor in Honorius' name. Accordingly he opened negotiations, and a meeting was arranged in Epirus. At the last moment, however, when on the eve of starting, a peremptory order from Honorius forbade his leaving Italy—at whose instance is obvious. Patriotic feeling (so called) was strongly roused by the rumour of these negotiations. One more false step completed his ruin.

Murder of Stilicho.—On the death of Arcadius in A.D. 408, Honorius resolved to visit Constantinople, and set in order the affairs of the Eastern Empire on behalf of the infant Theodosius. In view of the difficulty and expense of so long a journey, Stilicho strongly urged Honorius to stay in Italy, and offered to go himself in his place. Here was an opening little expected. "See," said his enemies, "the ambition of the man! Will it not be easy at Constantinople to make away with the helpless Theodosius? And then, as Emperor of the East, with Alaric as ally and lieutenant, perhaps he may return to conquer the West." The terror of Honorius, thus artfully excited, was increased by a military riot which broke out during his presence at Pavia, and in which high functionaries, courtiers, generals alike were massacred. Olympius seized the opportunity, and secured Honorius' signature to an order for the death of Stilicho. The regent was warned of his danger, but could hardly bring himself to believe in such treachery, although, after a night attack upon his camp, in which he barely escaped, he judged it prudent to retire to Ravenna and take sanctuary in a church.   From thence, like Eutropius, he was lured by false promises.   The officer in command of the troops sent to arrest him assured Stilicho that he was only charged to take good care of him ; but no sooner did the regent leave the church than the officer drew forth a second despatch, which he read aloud in the hearing of all, ordering the immediate execution of the " public enemy, Stilicho the patrician."   Friends, clients, soldiers closed round him at once as one man, and prepared to defend him ; but as noble in death as he had been in life, this " last of the Romans " refused to save his own life at the expense of others, and, kneeling down on the spot where he was, gave his neck to the sword of the execu-tioner (August, A.D. 408).

It is difficult to think with patience of such an ending of a really great life ; that the man who gave peace to Italy, and restored honour to her senate and glory to her arms, and twice saved Rome from capture, should have been deliberately murdered by those who owed him so much.   It was a fitting retribution that in one day 30,000 brave men, who under his auspices had fought and bled for Rome, marched off to join Alaric in Illyricum, and that three months afterwards Alaric was at the gates of Rome.

Reaction in Italy.—Then followed the hateful animosities of a time of " reaction," when it is thought " policy " to seize the utmost advantage of a brief superi-ority.   Stilicho's murder was followed by that of the wives and children of his barbarian soldiers, kept as hostages in the towns of Italy.   Serena fled to Rome. Eucherius, her son, was there beheaded before her eyes ; and her daughter Thermantia, whom Honorius had married after Maria's death, was repudiated and sent to her mother. A widespread confiscation followed of the property of his

friends and (as his enemies called them) "satellites,"
even the poet Claudian being involved in the persecution
and reduced to penury. Religious animosity again blazed
out, now the strong hand was removed, and Catholic
bishops and fathers acquiesced in a "persecution" which
tended to unity. Nor did a spurious and exclusive
"patriotism" forget to avail itself of so useful a handle
as this religious bigotry. Non-Catholic officers—that is,
nearly all the barbarians—were forbidden to appear at
court in the military belt which was their badge of office;
and when they resigned rather than submit to such a
slight, Romans and Italians stepped with light hearts
into their places. But the effect of all this was fatal—
disorganisation, fear, and enmity, in the face of dangers
more terrible than any which had yet threatened Italy.

Alaric Marches on Rome—A.D. 408.—Alaric had
been joined by thousands of veteran barbarians, whose
best feelings had been outraged by the slaughter of their
wives and children. These men clamoured for revenge.
His army was further strengthened by large reinforcements
from the Danube. He was in a position, therefore, to
influence the politics of the Empire, whose ally he claimed
to be; and a man of his ability and ambition could not
fail to see how great was the opportunity. His demands
were moderate, extending only to the payment of expenses
incurred in preparation for the campaign proposed by
Stilicho in Gaul or Greece. But this foolish court, wrapt up
in petty party questions, which had lost its best troops and
offended its best generals, mistook his modesty for weakness, and ignored his demands; and when the offended
king revenged himself in his own way and appeared suddenly in Italy, it was helpless; and, while covering
Ravenna with troops, left Italy and Rome to their fate.
Aquileia, Altinum, Cremona being passed and the Po

crossed, Alaric vainly offered battle to the Imperial troops at Ravenna; and after ravaging the coast of the Adriatic as far as Picenum, struck up into the Apennines, and following the Flaminian Way, arrived without opposition beneath the walls of Rome.

First Siege of Rome.—It was more than 600 years since a foreign enemy had been there, and Hannibal had advanced so far only to retreat. It is hardly strange that Alaric, as he approached the sacred city, should have been torn by conflicting feelings, and even have doubted whether to spare or to destroy. To the city itself his sudden appearance was like the falling of a thunderbolt in a clear sky. So utter was the disorganisation throughout Italy, so indolent and careless the Government, that the Romans knew nothing of an invasion of the Visigoths till the fugitives told of their approach, and could only account for their unopposed advance by the supposition of " treason." A victim was demanded, and found in the hapless Serena, who was accused, found guilty, and strangled. But neither god nor demon was propitiated by the sacrifice, and the blockade continued. Ere long scarcity became absolute famine, and famine was followed by pestilence. At last, abandoned by the Imperial Government, the Senate resolved to throw themselves on the clemency of the Gothic leader whoever he might be—for even of this they were ignorant. Two ambassadors were despatched with orders to say that the Romans wished indeed for peace, but were ready for war,—an innumerable multitude ready armed. " So much the better," broke in Alaric, with a laugh; " the thicker the hay, the easier it is mown." As for conditions of peace, he demanded *all* the gold, silver, movables, and foreign slaves to be found in Rome. " And what then, O king," asked one of the amazed ambassadors, " wilt thou leave us for ourselves ? "

"Your lives," he answered. The discovery that it was Alaric before the walls redoubled the terror of both Senate and people. A second embassy was sent without delay to obtain, if possible, less rigorous terms; and Alaric at last consented to accept 5,000 ℔ of gold, 30,000 ℔ of silver, 4,000 silken robes, 3,000 purple cloths, 3,000 ℔ of spices. It was the last drop in the cup of Rome's misery, half pagan as she was, that to raise this sum it was necessary to strip the temples and the statues of the gods, and even to melt down the statue of "Virtus." Well might the pagan historian say, "All was over."

Negotiations for Peace.—The withdrawal of Alaric from Rome was followed by protracted negotiations for peace, in which, as before, his real or studied moderation only invited insult from the contemptible favourites of Honorius. His demands were limited to the office of master-general of the West, an annual subsidy of corn and money, and a kingdom to be carved out of the provinces of Dalmatia, Noricum, and Venetia; and three senators were sent at his request to Ravenna from Rome to conclude the treaty. One of them was named Priscus Attalus, an Ionian by birth, and afterwards for a short time Emperor. Affable, brilliant, eloquent, yet unstable, ambitious, and spoiled by success—a freethinker and a master of erotic poetry—this man was no bad type of the noblemen of the day. The court party at Ravenna entertained the ambassadors, ridiculed their fears, and finally sent them away empty. Not long afterwards a second embassy was sent for the same purpose, one member of which was Pope Innocent. Meanwhile a chamber revolution at Ravenna had replaced Olympius by a certain Jovius as chief favourite. This man was personally acquainted with Alaric, and trusted to being able to arrange matters in a personal interview. They met at

Ariminum.   Alaric demanded, as before, the master-generalship, and Jovius pressed Honorius to bestow it. The Imperial answer was brief, but to the point.   Jovius, as præfect, might arrange as he pleased about pensions and supplies, but that neither to Alaric nor to any of his race should ever be given any military function or dignity whatsoever.   Alaric's answer was equally pithy.   The "route" was given for Rome.

Second Siege of Rome—A.D. 409.—This time, however, instead of assaulting the capital he seized the "Port" of Ostia, the granary of Rome—a magnificent harbour with three great basins, the work of the Emperor Claudius, to which the corn of Africa was brought, and stored ready for transport in barges up the Tiber. Master of Ostia, he was master of Rome; for without Ostia Rome must starve.   The Senate obeyed Alaric's instructions, and elected the præfect Attalus Emperor in the room of Honorius; and the new Emperor at once named Alaric master-general of the armies of the West. The nominee of the Senate was accepted without difficulty in the greater part of Italy.   But the elevation of Attalus to the Empire was as degrading to the West as that of Eutropius to the consulate had been to the East; and ere long his evident incapacity made his cause so hopeless, that he was thrown over by his patron, publicly despoiled of the Imperial insignia, and contemptuously allowed to retire into private life.   His purple and diadem were sent by Alaric as a pledge of reconciliation and friendship to Honorius.   And now it might have seemed that the last real obstacle to peace was removed, and that Italy would now have rest.   But while negotiations were still pending with the court of Ravenna, Alaric learned that a personal enemy of his own, Sarus the Goth, who but a few days before had attacked his escort and nearly succeeded in seizing himself, was closeted with Honorius. The inference to Alaric seemed obvious that a plot was on foot of which he was the object, for the experience of the last five years had made him suspicious. Infuriated at this last proof of Imperial perfidy he hesitated no longer. Once more the Visigoths were marching upon Rome, and the fate of Rome was sealed.

Third Siege and Sack of Rome—A.D. 410.— Senate and people alike knew now that there was no hope save in themselves. And for a while behind the shelter of Aurelian's walls they stoutly resisted all attacks; but famine is a foe whom none can resist, and a pitiless blockade brought famine and pestilence in its train. The suffering was awful. At last, on the night of August 24, by some unknown hand, the Porta Salaria was opened from within, and the Goths marched in with braying trumpets and savage shouts. The adjoining houses were fired at once, and the flames told the secret to the startled city. It is said that as Alaric passed the gate an inward terror troubled him; for to him, like many another barbarian, the name of "Rome" had been a fascination,—Rome, the capital of the world, the city of the apostles. He gave strict orders, therefore, whatever else was done, to spare the churches of St. Peter and St. Paul. The flames meanwhile marched as fast or faster than the Goths, and often parents and children had much ado to escape in time from their houses into the streets. And in the streets was a foe hardly less cruel than the fire, already drunk with lust and wine. Children and elders, women and men, poor and rich, all fared alike. As if to add to the horror of the scene, a terrific storm burst over the capital, and the lightning flash which revealed the surging crowd below, struck house, or temple, or statue, strewing the very Forum with ruins, and seeming to presage to the affrighted pagans the departure of the gods themselves. Amid the awful terrors of that night—violence, rapine, and murder—two places of refuge alone gave effectual protection to the fleeing crowds, the two churches named above, which were thronged with ever-increasing numbers, — even pagans in their extremity bartering honour for safety, and assuming for the nonce the guise of Christians. But indeed the sack of Rome was the extinction of paganism, whose centre and focus was thus destroyed. The estates of the Roman patricians were desolated; whole families were carried into exile; many of the old ancestral houses disappeared for ever; and the coasts of Italy, Africa, and the East swarmed with the fugitives. But Christian Rome rose on the ruins of pagan Rome; and Alaric was an unwitting instrument in the elevation of the Bishop of Rome to power. Henceforth beyond dispute the greatest man in Rome was the Pope.

Death of Alaric — A.D. 410.—For three days and nights the sack of the city lasted. Then the Goths marched southward, and ravaged Campania, Lucania, and Calabria. The sight of Rhegium in flames might even warn the Sicilians of what they had to expect. But if (as is said) Alaric really contemplated the conquest of Sicily as a step towards the conquest of Carthage, his wishes were effectually prevented by the destruction of his fleet of transports in a sudden storm, and by his own premature death, the cause of which is unknown. He was honoured by the Goths with a worthy burial. Fearful lest vengeance should be wreaked on his remains if the place of his burial were known, they diverted the little river Basentinus from its course; built in its bed a royal sepulchre, filled with treasures and spoils from Rome; placed therein the dead hero; and after turning the river into its old course, slew the captives who had performed the work.   A worthy end of a life so strange and wilful !

Succeeded by Ataülf and Wallia.—After his death the Visigoths chose Ataülf his brother-in-law as king, who married Placidia, the daughter of Theodosius by his second wife Galla.   He entered into an engagement with Honorius to carry out what had been proposed before, and led his people over the Alps into Gaul and Spain to fight the Vandals and Alani, who (since A.D. 406) had overrun those provinces.   Ataülf was assassinated at Barcelona in A.D. 415; but his work was carried on by his successor, Wallia, under whose auspices the Visigoths were settled in Aquitaine (A.D. 419), their final home, and the royal residence fixed at Toulouse.   They were a new and powerful influence in the Roman province of Gaul, and largely affected its subsequent history.

GENSERIC AND THE VANDALS—A.D. 423-533.

Events following the Death of Honorius—
A.D. 423.—Honorius died in A.D. 423. The fifty-three years
which elapsed between his death and the destruction of
Italian independence were years full of trouble and disgrace. Italy was nominally ruled by a succession of
cyphers, puppets in the hands of men stronger than
themselves. Mœsia, Thrace, Illyricum, Gaul, and even
Northern Italy, were overrun by the Huns. Africa was
conquered by the Vandals. Rome was twice pillaged.
It was a time of blind confusion, when law meant the
will of the strongest, and every man's hand was against
his neighbour. The first part of this chapter will be
devoted to giving a brief sketch of Italian history during
these years, in order to show clearly the crippled state of the
Empire, which had to sustain a desperate struggle with
Genseric in the south and with Attila in the north almost
at the same time. In the latter part will be narrated the
attack of Genseric on Rome.

Valentinian III.—A.D. 423-455. — Honorius was
succeeded by Valentinian III., a child of six years old,
the son of his half-sister Placidia, who became regent.
Placidia had had a wide experience of life. Married to
Atäulf the Visigoth, whom she accompanied to Gaul and

Spain, she returned after his murder to Italy, and married Constantius, by whom she became the mother of Honoria and Valentinian. On his death (A.D. 421), and in consequence of a quarrel with Honorius, she withdrew to Constantinople, where the kind conduct of Theodosius II. (A.D. 408–450) doubtless induced her to think of the marriage afterwards arranged between Valentinian and Eudoxia. Moreover, Western Illyricum was ceded to the Eastern Empire, in acknowledgment of her courteous reception and of the aid given her in securing her son's position. A woman in power, however, has always a difficult place to fill; and Placidia was no exception to the rule. She was jealous of all rivals, and studiously asserted her own supremacy at her son's court, even when he was nominally Emperor. Nor was her task rendered more easy by the mutual jealousy of Aetius and Boniface, the foremost soldiers of the day. The latter had proved his fidelity; the former had shown himself an untrustworthy time-server. Yet Placidia allowed herself to be cajoled by Aetius into the belief that Boniface was a dangerous conspirator. She ordered him to return from Africa, while at the same time Aetius persuaded him that to obey orders and leave Africa was equivalent to a sentence of death. Fearing the consequences of disobedience, Boniface looked round for an ally, and seemed to find one in Genseric the Vandal, ruler of Spain. It was a fatal alliance, fraught with bitter results to himself, the province, and the capital; and it indirectly precipitated the attack of Attila upon Gaul. From this last evil, indeed, Italy and the Emperor were saved by the courage of Pope Leo and the tactics of Aetius; yet in his case, as in Stilicho's, although the Church claimed for Leo all the glory of the victory over "the scourge of God," Valentinian was none the less jealous of the real victor's reputation. Aetius was murdered by the Emperor's own hand. Retribution, however, followed close upon the act, for the Emperor was assassinated by two of Aetius' domestics at the instigation of his successor on the throne (March 16, 455).

Petronius Maximus—A.D. 455.—This successor was Petronius Maximus, a Roman senator, who lived scarcely three months to enjoy his triumph. He had compelled Eudoxia, Valentinian's widow, to marry him; and she, enraged at the insult, and hating the man who had instigated her husband's murder, made secret overtures to Genseric in Africa, and besought him to set her free. Thus she avenged Valentinian, it is true, but she ruined Rome. Maximus was torn to pieces by a street mob, and Rome was sacked.

Last Twenty Years of the Western Empire —A.D. 455–475.—Of his eight successors on the Imperial throne, it is hard to say which was least worthy. Avitus (A.D. 455), Majorian (A.D. 457), Severus (A.D. 461), Anthemius (A.D. 467), Olybrius (A.D. 472), Glycerius (A.D. 473), Nepos (A.D. 474), and Romulus Augustulus (A.D. 475) — it is a mere string of names! One name, indeed, there is which does not figure in the muster-roll of Emperors, yet towers above them all, that of Ricimer. Like almost all the military men of the fifth century, he was a barbarian. His father was of the royal family of the Suevi; his mother's father was that Wallia who had settled the Visigoths in Aquitaine. And if it seems strange that this man should have been paramount for some sixteen years, and have actually nominated three Emperors, and yet not have seized the Empire for himself, we may remember that during 500 years of Imperial history no barbarian had dared to sit on the Imperial throne, with the one exception of Maximin the Goth

(A.D. 235), who, nominated Emperor by soldiers in revolt, was never recognised by the Senate, and never set foot in Italy. Ricimer has been compared to Sulla—a comparison hardly fair to the former. Though hard and unscrupulous, he was not cruel in cold blood. Glycerius was nominated by Gundobald the Burgundian; Anthemius and Nepos were Greeks, appointed by the Eastern Emperor Leo; Romulus by his father Orestes, who claims something more than a mere passing notice. In a period rife with adventurers, no life perhaps presented stranger contrasts than his. He was born at Pettau in Illyriu,—a man (like Rufinus) supple rather than able, and possessed of more experience than honesty. While Pannonia was Roman, he was Roman also; when Aetius permitted its occupation by Huns, he ceased to be Roman, and served Attila faithfully as secretary. On Attila's death he repaired to Italy, once more a Roman, there to spend his share of the pillage of the Empire; and he knew how to wait upon events. When a hard fate compelled Nepos to abandon Auvergne to the Visigoths, already in possession of Aquitaine and the greater part of Spain—in other words, to abandon the provinces beyond the Alps, except Narbonne—Orestes skilfully fomented the general discontent. When Nepos fled from Italy to escape the vengeance of the army, Orestes made no sign, but waited patiently till events (as he foresaw) should throw the Imperial power into his hands. Then he placed his son, a mere boy of thirteen, upon the throne, the more easily to retain the reins of power himself. But, like many another, he found it easier to raise than to rule the storm; and the same military discontent, by which he had raised himself to power, was as fatal to him as to his predecessor. As their reward for serving him, the army demanded *one-third* of the land of Italy; and when Orestes shrank from bringing misery so great on an unoffending people, they transferred their allegiance to a man not less able and much less scrupulous, Odoacer, son of Edecon, the Herulian. Orestes fell, and with him the independence of Italy.

The Transition—A.D. 450–500.—The last fifty years of the fifth century were indeed a strange period—a time of transition, full of odd contrasts and surprises; when the old *forms* of government and of nations were slowly passing away, while the *spirit* of Imperial Rome, her language, laws, and thoughts, were slowly modifying the character of her barbarian conquerors. Amid the general confusion, however, one body of men beyond all others challenges our admiration, the Christian bishops and clergy —the only men (not barbarians) who showed courage in danger, the only men who seem to have had "ideas." Among so many it will suffice to name Innocent and Leo of Rome—Augustine of Hippo—Epiphanius of Pavia— Anianus of Orleans—and, not least, that Severinus who, by the simple exercise of courage, wisdom, and charity, reduced order out of chaos in Noricum, and became saint and teacher, ruler and judge alike of Romans and barbarians.

The Vandals.—The history of the Vandals in connection with the Empire is even more dramatic than that of the Huns. The mere extent of country which from first to last they traversed is as marvellous as the wanderings of the Arabs in the seventh century. And the way in which their name and nation vanished in the sixth century is not less wonderful than the similar fate of the Carthaginians whose land they had possessed, or of the Ostrogoths in Italy. One province of Spain alone recalls their name, Andalusia.

Their Migrations—A.D. 330–429.—In Chapter III. it was related how the Vandals had gradually worked their way southwards from the region of the Elbe and

Vistula, until Constantine settled them in Pannonia about A.D. 330. There for seventy years they remained, and were converted to the Arian form of Christianity; until at last, compelled by hunger or by pressure from other tribes, they joined the Suevi and Alani in a sudden descent upon Gaul (A.D. 406), at the same time that Radagaisus was threatening Florence and Rome. Their coming was as that of a swarm of locusts, and resistance was hopeless. From Mainz and Strasburg to Amiens and Tournay, and thence southward to Aquitaine and Narbonne, the whole country was swept by them. But in less than three years, being hard pressed by another Constantine, whom the legions of Britain had named Emperor, and who was supported by the Frank confederation, they crossed the Pyrenees into Spain (A.D. 409), and repeated on Spanish soil the devastations they had already caused in Gaul. Spain has gone through many a fiery trial, but never a worse one than that of the opening years of the fifth century. Army after army, enemy after enemy marched through, fought in, and lived upon the unhappy country. The three confederate nations divided the land between them,—a division recognised by the Emperor Honorius in A.D. 412. But that this was a concession wrung from weakness, and not an honourable recognition of accomplished facts, is clear from the insincere reservation accompanying it, that the ordinary legal prescription of thirty years constituting ownership was not to apply to the case in question! This was bad; but it was worse when Roman jealousy of any government better and abler than its own (and under Vandal rule Spain had become fertile and Spaniards rich and contented) brought Visigoths from over the Pyrenees to fall upon the Vandals, no doubt with the secret hope that both would at least be weakened in the struggle, and one might perhaps be destroyed (A.D. 416). The Vandali Silingi were indeed destroyed, and the Alani so roughly handled that they united themselves to the rest of the Vandals (whose king took the title of King of the Vandali and Alani), and retired to the south, while the Suevi were confined to the north-western districts. Spain returned once more to at least a nominal allegiance to Rome; and Wallia the Visigoth was rewarded by the honour of a "triumph" in Rome, and by the grant of Aquitaine,—a grant which formed the basis of the great Visigothic kingdom, that eventually included all the south of Gaul and nearly the whole of Spain (A.D. 470). But the allegiance of Spain to Rome was brief, and in fifteen years the Vandals were once more masters of the country (A.D. 423). Roman perfidy, moreover, seems to have called out all the worst side of what had been a noble character, and the six years which ensued were marked by a ferocity justifying perhaps the use of the term "Vandalism." The country was pillaged, and the Catholic clergy and people persecuted.

Genseric King—A.D. 428.—This pillage and persecution appears to have been due to a man whose name aroused as much horror as that of Attila the Hun. This was Genseric (or Gheiseric), the bastard half-brother of Gonderic, who reigned until A.D. 428. He was short in stature, and had been lamed by a fall from his horse. A man of few words and powerful intellect—of rare self-command, but terrible when roused, his character seems to have made a profound impression on his contemporaries. Scorning luxury and indulgence, yet devoured by avarice, he had one passion and one purpose in life, *gold;* and in pursuit of it he was impassive, cold, pitiless. And in this respect he compares badly with Attila, who at least had the instincts of a warrior and conqueror, who loved the fever of battle and the glory of victory as other men love peace, while Genseric was a mere robber and pirate. The one would have sighed with Alexander for more worlds to conquer, the other for more towns to pillage.

Invasion of Africa—A.D. 429.—Genseric succeeded his brother Gonderic in A.D. 428. He had already become aware that it would be more difficult to hold than it had been to conquer Spain. The population itself was quite Roman in feeling, and would resent the rule of a barbarian; while the Visigoths lay close to his northern frontier, a nation stronger than his own, and more friendly with the Empire. To remain in Spain, therefore, was to remain in presence of a constant danger. Meanwhile across the water lay the province of Africa, fertile, rich, and as yet unpillaged. The strait was but twelve miles across. And there were allies whose assistance would be of value, and who would welcome him with joy as a deliverer, — the Moors, utter savages, who had been irritated but never subdued by the civilised arms of Rome; and the heretics called Donatists, the "Puritans" of the early Church, whose bishops almost equalled in numbers the Catholic bishops; but who, since the conference of Carthage (A.D. 412), had suffered a rigorous persecution. Moors and Donatists alike, therefore, would welcome Genseric as a deliverer; and that the latter were right in so doing is proved by the fact, that for 100 years, the duration of the Vandal empire, they enjoyed perfect peace. At this juncture it was, while the Vandal was still hesitating, that a strange chance gave him the opportunity he required. Boniface, Count of Africa, had been made the victim of a plot (as we have seen), and recalled from his province by Placidia. Believing that his life was in danger, he looked round him for allies; and as Vortigern (if we may believe tradition) summoned the Jutes to aid him against the Picts (about A.D. 445), as Narses sum-

moned the Lombards into Italy (A.D. 567), as legend says
Count Julian summoned the Arabs into Spain to avenge his
daughter's wrongs (A.D. 710), so now Boniface summoned
the Vandals to come and help him.   And the barbarians
who came to help remained to occupy.   In A.D. 429 the
Vandal nation crossed the straits, numbering, it is said,
only 50,000 effective warriors,—a number, however, soon
swelled by the allies already mentioned.   Their crossing
was the signal for a general flight.   Before Moorish horsemen and pitiless Vandals, still more before the dreaded
vengeance of religious foes, who had suffered and now
burned to avenge, all of the Catholic population who
could escape fled pell-mell to the oases of the desert or the
caves of the Atlas.   All too late Boniface discovered the
treachery of Aetius, and too late tried to negotiate with
the ally whose aid he had implored.   In vain he rallied
round him the garrison of Carthage and of a few other
towns.   Genseric turned a deaf ear to all representations,
defeated Boniface in the field, and overran the whole open
country; and Carthage, Cirta, and Hippo were the only
cities that stood up out of the waves of invasion that
surged around.   Africa now suffered what Greece and
Italy had suffered from Alaric, and Gaul from Ataülf, and
Spain from Wallia and Gonderic; and without crediting
all the stories suggested by passion or fanaticism, we may
imagine it was a time of terrible misery.   Even Rome
felt the blow in the loss of her annual store of corn.
Boniface meanwhile was besieged in Hippo, a maritime
colony some 200 miles westward of Carthage, of which
Augustine was at this time the bishop.   This greatest
bishop of the African Church died in the third month of
the siege (August 28, 430); and of him, if of any man,
we may truly say that he was taken away from the evil
to come.   The long peace which his province had enjoyed,

ever since the battle of Thapsus (B.C. 46), was now ended; and with the Vandal conquest began a series of troubles —of Arian persecution, of conquest and reconquest—until the strong arm of Mohammedanism wrested it from Christendom (about A.D. 650–700) and from civilised Europe. The siege of Hippo was protracted for fourteen months, until the Vandals were obliged to relinquish their efforts; and at Placidia's urgent request, reinforcements were sent to Boniface from Constantinople, under the command of Aspar. A second battle was hazarded, followed by a second defeat, which determined both Aspar and Boniface to abandon Africa at once (A.D. 431). Boniface returned to Italy; but it was only to end an unfortunate life by a dishonourable death. The enmity between himself and Aetius burst into an open flame, and their private quarrel was decided in a bloody battle, in which Boniface received a mortal wound from his enemy's hand, and died in a few days; while Aetius was obliged by Placidia to withdraw into Pannonia. Thus did a fatal jealousy rob the Empire of the invaluable services of two able generals at the very moment when most she needed them. However, it was not until A.D. 439 that the conquest of Africa was completed by the surprise of Carthage, so turbulent were the subjects, so numerous and dangerous the domestic enemies of Genseric. On October 9 Carthage was taken, a fitting retribution, it was said, for almost unexampled corruption; and when the rumour reached Italy of what had happened within but a short distance of her own coast, when a bishop of Carthage (with the strangely Puritan name of " Quod vult Deus") and many of his clergy, embarked on crazy vessels and, tempest-tossed, were eventually stranded on the coast of Italy, it might well have seemed to Rome that her hour too was coming.'

The Vandal Kingdom—A.D. 430–533.—Under the

rule of Genseric Africa threatened to relapse into something like barbarism.   Civilisation and Catholicism alike were in danger.   The Mediterranean once more swarmed with pirates; no island, no harbour, was safe from their attacks; and at last even an army from Carthage was seen encamped in the Forum and occupying Rome for fourteen days!   But before this occupation the prosperity of Rome was utterly destroyed by the severance of Africa from the Empire.

Rome Sacked by Genseric—A.D. 455.—Master of Africa and the Mediterranean, it is little wonder that Genseric's thoughts should have turned to Rome and the treasures of Rome.   Cut off from their usual corn supply, and wounded by the loss of their far fairest province, it is little wonder, on the other hand, that the Italians should have longed to recover it.   And the two enemies, face to face, each with injuries to avenge, would doubtless have met sooner had not the special difficulties of each at home occupied their attention for some five years.   Rome was doing battle with the Huns, Genseric was pacifying a turbulent population.   At last (A.D. 455), when Valentinian had been murdered, and Maximus, from passion or revenge, had forced the widowed Eudoxia to marry him, she, remembering her royal birth and indignant at the outrage, yet unable to hope for any aid from Constantinople (for her father was dead, her mother in a disgraceful exile, and the Empire in the hands of a stranger), appealed secretly to Genseric, as the Princess Honoria had appealed to Attila,[1] and within three months the Vandal was at the mouth of the Tiber.   Maximus was at once murdered by the mob in the streets, and three days afterwards Genseric was at the gates of Rome.   Once more it was a priest who alone did not fear.

[1] See next chapter.

Once more the same Leo, bishop of Rome, who had arrested Attila's progress on the frontiers of Italy (A.D. 452), sallied forth at the head of his clergy to intercede for the city (June 14, 455). But it was little that he won from the hard heart of Genseric. The lives of those who offered no resistance were to be spared; the buildings were to be saved from fire, and the captives from torture. And this was all. Rome and its inhabitants were delivered over for fourteen days to the tender mercies of Vandals and Moors, and everything of value which had been left by Alaric, everything which Christian devotion or patrician luxury had accumulated since Alaric's departure, was swept off and carried to Carthage. And thus it was, by a strange catastrophe, that a fierce barbarian, whose forefathers lived on the shores of the Baltic, compelled Rome to surrender, and carried to Africa the spoils of two religions not his own. From the Temple of Peace he bore away the gold table and the seven-branched candlestick which Titus had brought as trophies from the sack of Jerusalem (A.D. 70); while he stripped the Capitoline Temple of its yet remaining statues of gods and heroes, as well as of its costly gilt bronze roof, on which Domitian alone is said to have spent more than £2,000,000. Last, but not least, the Vandal fleet conveyed to Carthage the occasion of all this misery, the Empress Eudoxia, and her daughters Eudocia and Placidia, accompanied by hundreds of captives of both sexes. But the fate of Eudoxia, who, if a prisoner, was treated honourably, and whose elder daughter was married to Genseric's son, Huneric, was happy compared to that of the innocent Romans whom she had brought to ruin. They were divided as booty or sold as slaves—husbands torn from wives, and children from parents—a hard fate, only mitigated by the charity and self-devotion of Deogratias, bishop of Carthage. Yet if the sack of Rome inflicted loss upon the Christians, to the pagans and to paganism it was destruction. Genseric completed what Alaric had begun, and by a strange fatality, even the ship which bore the statues of gods and heroes, the last relics of pagan Rome, to Carthage, foundered at sea.

Policy of Genseric.—The object of Genseric in taking Eudoxia and the other captives to Africa was booty. Princesses at least must have considerable property, he thought, and be worth a ransom—probably also must have dowries. Hence the marriage of Eudocia to Huneric. And further, now that Eudocia and her mother were connected with him by marriage, any refusal to ransom the one or dower the other, would be a direct insult to himself, and serve as an excuse for appealing to arms. On the other hand, the Eastern Emperor, Marcian, was equally anxious to obtain their release, and alternately tried threats and cajoleries upon Genseric. But the latter was imperturbable. Whether it was to be war or peace between them, he cared not; but he did care for the dowry of his daughter-in-law and the ransom of her mother and sister. For seven years these negotiations lasted. In the end, by the intervention of a Roman senator, Olybrius, the lover and afterwards the husband of Placidia, the Court of Constantinople was induced to pay the sums demanded, and the mother and daughter were set free. Olybrius and Placidia were married. And now Genseric put in a second claim, which was almost comical. He demanded that Olybrius should be made Emperor of the West, adding that he could think of no other reason why his demand should be refused, except a desire to insult himself, and in that case he should know how to act. At this juncture Majorian might have been formidable as an antagonist, but Majorian was dead, and the feeble Severus was already tottering.

On Ricimer's refusal to accede to Genseric's proposal, the Mediterranean was at once covered with piratical fleets, which penetrated to every corner, and by Genseric's orders everywhere raised the same war-cry, " Olybrius, for Emperor of the West !"

Expedition against Carthage—A.D. 468.—In this extremity Ricimer appealed to the Eastern Emperor Leo to nominate an Emperor in the West, and to join in an expedition to curb the insolence of the Vandals. Leo nominated Anthemius, and showed his further good-will by immediate preparations for an invasion of Africa. No less than 1,113 ships were equipped in the Golden Horn, manned by 7,000 marines, and able to carry 100,000 men; large sums of money were provided to meet current expenses, and the only question was as to the general. Had the right man been appointed, the Vandal power might have been crushed sixty years before it really was, and the combined action of East and West, at once harmonious and successful, might have deferred if not prevented the destruction of Italian independence.

Basiliscus its Leader.—The right man would have been Marcellinus, a general trained under Aetius, nominally governor of Dalmatia, in reality almost an independent sovereign. But once more jealousy and political intrigue ruined a good cause. Ricimer in the West threw every obstacle in the way of his appointment as commander-in-chief, and would now neither countenance the expedition himself nor allow Anthemius to do so. In the East—equally anxious with the West to see Marcellinus in chief command—two men intrigued to prevent it; one who did not wish the expedition to succeed, another who was convinced that its success depended on himself. And the former used the latter as his tool. The former was Aspar the Goth, the latter was Basiliscus, brother of the Empress Verina.   Aspar was afraid that a successful war would diminish his own influence at Court, while he foresaw that the incompetence of Basiliscus would ensure failure.   Accordingly, he used all his great influence, and with success, to secure the appointment of Basiliscus; while, feigning to see in it a mere religious quarrel and not a national war, he entreated the good offices of Basiliscus for his Arian friends and kinsmen the Vandals, whom he was about to attack and conquer. The expedition was well provided, well officered, and well concerted.   Nothing but the mingled folly and treachery of Basiliscus prevented its succeeding.

Defeat of the Expedition.—The Western fleet or right wing of the expedition was to set out from Italy under the command of Marcellinus, and to clear Sardinia of Vandals : the left wing, under Heraclius, was to pick up the garrisons of Egypt and Cyrenaica, and to fall upon Tripolis, and thence to march upon Carthage by land ; while the centre, under Basilicus in person, was to join the right wing off the coast of Sicily, and attack Carthage from the sea.   The force at command was overpowering. The right and left wings succeeded with ease in effecting the first steps in the campaign.   The right wing and the centre united off the coast of Sicily : and Heraclius was on the march for Carthage.   Even Genseric, we are told, was discouraged, and a bold attack might have carried the capital, and ended the war at once !   Not once or twice only in history, however, discretion has falsely seemed the better part of valour.   Carthage lay at the south-west corner of an immense gulf, facing nearly due north, the north-western and north-eastern extremities of which were named respectively the promontories of Apollo and of Mercury (Cape Farina and Cape Bon). Just to the west of the latter, and immediately within the gulf, was a small town with an open roadstead, exposed especially to gales from the north-west and west. From hence to Carthage was about thirty-five miles direct. In this roadstead Basiliscus cast anchor, afraid to attack without feeling his way, and anxious to hear tidings of Heraclius. Presently an envoy from Genseric presented himself. He represented his master as eager for peace, but afraid of his people. He asked, therefore, for five days' truce, that Genseric might consult their wishes, handing Basiliscus, at the same time, a large sum of money as an earnest of his master's good-will. Basiliscus remembered Aspar, and was completely deceived. He took the money and granted the truce, and relapsed with his army into fatal security. To Genseric, meanwhile, time was everything, and during those five days every nerve was strained to prepare for the change of wind to west which might be expected. On the 5th day the wind changed, and Genseric was ready. At nightfall two fleets issued from the harbour before the wind, one of men-of-war amply equipped and manned, the other of boats and smaller merchant vessels filled with combustibles. As they drew near the doomed fleet of their enemy no watchfires, no sentinels, were to be seen. Fleet and army alike were wrapped in profound slumber. At a signal the fireships were cast loose, and driving before the wind presently became entangled with the nearest Roman ships : and the horrified Romans awoke to find that all was lost. The flames spread unchecked, until the whole bay was illumined : there was no possibility of concerted action, and individual effort was useless : while the confusion was increased by the Vandal men-of-war sailing along the burning line, and showering darts and arrows on any who were bold enough to try and meet the peril. Even Romans of Rome's palmy days might have been awestruck by such sights and sounds: and the Romans of the later Empire were no heroes.   Basiliscus fled under cover of the night: many followed his example; some few cut their way in despair through the enemy's line.   When the relics of the fleet and army were reviewed in Sicily, it was found that more than half had been sacrificed by their own supineness, and the treachery of Basiliscus.   Even yet, however, much might have been done with an army of 50,00ʋ men, and a fleet of more than 500 vessels, had a man like Marcellinus been placed in command.   But it was not to be.   Marcellinus was murdered in open day—men said, at the order and by an agent of the jealous Ricimer. The forces of the Western Empire were recalled.   At the news from Carthage Heraclius in Tripolis halted, and retraced his steps.   And lastly Basiliscus slunk back to Constantinople, a disgraced fugitive, and sought asylum from popular vengeance in the Church of St. Sophia.   The intervention of the Empress Verina alone enabled him to retire in safety to an obscure town in Thrace.

Decline of the Vandal Power.—After this victory, so unexpected and so crushing, Genseric became undisputed master of Africa, Tripolis, Sardinia, even Sicily, until his death in A.D. 477, and hardly a coast of the Mediterranean was safe from the Vandal fleets.   Owing to his energy and ability for command, the Vandals, in the middle of the fifth century, became the foremost barbarian nation within the Roman Empire, and might have seemed destined far more than Franks or Visigoths to found a permanent kingdom.   But Genseric may be compared to Epaminondas the Theban, whose death put an end to the glory of his nation, which his life had won. And after his death the declension of the Vandal power and name was so rapid, that only fifty years afterwards

Belisarius destroyed the kingdom without difficulty in a campaign of less than three months. The story of this campaign, and the account of the causes of Vandal weakness, will be reserved for the chapter on Justinian's reign.

CHAPTER VIII

ATTILA AND THE HUNS.

King Attila.—Of all the characters that played a part on the stage of Roman history in the fifth century, not one is so weird, or so hard to grasp as that of Attila. As in a dense mist, some half-seen approaching figure looms larger than human, yet dim and undefined, so is Attila a shadowy figure, half-revealed by contemporary history, half-obscured and distorted by dim traditions, which in after ages gathered round his name. That he was really *terrible* is seen in history. That he was also really *great*—great out of all proportion to the results of his brief career—is evident from the fact, that numerous peoples, Romans, Gauls, Franks, English, Scandinavians, Goths, and Hungarians, seized upon his name—as afterwards on that of Charles the Frank—and preserved it in their songs and legends. It is a strange medley of historical and traditional evidence, from which we have to infer the man as he was—history dating from one hundred years later; traditions as shifting and diverse as they are interesting. One " precious fragment," however, remains to tell us, at least, what one man saw with his own eyes, and thought of what he saw. In A.D. 449, a certain Greek, named Priscus, was attached to an embassy from Constantinople to the Court of Attila. He traversed a large part of the Trans-Danubian provinces, and saw much both of Attila and his chief wife, and of the manners and customs of the Huns. His description of what he saw has been preserved almost entire, and is singularly vivid. Attila himself he represents as a silent, reserved, resolute, and ambitious man; able to conceive and energetic to carry out vast schemes of conquest; and skilled in the secret of gaining the loyal obedience of even enemies—indisputably, a master of men.

The Traditions about Attila.—On this commanding figure, which dominated the minds, and awed the imagination of a whole Continent, converge a multitude of side-lights from all sorts of local traditions, and national folk-lore. Not only are these of interest in themselves, but of great use in illustrating the story of Attila; although, of course, their value varies in proportion to their remoteness in time and place from the time and place of their subject. An Italian legend on the one hand, and a German on the other, may be of equal value from different points of view; but a Scandinavian or an English tradition will be worth less than a German, and a Hungarian worth less than a Scandinavian. Lastly, each set of traditions has its distinctive type and character, due to assignable causes.

Gallo-Roman and Italian Traditions. — The Latin traditions about Attila owed their special character, partly to the fact that the communities which suffered from his arms were Christian, partly to the accident that the most dramatic situations in the tragedy were sustained by Christian priests or saints. As Anianus at Orleans, and Lupus at Troyes, and Geneviève at Paris, so Leo at Mantua was the prime agent in a great deliverance. In the fifth century the gratitude of a Christian province for such deliverance took the shape—not of thanks and honours to military genius, which had laid the spectre of Hunnish invincibility—but of overflowing, almost abject reverence for the saintly men and women, who by death or unworldly calmness in the presence of danger had moved an Attila to mercy. Every district, every city, began little by little to claim some special part for itself in the awful horrors, from which, as by the finger of God, Gaul and Italy had lately been saved ; and some special glory for its own saint or prelate. Thus a mass of traditions was insensibly accumulated, which (however unhistorical) exactly chimed in with the notions and wishes of the time : and the idea was developed and fostered by the teaching of the Church, that Attila had been an agent of God's wrath against men, a " scourge of God," while holy men and women were agents of His pity, to intercede and save them from extermination. All things were double, one against the other ; on one side war and rapine, on the other peace ; on one side the scourge, on the other the intercessor. What honour then could be too great for a Church, whose ministers were so favoured of heaven—for a Geneviève, who (legend said) had saved Paris from capture ; for an Anianus, who had rescued Orleans ; for a Lupus, who led a host of Huns harmless through the streets of Troyes—harmless, because a veil was before their eyes, and they seemed to be marching through woods and meadows ; for a Leo, whose intercession saved Rome from pillage by the heathen ! There was but little room left for the recognition of such a trifling accident as the winning of a great battle. To the fifth and sixth centuries the conference of Mantua between Attila and Leo seemed as much more glorious than the victory of Chalons, as the prayers of Leo seemed greater than the genius of Aetius. The glory of Attila's repulse was thus transferred by religious sentiment from the warrior to the priest, and the story was coloured accordingly. When a hermit salutes Attila by the title of "Scourge of God," and predicts his defeat at Chalons; or when the two apostles, St. Peter and St. Paul, stand behind Leo in his embassy to Attila, and with silent gestures, and drawn swords, threaten the great king, if he spares not Rome, it is no longer sober history we are dealing with, but history transfigured by religious sentiment.

East German or Gothic Traditions.—The German traditions were very different from the Latin. Their theme is not the "scourge of God," nor their burden a tale of carnage and misery. But they tell of a great king, wise and magnificent; a hard fighter and a deep drinker; whose court was hospitable, splendid, and joyous.

There are two causes which seem to have left this deep impression on the legends of the Germans. Almost without exception they had been Attila's vassals. But the vassalage had been such as to soothe rather than wound their pride. It had brought with it conquest and glory. It had been shared with all the other nations of Central Europe. And the Ostrogothic chiefs, in particular, had been admitted to Attila's counsels, and intrusted with the command of his armies. Further, the series of wars and Gothic conquests, which followed Attila's death, was identified with his name and memory. Odoacer, who ruled Italy for fifteen years, was son of that Edecon who had more than once been Hunnish ambassador to Constantinople; and Odoacer himself had served in Attila's armies. Theodoric, who founded the kingdom of the Ostrogoths, and governed Italy for thirty years, was a son of Theodemir, Attila's chief counsellor. Thus, though dead, the memory of the great "King Etzel" seemed yet to survive in the exploits of his captains and their children. Tradition, however, is careless of truth. Ere long Ostrogothic vainglory coupled together the names of Ermanaric, Attila, and Theodoric, as a glorious trio of contemporaries, to do honour to the royal race of the Amali; forgetting that Attila was born twenty-five years after Ermanaric's death, and that he died when Theodoric was only eight years old. It is instructive to note this confusion, and its probable origin. Every good Goth or Frank knew by heart the songs that celebrated the deeds of his fathers and his people, the Iliad of his race. They were sung at every feast by bard and poet. But of all their heroes Theodoric was the greatest, the worthy peer of heroes as great as himself, even though they were not Ostrogoth, but Visigoth and Hun. The combination was as easy, as it seemed natural and legitimate.

West German and Scandinavian Traditions.— Nor is it wonderful that the glorious deeds of the fifth and sixth centuries, their most glorious epoch, stimulated the ideas of Gothic singers; and that the sixth century saw rise a cycle of legend, which gradually passed from Eastern to Western Germany, and thence to Scandinavia, Iceland, and England, in which Attila figures largely, while Theodoric is the hero. And there is nothing singular in this passing on (as it were) of tradition from one people to another. The songs of the Lombards in honour of Alboin were current not only in Lombardy, but among Bavarians and Saxons. Not seldom one king would send to another king his own favourite harper or singer (as Theodoric to Chlodwig the Frank), who would of course carry with him his own special songs. The English Alfred, the Frank Charles, the Scandinavian Scalds were all devoted to these glorifications of ancient heroes, all dwelt with equal delight on the exploits of Theodoric and Attila. Thus, in Northern and Western Europe the popular songs of the ninth century repeated the same story, though in a different shape. In the latter, as in the earlier form, the mysterious king "Etzel" or "Athel" still figures—no longer, however, as the friend of Theodoric and Italian heroes, but in connection with Walter the Visigoth and Sigurd the Netherlander, veritable German heroes. He even woos and wins the fair Gudrunn, when Sigurd, her lord, had been slain by the wicked wiles of Brunehild—wins her, however, to his own sorrow, for she bids her first lord's murderers and all their followers to her new lord's court, and there one and all are slain, including Queen Gudrunn herself.

Nibelungen-lied.—Thus far, then, the legend was a genuine tradition, passing from mouth to mouth. Towards the end of the tenth century, however, a certain Pilgerein or Pilegrin, bishop of Passau, and apostle of the Hungarians, collected the various popular songs concerning Attila, which were floating about Germany, and threw them into the form of an epic poem written in Latin. This was practically the first edition of the famous "Nibelungen-lied" (Song of the Nibelungs) and determined the character of all after legends respecting Attila. The song is the story of the curse, which clave to all who had aught to do with the hoarded treasure of King Nibelung of the Nibelungen land—a curse which lighted upon Sigurd and Hagen, and Gunther and Gudrunn, and even involved King Etzel himself in trouble. In fact, the whole catastrophe of the tale turns upon Attila's second marriage.

Hungarian Traditions.—Lastly, there is a whole cycle of Hungarian traditions gathered round three great heroes—Attila, the common ancestor and glory of all Huns;

Arpad, founder of the Magyar kingdom (about A.D. 930); Stephen, apostle, saint, and king (A.D. 1000): but it is the name of Attila again which predominates; who invades Italy; who is forbidden, not by Leo, but by Jesus Christ himself, to disturb the repose of His apostles in Rome; who has two wives, Honoria the Roman, and Chriemhild (*i.e.* Gudrunn), the German; and whose death is connected with his marriage to a third wife, daughter of the king of the Bactrians.

Summary.—Such is a short sketch of a very wide subject. Its interest lies in the fact, that the name of Attila became the common stock of European legend for centuries after his death; and in the inference to be drawn therefrom, that none but a man of commanding greatness could have left this indelible mark upon his own and succeeding ages. And if it be asked why, if he were so great, the results of his efforts were so small, the answer would be twofold—first, that the tribes over whom he ruled, and especially the Huns themselves, were hardly in any sense civilised; and, secondly, that the jealousy between the two great divisions of his Empire, the Aryan and Turanian, which was repressed with a strong hand while he lived, burst out after his death, and destroyed for a while the Empire which he had consolidated.

State of Central Europe—A.D. 400–450.**—**It has already been told how, at the beginning of the fifth century, Italy, Gaul, Spain, and Africa, suffered from barbarian inroads—from Visigoths, Vandals, Alani, and others. The Italian or the Gaul, who writhed beneath their violence, never suspected of course the cause which brought on him and his such woes from beyond the mountains. But in fact his enemies were fleeing from enemies more terrible than themselves. A great wave of Huns, with their subject-allies, was sweeping into and over the east of Europe, driving all before them; and the valley of the Danube was like an ant's nest, disturbed and up-turned, where all is confusion and agitation and hurrying to and fro. The first glimpse we obtain of these Huns shows us hordes of savage horsemen preying on the industry of others, trampling out the faint traces of civilisation which were just beginning to show themselves, and reducing all with whom they came in contact to a state of nomad barbarism like their own. Year by year they pressed further westwards, led by four kings or chiefs, one of whom was Moundzoukh, the father of Attila. Year by year they drew nearer to the frontier of Rome. And Rome soon learned both to fear and to use the swords of the fierce horsemen, who would sell themselves to any bidder. It needed but a strong hand to reduce these restless hardy men to order and obedience, and a strong head to guide them, and then Empire was assured.

Attila, King—A.D. 435.—Both were united in Attila, who succeeded to the chief power about A.D. 435, and having rid himself of his brother Bleda, gradually laid a firmer and firmer grasp on all the Hunnish tribes of Eastern Europe, preparatory to reducing the Teuton and Slave populations in the North and West. And, if we may believe Norse tradition, he pursued his conquests as far as the Baltic, and in a very few years was master of all Europe north of the Danube and east of the Rhine, with the exception of Scandinavia and the country between the Lower Rhine and the Elbe. "Barbaria" and "Romania" were once more face to face; but the latter was no longer united, the former was no longer divided. And weakness on the one side was quickly followed by encroachment on the other.

Gradual Encroachments.—Already in A.D. 435 the Treaty of Margus, dictated by Attila, had shown what the Roman Empire might expect at his hands. He demanded an instant cessation of alliance between the Empire and the Trans-Danubian tribes; the immediate extradition of all Huns within the Empire; the restoration of Roman prisoners who had escaped unransomed; and a large increase of the "subsidy" or "aid," or whatever other euphonious name they might choose to give to the "*tribute,*" paid to himself. And in A.D. 441 and A.D. 446, on the pretext that the Bishop of Margus had surreptitiously rifled the tombs of the Hunnish kings, he had crossed the Danube, pushed as far as Thermopylæ, defeated two Roman armies, and ravaged seventy cities, allowing himself finally to be bought off.

Embassy to Constantinople.—Again, in A.D. 449, an embassy was sent to Constantinople with demands more urgent than before. Attila claimed by right of conquest all the Cisdanubian provinces within five days' march of the river. He required that future ambassadors sent to his court should be men of the highest rank only. He renewed his complaints about the refugees, with no indistinct threats of war. War indeed was what he wanted—war leading to conquest and aggrandisement. And the Eastern Emperor, Theodosius II. (A.D. 408–450) was no match for Attila in either firmness or policy. They were almost a ludicrous contrast. The one by his very personal characteristics, by his broad chest and deep sunk restless eyes, by his mingled simplicity and love of splendour, by the alternate ferocity and placability of his temper, by his subtle and persistent policy, by his wisdom, and justice, and generosity, challenged the awe and admiration of mankind. The other was at fifty as much a child as he had been at fifteen—regular in his studies and devotions, lavish in his expenses, willing to abandon the cares of State to any one, sister, wife, or favourite, if he himself might only be let alone. It was the fable of the lamb and the wolf repeated.

Counter-Embassy.—The reigning favourite at Constantinople was the eunuch Chrysaphius. This man flattered himself that he had successfully bribed Edecon, one of the Hunnish ambassadors, to assassinate Attila. In reality, Edecon had betrayed the plot to his master. However, Chrysaphius, himself deceived, persuaded Theodosius to send a counter-embassy to Attila with an evasive if not imprudent answer, practically shelving his demands. What need of courtesy to a barbarian, who would shortly cease to trouble them? The three ambassadors, Maximin, Vigilas, and Priscus, already mentioned, set out with Edecon and Orestes, who were to return with them. They crossed the Danube, and after some days' journeying, unexpectedly met a deputation similar to their own, despatched by Valentinian III., the Western Emperor, to Attila. They, too, had a difficulty of their own to arrange, connected with certain vases or sacred vessels, which had been secretly withdrawn from Sirmium before its pillage, but which Attila had heard of and now claimed. The irony of Fortune could hardly farther go! The answer of Attila to the joint deputation, given after some delay, was couched in similar terms. To the West it was, "The Vases, or their holder, or war." To the East it was, "The head of Chrysaphius, or war." Such an answer from such a man seemed to echo back and to force into relief all the vague presentiments and forebodings which were, so to say, in the air (A.D. 450), and were aggravated by a curious succession of natural phenomena, an eclipse, a comet, and shocks of earthquake. Tribe after tribe was known to be gathering on the banks of the Danube. East and West alike were sitting as in mute despair, expecting where the blow would fall, when on the same day at the same hour, (so runs the story), a courier demanded audience of Theodosius in the East and Valentinian in the West, and each delivered his message in the same terms:—" Attila, my master and thine, bids thee prepare him a palace, for he comes."

Attila demands the Princess Honoria.—But a more precise demand was yet to follow. Fifteen years before, Honoria, sister of Valentinian, in a fit of romantic folly, or wearied with the monotony of life, had sent a ring to Attila and offered him herself. For fifteen years Attila had left the offer unnoticed, though he kept the ring. And now suddenly a formal request was made, that his bride might be sent, and with her, more important still, her dowry.

Alliance with Genseric and the Franks.—At this juncture fortune gave Attila two allies, and an opportunity which he was not slow to seize. These allies were Genseric the Vandal, and a Frankish prince. The former had deeply insulted Theodoric the Visigoth by mutilating his daughter, his own son's wife, on some fancied slight, and then sending her home. The latter had been driven from his country by a domestic revolution on his father's death, and besieged Attila with entreaties to restore him to his father's throne. Genseric, fearing that Theodoric would revenge himself for the insult (as in fact he did) by an immediate alliance with Rome, and preparations for war, concluded on his part an alliance with Attila, by which it was agreed that a simultaneous attack should be made on Italy and Gaul— an attack, however, which, as far as Italy was concerned, was deferred for some five years by Genseric's own difficulties in Africa. Attila meanwhile prepared with vigour to restore his Frank ally, and to attack his Visigothic enemies, whom, at the same time, he tried to cajole with fair words. Now, as always, his words were ambiguous. Whether Romans or Visigoths were his friends or enemies he left uncertain. One thing only was certain, that devastation and misery were in store for whomsoever he should attack. Only once before in history had such "numbers numberless" been gathered in one host, and the description of their names and arms rivals that of Xerxes' army as given by Herodotus. The lowest estimate reckons 500,000 fighting men.

Attila invades Gaul—A.D. 451.—By the beginning of March Attila was on the Rhine. Resistance seemed hopeless. Town after town was taken or surrendered—Spires, Worms, Strasburg, Metz, Rheims, Arras. All alike were pillaged. Officials, civil and military, fled. In the general panic one class of men alone remained at their posts, the priests, discharging ecclesiastical, civil, and even sometimes military functions, and earning for their order a well-deserved renown—for themselves too often a crown of martyrdom for their bold obedience to duty. Both history and tradition unite to honour also a woman, St. Geneviève, who saved Paris—not indeed, as legend says, by resisting an assault, but, when the men had resolved to abandon the city, by persuading their wives to refuse to acquiesce, and to shut themselves into the church of St. Stephen. The baffled husbands were forced to yield; and as Geneviève had ventured to predict, Attila passed Paris by. The Paris of those days was comparatively unimportant; and Attila had other projects in view. To a leader, the strength of whose army was horsemen, the great plain of Central France promised to be at once a forage ground and a battle field; and towards that the king now directed his march from Metz. In twenty days he was before Orleans (beginning of May).

Siege of Orleans.—The situation of Orleans is re-markable. In ancient Gaul, as in mediæval and modern France, it has always played an important part, and a glance at a map will shew why. Lying on the right bank of the Loire, where the river bends to the west-ward—commanding, therefore, the valleys west and south, and (as it were) barring the way from the north—whether known as Genabum, or Aurelianum, or Orleans, from the days of Cæsar to our own days, the city has been a famous centre, both commercial and strategic. As in the fifteenth century against the English, as in the nineteenth against the Germans, so in the fifth against Attila, Orleans made a vigorous resistance, and formed the turning point of the struggle. To one man belongs the glory of this resistance, Anianus, (St. Agnan), Bishop of Orleans, who was as good and self-devoted as he was full of vigour and resource. As the Huns were approaching, he hurried to Aetius at Arles, and urged him to march without delay. The city could hold out until June 23rd, and no longer. Then he returned with all haste to animate the citizens by his courage and his presence. Meanwhile, Aetius had no easy task before him. The relief of Orleans was a pressing necessity; but Valentinian had retained in Italy all but a handful of troops, the Burgundians had been defeated, the fidelity of the Alani was more than doubt-ful, and the Visigoths sulkily refused to move a finger. It was Roman folly, they said, which had brought them into this difficulty; and the Romans must meet it as best they could. In this crisis he had recourse to a man, whose influence with Theodoric was greater than any man's, the Senator Mecilius Avitus, afterwards Emperor (A.D. 455–6). Avitus was a strange mixture of the soldier, statesman, student, and man of pleasure, who had sustained each character with equal success, and captivated the barbaric imagination by the elegance of his life. And now this influence was turned to good account. Where Aetius had failed, Avitus succeeded. Theodoric issued the order to march, and the junction of the Roman and the Visigothic forces seemed to assure victory beforehand.

Relief of Orleans.—But they were only just in time. It was June 23rd, and no signs of relief were visible to the hard-pressed town. A messenger was sent in hot haste to Aetius, warning him that to-morrow would be too late. Still no help came; and at last the city was forced to surrender at discretion to an enemy irritated by protracted resistance. The Huns entered Orleans, and the pillage began. But "when the night is darkest, dawn is nearest." A sudden cry of panic, and a sudden retreat of their enemies told the trembling city that help was at hand; and the Roman and Gothic forces were attacking the Huns, even before they could extricate themselves from the narrow streets. Orleans was saved, and Attila in full retreat eastwards. But Aetius wasted no time in idle rejoicings. A hot pursuit was at once begun; and ere night-fall the Roman van-guard of Franks had overtaken the Gepidæ, Attila's rear-guard, at the confluence of the Seine and the Aube, and at once attacked them. The battle raged all night, and at dawn 15,000 men lay dead upon the field. But the struggle had been worth while. Attila had had time to concentrate his forces on the chosen spot, where he resolved to fight out the contest for Gaul—a level country intersected by rivers, and bounded by mountains on the north and east. In this vast "Campania," as it was called, (Champagne) and at a spot (Durocatalaunum, Châlons) where two Roman roads diverged to the north-east and south-east, offering means of retreat, if necessary, Attila took his final stand.

On the same day the army of Aetius encamped opposite to the Huns. The battle of Châlons has well been called one of the "decisive battles" of the world; for the question at issue was nothing less than the question, what race in particular should enter upon the rich inheritance of Roman civilisation, language, and law—whether it should be German or Hun, Aryan or Turanian. The victory of Aetius did, in fact, secure to Europe all that is contained in the words "Christianity" and "civilisation." By the victory of Attila the settlement of Europe would have been indefinitely postponed, and Roman civilisation possibly lost for ever.

Battle of Châlons—A.D. 451.—In the host of the Huns there was general discouragement, even Attila being moved by adverse prophecies and omens to forebode defeat. Accordingly, he delayed the action till as late in the day as possible; nor was it till three in the afternoon that he led his army from their encampment of waggons. His Huns he posted in the centre under his own command, the Ostrogoths on the left wing, the Gepidæ and other subject tribes on the right, his object being to break the Roman centre, and at the same time to secure his own retreat to his camp, if needful. Aetius' tactics were skilfully directed to meet the very thing which Attila had in view. The centre he left to take care of itself, posting there the smaller tribes, and those whose fidelity was doubtful, while he opposed the Visigoths to the Ostrogoths, and himself took the command of the left wing against the Gepidæ. That his own centre would be overpowered and pushed back was clear; that his own right and left wing would defeat their opponents was probable; if so, his victory was assured. Visigoths and Romans would wheel round and charge; and no people so wayward and unstable as the Huns would withstand a simultaneous attack on each flank. All happened precisely as he had foreseen. The Alani and Burgundians were no match for the Huns, though they fought bravely: the Visigoths, (though their king Theodoric was slain), after a fierce struggle, defeated their kinsmen the Ostrogoths, and instantly fell on the flank of the Huns, while the Roman left under Aetius did the same. Thus assailed, Attila was unable to hold his ground, and slowly retreated to the circle of waggons, whence a ceaseless shower of arrows was kept up, warning the pursuers not to presume too much upon their victory: and when next day a ceaseless din of arms and blare of trumpets was heard from the Hunnish camp, it seemed as if some sudden blow were in preparation. Accordingly, a council of war was held; and the Romans and Goths agreed to sit down and blockade Attila in his camp, and starve him out. But Thorismond, the Visigoth, was anxious to return southwards, now that his father was dead, in order to secure his own position—as anxious, indeed, as Attila was to retreat before his forces were utterly demoralised by confinement and inaction. The temper of barbarians is proverbially fickle. Aetius, therefore, judged it prudent to let the Visigoths have their way, and to withdraw his opposition, although their desertion was fatal to complete success. For no sooner was it discovered in Attila's camp that the Visigoths had set out on their homeward march, than Attila also broke out, and began his eastward journey, while Aetius did not feel himself strong enough to do more than follow at a safe distance, and prevent plunder. Attila recrossed the Rhine, and Gaul was saved, if not from a passing devastation, at least from ruin; but the glory of his repulse, as we have seen, was not for Aetius. The Visigoths disputed with him the honour of the victory; while the Court of Ravenna accused him of treason, in letting Attila escape—a charge repeated with dangerous emphasis, when the Huns threatened Italy in the very next year.

Attila threatens Italy — A.D. 452. — This jealousy felt towards Aetius made his task in protecting Italy, Ravenna, Rome, doubly difficult. He had no longer barbarian auxiliaries, scarcely even patriotic spirit to fall back upon; and when in despair he proposed at least to save the Emperor by conducting him to Gaul, a general chorus of indignation at once proclaimed it an impossibility. All he could do, therefore, was to make the best use of the resources at hand. To protect Ravenna and Rome at the same time was impossible, so he abandoned Ravenna to its fate. The Emperor took refuge in Rome. All troops, save a few garrisons, were withdrawn to the south of the Po, and a large camp was formed on the northern slope of the Apennines; and there, as the year before, behind the Loire, he prepared to make a last desperate struggle for his sovereign and the capital, sending urgent demands meanwhile to the Eastern Emperor Marcian (A.D. 450–457) for reinforcements against the common enemy. But they were never needed. Attila had set out in the winter from Hungary, seized Sirmium, crossed the Julian Alps, and, after a three months' siege, had taken and so cruelly devastated Aquileia, that 100 years later its site could hardly be identified. From thence, and from many another town, the inhabitants fled in panic to what seemed a safe retreat, the archipelago of islands on which Venice afterwards arose, but which at that time was haunted only by sea-birds. Venetia was overrun; Milan and Pavia were sacked. But the delay before Aquileia had been fatal. It was now the heat of summer, and fever and pestilence appeared. Attila himself indeed was anxious to march on, to force Aetius to fight, and then to grasp the glorious prize of Rome; but his army was already laden with booty, and remembering with dismay the awful fate of Alaric, who had broken the spell of Rome's inviolability, and paid for his temerity with his life, they were eager to return.

Embassy from Rome to Attila.—At this juncture a solemn embassy from Rome arrived in Mantua, headed by Pope Leo, and sought an interview with Attila. It was granted. And the king, flattered by the thought of thus seeing Rome and her pontiff sueing for peace and of humiliating his enemy Aetius, granted the peace that they asked for, and promised to quit Italy on condition of an annual tribute (July 6th, 452). One right he still reserved to himself, as though loth to part with a ground for complaint—the right to Honoria and her dowry.

Attila leaves Italy.—And so the mighty conqueror went his way, never again to trouble the peace of Italy —the conqueror, as his soldiers said, "invincible by men, but whom two wild beasts had overpowered," meaning Lupus at Troyes and Leo in Italy. And as he went, so runs the story, a warning was sent to him from heaven of impending doom; for, as he was about to cross the river Lech (Lycus), a strange female figure, as though inspired, seized his horse's bridle and thrice cried aloud in awful tones, "Attila, back" (Retro, Attila). And indeed the doom was very near.

Marriage and Death of Attila—A.D. **453.—**He took to himself in the following year a new bride, named Ildico or Hildegonde, probably a prize of war, whom tradition variously describes as a Frank, a Burgundian, and a Bactrian. Be that as it may, on the morning following his marriage, Attila was found dead in his bed, wallowing in his own blood, and the young bride seated by the bed and bathed in tears. An ignoble end to a

life of conquest and glory, the more so as it was never
known whether he had died of apoplexy or been murdered
by his new wife, in vengeance for some insult to herself
and her people.   Surely Attila should have died on the
field of battle, and in the rapture of victory !

CHAPTER IX

THE "CHANGE OF GOVERNMENT"—COMMONLY CALLED THE FALL OF THE WESTERN EMPIRE—A.D. 475-526.

Results of Attila's Death—A.D. 453.—Attila was dead. And the strong will which for twenty-five years had known no check was not obeyed a single day after his death. A quarrel for power broke out at once among his sons, necessitating a division of his Empire, of its soil and people and flocks. Among a nomad people, however, this is no easy task; there are no natural frontiers; the population is ever on the move. The passions of the Germans, too, were aroused by the idea of being counted and told off like so many cattle. The example of revolt, begun by the Gepidæ, was speedily followed by the Ostrogoths and other German tribes; and the question was fought out in the plain of the Netad (a tributary of the Danube), whether Germany should be ruled by Germans or by Huns, should be Aryan or Turanian. It was settled by the defeat of the Huns. The Gepidæ occupied what is now Hungary as the fruit of their victory. The Ostrogoths occupied Dalmatia, Noricum, and Pannonia, an encroachment connived at by the Eastern Emperor Marcian, in return for which they were supposed to be in alliance with the Empire, and to furnish contingents to its armies. Other German tribes, the Herulians, the Rugians, the Sueves, seized the country lying between the Danube and the Alps; while the Lombards (Langobardi) moved southwards from the Elbe and took possession of what is now Bohemia. Thus once more was unhappy Italy threatened by a new series of barbarous foes.

Attila was dead; but his influence and spirit lived after him. Italy was presently overrun by crowds of barbarians, singly or in bands, who flocked there to make their fortunes, as vultures flock to a dying carcass. For the Western Empire was nodding to its ruin. Aetius fell by the hand of Valentinian (A.D. 454), and with him fell the only clear head and strong arm, which could have warded off coming evils: for it is hardly exaggeration to say, that after his death there were no more Emperors of the West deserving of the name. Political power was wholly in the hands of barbarian adventurers, many or all of whom had known Attila, and in one way or another served under him.

Orestes the Pannonian.—Foremost among these was that Orestes, the Pannonian, who has already been noticed (chap. vii.) He had been secretary to Attila, and more than once ambassador to Constantinople; and when the great king was dead, he offered his services to the Emperor of the West, and speedily rose to be patrician and master-general. The Empire meanwhile was rapidly falling from bad to worse. Britain, Spain, and Africa, were lost. The Mediterranean was swarming with Vandal pirates. Dalmatia was independent, and Gaul practically the same, with the exception of Narbonne and Auvergne. Ricimer was dead; Constantinople was far off; and there seemed no man able or willing to hold the reins of power. At this crisis, moreover, the reigning Emperor was a Greek (Julius Nepos, A.D. 474), a nominee of the Eastern Emperor Leo (A.D. 457–474), and consequently unpopular as a semi-foreigner. A man of high virtue and considerable talent, his lot was cast in unhappy times; for the sole event with which his name is coupled was the compulsory cession of Auvergne to the Visigoths. Orestes was the officer charged by Nepos with the unpleasant duty of handing over the province to its new masters, and a large body of troops was told off for the purpose and placed under his command. But the cession cost Nepos his crown. General and troops alike fretted under the duty imposed upon them; and, instead of crossing the Alps, they marched as with one mind upon Ravenna, and Nepos had no alternative but to flee. He hastily embarked on board ship, and crossed the Adriatic to Dalmatia, where, six years later (A.D. 480), he was assassinated by order of Glycerius, his predecessor on the imperial throne, who had himself been ousted by Nepos.

Romulus Augustulus—A.D. 475.—Orestes entered Ravenna as master of Italy on March 28, 475; but, contrary to all expectation, he steadily refused the purple for himself, too cautious perhaps to run so great a risk uselessly. For time was in his favour: the longer the delay the greater was the confusion. At last an interregnum of seven months was finished by what Thierry calls a "coup de théatre." On October 29th, a body of soldiers marched to the house of Orestes, seized his young son, aged fourteen, named Romulus Augustulus, and saluted him as Emperor. Their choice was accepted by the army and the country, and thus by a strange accident the last in the long line of Roman Emperors of the West bore the name at once of the founder of that Empire and of the founder of Rome itself. Nor was this all. The traditions of long years, the forebodings of seers and poets, tended to the conviction that Rome's destined twelve ages of Empire, typified by the twelve vultures of Romulus, were either completed or fast bordering on completion. The end at last seemed approaching.

Downfall of Orestes and the Emperor — A.D. 476.—The ruin of Orestes began from the moment when he appeared to have gained his object; for he had to satisfy the demands of those who had lifted him to power.   And those demands were for nothing less than a third of the soil of Italy.   Was the claim indeed so unreasonable? They had deserved well of Orestes.   Other tribes and nations, like themselves, had been allotted land within the Roman Empire.   Visigoths and Burgundians in Gaul had laid hands on two-thirds of the soil; were they not moderate in only claiming one-third? To themselves, no doubt, they seemed moderate enough; but Orestes could realise what such a confiscation implied, and was not so hard-hearted or unscrupulous as calmly to inflict so much suffering on an unoffending people.   He refused the demand.   The refusal at once resulted in a meeting; the meeting in a revolt; and the revolters had no difficulty in finding a leader in Odoacer (or Otochar), the Rugian, son of Edecon, whom Attila had often employed, like Orestes, as ambassador to the court of Byzantium.   The dreams of ambition had already been aroused in his mind by some words of St Severinus, whom he had visited in Noricum when on his way to Italy, foretelling his future greatness.   Young and energetic, he had soon forced his way to high rank in the Italian army; and being encumbered with few scruples, he readily promised to give what Orestes had refused, if his comrades would accept him as their chief.   They consented; and war was at once declared against the ungrateful Orestes.   From all the garrisons of Italy, and from the valley of the Danube, recruits flocked in to join the standard of Odoacer, whom accident and force of character thus enabled to verify the prediction of Severinus. Orestes threw himself into Pavia; while his brother Paulus prepared to defend Ravenna and the youthful Emperor. But it was too late. Pavia was blockaded by Odoacer for forty days, and at last fell, rather by treason from within than by force from without. The prayers of its saintly Bishop Epiphanius, glorious already for many a similar intercession, saved indeed the liberty and honour of many of its inhabitants, but Orestes was put to death (A.D. 476). From Pavia the victorious Rugian, already saluted as "king" by his soldiers, marched rapidly on Ravenna, defeated Paulus in the pine woods that covered the city in those days on the south and south-west, and entered the streets without resistance. Meanwhile, the trembling Romulus had thrown off the imperial insignia, and tried in vain to hide himself from the ruthless barbarian, who had slain his father, and would hardly hesitate to slay the son. Odoacer, however, was no mere butcher. Moved by the fears, or the youth, or the beauty of the lad, he scorned to take his life, and allowed him to retire with his whole family to the luxurious obscurity of the villa of Lucullus on the promontory of Misenum in Campania,—once the home of Marius, and then of Lucullus, and now of the last Roman Emperor of the West,—and yet to be, twenty years later, the final resting place on earth for 500 years of the body of the saint who had first warned Odoacer of his coming greatness.

A Change in Form of Government.—Thus ended the long roll of Roman Emperors in the West for 325 years. An Emperor, indeed, there was at Constantinople, and continued to be for nearly 1000 years, but his power in the West and over Italy was partial and temporary, where he was regarded with jealousy as an alien. Rome

saw not another Emperor until the day when Pope Leo
III. crowned Charles the Great Emperor in the basilica
of St. Peter, and the Empire revived to attempt once more
the great work of "Union," of Roman and Teutonic amal-
gamation (Christmas Day, A.D. 800).   But we must not
confound two different things.   Empires can exist without Emperors, and there is no special virtue in a name.
Although, there was no Emperor, the life of Rome and
Italy continued much the same as it had been for the last
fifty years ; indeed, it is remarkable how little noise among
contemporaries this revolution produced, of which later
historians have made so much.   It was a change in the
form of government, long foreseen ; and whatever change
it produced among the governed was certainly a change
for the better.   It would be idle to compare the vigorous
reigns of Odoacer and Theodoric with the anarchy preceding them ; and it may well be doubted, on the other
hand, whether the effect of the revolution on the ordinary
life of an Italian was comparable to that produced by the
Protectorate of Cromwell in England or by the Great
Revolution in France.

Odoacer " King "—A.D. 476.—Odoacer was "king,"
and for fifteen years he ruled Italy strongly and well.
He respected and enforced the Imperial laws ; he retained
the Imperial officers, consuls, præfects, and the like.
Though an Arian, he granted toleration to the Catholics.
He protected the Italian frontiers from the barbarians of
Germany and Gaul.   He even crossed the Adriatic to
recover Dalmatia, and passed the Alps to reconquer Noricum.   But years of decay are not to be repaired by so
brief a period of peace; and the state of Italy was only
less miserable than it had been.

Difficulties in and out of Italy.—Ever since the
days of Tiberius, slavery and absenteeism had been work-

ing their deadly effect. Population had steadily declined,
as the means of subsistence became scarcer, and had been
further diminished by the incessant wars and disorders
of 200 years; while the loss of Egypt and Africa had suddenly cut off the ordinary supply of corn for the great
cities. Pope Gelasius now repeated the complaint made
eighty years before by St. Ambrose, that whole districts
in the Romagna and Tuscany were ruined and depopu-
lated. And now, to crown all, one-third of the soil was
wrested from the impoverished landowners, and bestowed (as in the times of Sulla and Augustus) on rude
soldiers, who did not, like the Visigoths in Gaul, bring
wives and children and cattle with them, and so form a
genuine "colony," but being unused to husbandry and
settled life, soon tired of their bargain, and abandoned
or sold what they did not care to keep. It seemed,
therefore, that many a farmer had been ruined to no
purpose; for the soldiers who dispossessed them were soon
as poor as they—men to whom revolution could mean
nothing but gain, and who were, therefore, ripe for revolution. For the moment, however, the danger was
evaded by the astuteness of Odoacer. There were two
quarters from which he might anticipate interference—
from the Visigoths in Gaul, and from Constantinople.
The former he pacified by ceding to them Narbonne, the
last relic of Roman dominion beyond the Alps. The
alliance of the Emperor Zeno (A.D. 474–491) he won by
a deeper stroke of policy. Zeno was very anxious to
interfere in the West, and there were two men at least
who were equally anxious to aid him in so doing. One
of these was Julius Nepos, the ex-Emperor of the West,
who had fled to Dalmatia, and was eager to regain his
crown; the other was Theodoric the Ostrogoth. Theodoric was the son of Theodemir, of the royal race of the

Amali (the Immaculate), and had been brought up as a hostage at the Court of Byzantium. Educated, indeed, he was not; for he never even learned to write; but contact with civilisation awoke and stimulated his native genius, and produced that happy combination of energy and wisdom, of power of will and respect for law, which marked soon afterwards his peaceful reign in Italy. As yet, however, all this was in the future, and Theodoric was only an ambitious man, with a consciousness of latent power which he longed to use—a dangerous enemy, however, should opportunity offer.

Odoacer Subordinate to the Emperor.—With this trio of unquiet spirits Odoacer had to cope—with Zeno, jealous of the independence of the West; with Nepos, ever importuning him to act; with Theodoric, eager for some field of action. And Odoacer was equal to the occasion. He too had an ex-Emperor in reserve in the person of Romulus Augustulus. At Odoacer's dictation, Romulus instructed the Roman Senate to send an embassy to Constantinople, declaring that Italy was weary of two Emperors, and asking Zeno to resume the Imperial power, and to name Odoacer "patrician" and representative of the Emperor in Italy. At the same time, as though an affirmative answer were certain, the Imperial insignia, diadems, and purple, the heirlooms of four centuries, were dispatched to Constantinople to adorn perhaps some cabinet of curiosities in the Imperial palace. Zeno graciously accepted the present, and assented to the petition as far as regarded Odoacer, while reserving the rights of Nepos—a reservation which the patrician wisely ignored, and which was rendered useless by the murder of Nepos (A.D. 480). For a time Odoacer was master of Italy. And to Italy he presently added Sicily, which he bought from the Vandals.

Theodoric sent to reduce Italy to Obedience —A.D. 488.—But it was only for a time. After a peaceful reign of some ten or twelve years Odoacer was vanquished, and Italy oppressed by a sudden irruption of Theodoric and the whole Ostrogothic nation. It would be alike useless and wearisome to narrate in detail the varying relations of Zeno and Theodoric, and the wretched intrigues and cabals of the Eastern Court. Suffice it to say that, after a dozen quarrels, and as many reconciliations, the enmity and the friendship of the Ostrogoth became equally burdensome to the Emperor of the East, who welcomed greedily, at last, a proposal made twice before and twice rejected, that Theodoric should release the province of Italy from the "oppression" (as it was styled) of the too independent Odoacer. That Theodoric was ambitious has already been said; but ambition was not now his only incentive. He was regarded as a natural leader, not only by his own Ostrogoths, but by many another people inhabiting the valley of the Danube; and while the Ostrogoths were chafing at the misery and inaction of their life in Mœsia, and bitterly exclaiming against their king's luxurious and ignoble life at court, Rugians, Herulians, and others were calling on him to avenge them upon the Italianised Odoacer, who had ventured to attack and defeat them on their own side of the Alps. Ambition, shame, and anger, therefore, combined to urge Theodoric to immediate action, while Zeno's assent relieved the East of a troublesome and domineering neighbour. The vast host, numbering (it was said) 200,000 fighting men, besides women and children, cattle and waggons, set out on its westward migration in the autumn of A.D. 488; and once again (as so often before, and so often since in her unhappy history) Italy was to be the prize of battle.

March of Theodoric—A.D. 488-9.—The line of march chosen by Theodoric was not the ordinary one by the valley of the Save and the Julian Alps, but the shorter and more southern road leading through Illyricum to Dyrrachium. He hoped thus to escape the hardships of a winter march over difficult ground; and knowing that there were vessels in abundance on the coast, he expected to be able to seize them, to transport his people across the Adriatic, while Odoacer was awaiting him in the North, and thus to be master of Central and Southern Italy, and perhaps of Rome, before his enemy could attack him. To this clever plan nothing was wanting but good fortune. When the Goths, however, arrived on the Eastern coast, they found all the vessels on which they had counted withdrawn, and the people bitterly hostile. To retrace their steps, or to follow the coast line and so march to Italy, seemed almost equal madness; while to remain in Dalmatia was certain destruction. The second alternative was finally adopted. And so in the dead of winter (A.D. 488-9) amid snow and frost, over mountain ranges, across rivers and torrents, in the face of enemies, and harassed by hunger and illness, the great host held its way obstinately northwards, until they struck the valley of the Save near Emona. They crossed the Alps, and halted to recover health and strength in the plain between the rivers Sontius (Isonzo) and Frigidus (Wippach) before attacking Odoacer.

Struggle between Odoacer and Theodoric—A.D. 488-493.—The struggle between Odoacer and Theodoric lasted for more than four years, and was marked by three desperate battles, and a siege of nearly three years—a struggle in which the material resources seem to have been mostly in Odoacer's hands, and only forfeited by his own recklessness, while it brought out into

strong relief the daring and energy of Theodoric, and
gave him without dispute the foremost position in Italy.
The first blow was struck by Theodoric (August 28,
489). Odoacer had formed an intrenched camp on the
Isonzo—as famous a battle field of Italy as Leipsic has
been of Germany—where Maximin had been defeated
and slain in A.D. 238; and Theodosius had conquered
Eugenius in A.D. 384; and Attila had destroyed Aquilcia
in A.D. 452. The intrenchments were carried, and
Odoacer fled to Verona. Theodoric lost no time in following his enemy. On September 27 a pitched battle
was fought on the east bank of the Athesis (Adige), in
which, after desperate fighting, the Goths were again victorious; the Italian centre was driven in and routed,
their right wing was pushed into the river, Verona was
taken, and Odoacer found refuge in Ravenna. Fifteen
years afterwards the plain was still white with the bones
of the dead, to whom the Ostrogoth had forbidden burial.
Theodoric now styled himself " King of Italy," and then
followed a paper war of proclamations, recriminations,
and appeals, each " king " striving to enlist on his own
side the hopes and fears of the people. The sympathies
of Italy were undoubtedly with Odoacer, rather than
with his antagonist. Theodoric had come unasked to
interrupt a period of unwonted peace; and as for Zeno,
who was this pseudo-Cæsar, that treated Italy and Rome
like a piece of private property to be passed from hand
to hand! In spite, therefore, of many just causes of
complaint, the Italians clung to Odoacer; until in a fit
of anger, because the Romans refused to admit him
to the city, and wished to stand neutral in the strife,
he ravaged the whole adjoining country, and alienated
the loyalty of his former friends. But for this he might
have weathered the storm; for what with the treachery

of allies, and the disparity of strength, Theodoric's position became so precarious, that he was reduced to ask for support from his kinsmen, the Visigoths in Gaul. Odoacer had even felt himself strong enough to besiege Theodoric in Pavia after sacking Milan. A third great battle, however, was fought between the rival kings on the Adda, near Milan (August 11, 490), in which the Ostrogoths were again victorious, and Odoacer again was forced to flee to Ravenna, with its sheltering marshes and pinewoods. Here for nearly three years he was blockaded by Theodoric—a blockade only interrupted by one spirited attempt (which failed) to carry off Theodoric bodily in the dead of night. Neither could exhaust the patience of the other; each was harassed by famine and disease.

Convention of Ravenna—A.D. 493.—At last, on February 27, 493, a convention was concluded, through the mediation of the Bishop of Ravenna, by which it was agreed that the two kings should share the kingdom of Italy, either dividing the territory between them, or ruling in turn after the ancient form of Consular Government. Theodoric entered Ravenna on the 5th of March, the two armies and the two kings occupying different quarters of the city.

Murder of Odoacer.—It was, however, only a brief truce. Between two such men, in such a position, peace was in fact impossible. Jealousy begot suspicion. There were meetings of officers, rumours among soldiers and townspeople. Mischief was evidently brewing, which nothing but loyal sincerity between Theodoric and Odoacer could prevent. And this was wanting. A few days after his entry into Ravenna, Theodoric invited Odoacer, his son, and principal officers to a grand banquet, at which they were all murdered in cold blood, Odoacer by

Theodoric's own hand. And these murders were followed by a general massacre of all Odoacer's friends where-
ever they were found. Theodoric was undisputed " King
of Italy."

It is difficult to form a just judgment of so dreadful a
beginning of a glorious reign. Murder is never defensible; but the *guilt* of murder varies indefinitely. Barbarians think lightly of bloodshed: and Theodoric was
more than half barbarian. In him lofty and almost
heroic aspirations, and an intellectual admiration of the
higher virtues of civilisation, were grafted upon the instincts of a savage. Attila was more merciful than Theodoric in his fiercer moods; while his justice, toleration,
and firmness as a ruler were worthy of Trajan. The
murder of Odoacer by Theodoric seems less odious in our
eyes than the judicial murder of Servetus by Calvin, in
the name of conscience (A.D. 1553), far less wicked than
that of the Duc d'Enghien by Napoleon, on the plea of
self-defence (A.D. 1804). A man must be judged by the
standard of his own day; and neither to the Italians,
who were familiarised with horrors by years of war and
revolution, nor to the Germans, who had been used to
human sacrifices, and still valued human life by a money
standard, would Theodoric's act probably have seemed
worse than a questionable deed wrought in self-defence.
Undoubtedly it is more to his glory to have risen above
the standard of his age in respect of toleration and political wisdom, than it is to his shame to have sunk down
to that standard in his regard for human life.

Prosperous Reign of Theodoric—A.D. 493–526.—
Theodoric was " King of Italy" during thirty-three years,
—the happiest thirty years which that country knew
between the age of the Antonines (A.D. 138–180), and the
time of Charles the Great (about 800). While acknow-

ledging in words a nominal dependence on the Eastern Empire, he was in reality an independent sovereign, and regarded himself as rightful heir of the Empire of the West—"hæres Imperii, semper Augustus." As Emperor in fact, though not in name, he addressed words of counsel, encouragement, or remonstrance to the neighbouring kings; while he carefully cultivated their alliance—himself marrying the sister of Chlodwig, and giving one daughter in marriage to the King of the Visigoths, and another to the King of the Burgundians. His sister married the King of the Vandals, and his niece the King of the Thuringians. His greatness is shown by these alliances, by the embassies which visited his court from far distant countries, by the memory that was long cherished of his name and deeds. He reduced to order the troubled districts of Pannonia and Noricum; he repulsed an attack upon Italy of the Emperor Anastasius (A.D. 509); he maintained a close friendship with the Visigoths, and even saved them from destruction at the hands of Chlodwig (A.D. 507). From Sicily to the Danube, from Sirmium to the Loire, the influence of Theodoric was paramount, and Italy for a generation was exempt from the ravages of war. That portion of the soil, which had been confiscated by Odoacer, was given to the Ostrogoths—no mere army of occupation, but a "people" with arms in their hands, men with wives and children and cattle, who meant to live in their hard-won homes. In the government of Italy he made little or no change; the functions and names of the old officials were carefully preserved; and he used the services of the ablest Italians in all but military duties. Rome and the great cities enjoyed in his reign order and plenty, while their works of art and famous buildings were carefully protected. But in nothing perhaps was the general prosperity more strikingly shown than in the sudden increase of wealth, and the great development of industry. Agriculture revived; mines were opened and worked; the Pontine marshes were drained and cultivated. These were the signs of government of a high order—so high, indeed, that we are driven to ask, *why* the work of a man so just and impartial, so wise and tolerant, was after all so transitory, that it was in part undone before his death, and that in thirty years hardly a trace of it was to be found? The answer to this question is threefold. Although Theodoric's avowed object was to fuse Teutonic vigour with Roman civilisation, a complete fusion of such diverse elements must be a work of time, and needs mutual intercourse, intermarriage, and community of religious faith to produce it; whereas the Ostrogoths in Italy were a distinct nation, an aristocracy of conquest, whose separation from the conquered was as jealously maintained as that of the Normans from the English by William the Conqueror. And they were Arians, whom good Catholics were bound to hate. If it required a century and a half to fuse English and Normans, Goths and Italians could scarcely be amalgamated in thirty years! For, deplore it as we may, religious differences are more indelible than any others; and, however they may be silenced for a while by a strong hand, are a constant source of danger. Men who feel sure they are right in their views are often strangely blind to the rights of others. Lastly, Theodoric's was a single life, and his work lacked continuity, which is indeed the special drawback of the rule of one man. The more we praise the wisdom which triumphed over exceptional difficulties, the more in such a case is it certain that the difficulties will recur, when the great man is gone, and the wisdom to cope with them is withdrawn.

Close of Theodoric's Reign—A.D. 523-6.—The last three years of a glorious reign were embittered by religious dissensions and political persecution. Five years before the aged and tolerant Anastasius was succeeded on the throne of Constantinople by the Dacian peasant Justin (A.D. 518), whose accession put an end to a schism of thirty-five years between East and West, and whose orthodoxy acknowledged the supremacy of the Roman See. It was the signal for a persecution of the Arians in the East, and even in Gaul. Italy alone was exempt. But Theodoric could hardly see unmoved the rise of a spirit, which he had done his best to hold in check; he was at once indignant and alarmed, and addressed strong expostulations on the subject to Justin. At the same time vague rumours began to reach Ravenna of a conspiracy against himself, involving the whole Roman Senate—rumours only too likely to be true, when their place of origin was Rome, and religious jealousy was running high. Theodoric's heir, too, was a child, whose only guardian would be a woman; while there was danger to be dreaded from the known ambition and orthodoxy of Justin's heir, Justinian. The future, therefore, looked doubtful enough to justify suspicion, which unhappily aroused the darker side of Theodoric's character. Summary and cruel vengeance was taken upon the leading members of the Senate. Boethius, the greatest of living Italians, was imprisoned, tortured, and beaten to death. Symmachus was executed. Even Pope John died in prison. But it is best to draw a veil over the last sad days of a really great man, in whom a fine intellect was enfeebled and a generous temper soured by unforeseen anxieties, and by what seemed to be the ingratitude of men for thirty years of uninterrupted benefits. No man is made better by despotic power, be he ever so good or able; and while we lament the fierce deeds which have left a stain upon his memory, we may well say of Theodoric, with the Gothic historian Procopius, that "though he was called a usurper and a tyrant, he was every inch a king."

CHAPTER X

THE EMPEROR JUSTINIAN—A.D. 527-565.

Contrast of East to West.—We pass abruptly from West to East—from a scene of vivid if rude and barbarous energy, to a life better ordered, yet on the whole less noble. Intrigue takes the place of war. The story of a Chrysostom or a Theophilus, a Eudoxia or a Eutropius, is repeated till we are weary, while barbarous chiefs patronise or tyrannise over a feeble Emperor, too weak to resist and too indolent to resent it. From Arcadius to Justin (A.D. 395–518) it is the same tale with slight variations, whose ignoble course it is as useless to follow as it is uninteresting to read. But in Justinian we come once more to a man whose thoughts and life affected all after ages. It is not with elected as it is with hereditary princes, who are for the most part cast in the same mould. Elected rulers are in the majority of cases "great men," embodiments in a sense of their own age, who represent in miniature, yet with definiteness, the vague and inarticulate tendencies of thousands of their fellows. Great men, as Carlyle says, are "profitable company."

Justinian.—And was Justinian great? Certainly, if the man who can conceive vast ideas and carry them to a successful issue be great, Justinian deserves the name.

To him was due the glory of the codification of Roman law, of the recovery of Italy and Africa to the Empire, of the repulse of attacks from Persians and Bulgarians. The character of Justinian was a strangely mixed one, it is true. It piques our curiosity. It is not necessary to believe half that the malicious "Anecdotes" of Procopius recount of the weakness of Justinian, or of the shameless vice of Theodora; and the deeds of his reign are before us to speak for themselves as to his energy, industry, and perspicacity. Yet he was at once rapacious and prodigal, ambitious and cowardly. Though a peasant born, and of barbarian blood, he had very little of barbarian independence or peasant hardiness, being guided by his wife's more masculine spirit. He had far-reaching ideas, and chose the fittest instruments to carry them into effect; but was too timid or too jealous to allow them independence of action. In an age of great warriors and ceaseless war, he had no military instincts, though (like Philip the Second of Spain) he serenely appropriated the glory and the fruits of struggles in which he took no part. However keen was his intellect, and incredible his energy, yet his character leaves on the mind an impression of pettiness; for he was neither liberal nor generous to his best friends —a man to be neither much loved, nor much hated, nor much respected, yet undeniably "great" intellectually.

Justinian's Rise.—The fortunes of Justinian arose out of the favour of his uncle Justin. The latter, born in Illyricum, and probably a Goth, had migrated to Byzantium about A.D. 474. He enlisted in the Imperial guard, rose rapidly from grade to grade, and on the death of Anastasius (A.D. 518) adroitly secured his own election as Emperor. Thus favoured by fortune, he lost no time in summoning to court his sister Beglenitza, her husband Istok, and their son Uprauda,—which barbarous names, too harsh for polite ears, were presently exchanged for Vigilantia, Sabbatius, and Justinianus. The young man, stimulated by the new and polished life around him, threw himself with ardour into his uncle's plans, and astonished his masters by his intelligence, curiosity, and untiring activity of mind. Poetry and music, law and theology, architecture and strategy—he studied, if he did not master them all. To Justinian knowledge was a passion. But there was a stronger passion even than knowledge, which mastered him before his uncle's death (A.D. 527), and to which he remained subject all his life. He fell in love with the famous dancer Theodora, whose dubious character and enchanting beauty were alike the talk of the town. But in spite of her repute, in spite of his mother and uncle, and in the teeth of the law which forbade such marriages, he married her, and remained her devoted husband ever after. She repaid him, indeed, with no small benefits. If her life had been vicious, if she was still a proud and domineering woman, yet she possessed a keen intellect, a powerful judgment, and a rapidity of decision, which more than once stood Justinian in good stead.

Description of Justinian.—Justinian was above middle height, with regular features and a high colour. His manner was self-possessed and gracious; his life was temperate, or even ascetic. Indolent and irresolute in action, he was restlessly diligent in business. Being troubled with sleeplessness, he devoted great part of the night to the affairs of Church and State, or paced up and down the galleries of the palace, shaping the great ideas which it was his good fortune to see realised. It is hardly strange that the popular imagination saw in him a demon in human form, who needed neither sleep nor food. He was an indefatigable builder both of palaces and churches, notably of the famous church of St. Sophia. He strengthened and increased the fortifications of the Empire, especially on the Danube and the Persian frontier. He had hardly mounted the throne before he began his great work of legislation, which both in importance and in the effects it produced, far surpassed the brilliant victories of his generals. It was a work much needed, to analyse and codify the mass of law and legal opinions which had grown up in 1000 years. The attempt had been made more than once, but with only partial success. It was reserved for Justinian to complete it. The matter was intrusted to a large commission, presided over by the famous lawyer Tribonian, and was begun in the Emperor's first year, A.D. 528. The first section of the business, the *Code*, was in fact a revision of the imperfect code published in A.D. 430 by Theodosius II., the lapse of a century having rendered addition and retrenchment alike necessary, and it was accomplished in fourteen months. This was followed by the *Digest* or Pandects, containing the gist of the opinions and writings of the most eminent Roman lawyers, the continuous labour of three years (A.D. 530–33). Most important of all were the *Institutes*, dealing with the elements or first principles of Roman law. These three—the Code, the Digest, and the Institutes, together with the Novellæ or successive supplements to the Code (A.D. 534–565)—formed the " Corpus Juris Civilis " (Civil Law).

The Nika Riot—A.D. 532.—In spite, however, of the unremitting efforts of the Emperor and of the glories of his reign, his home government was as weak as that or any of his predecessors or successors. One crowning instance will serve as a specimen—a mere city riot, arising from a trivial cause, which nearly cost him his throne. The drivers of the chariots in the Hippodrome were divided into " factions," distinguished by their colours—

the " white," " red," " green," and " blue." The " green " faction had been identified with the cause and the scarcely orthodox opinions of the late Emperor Anastasius; the " blue" was strictly orthodox, and devoted to Justinian. Hence between the two was bitter rivalry, extending, moreover, from the drivers to their relations and friends. The whole city was divided into hostile camps, until at last the " blues" ventured, under cover of favour at court, to proceed to open violence. They paraded the streets in bands at night. Ere long, joined by all the dissolute youth of a great capital, they plundered, beat, even murdered their enemies. The example spread. A dangerous spirit of lawless violence became the fashion. Terrorism was brought to bear on private enemies, on creditors, on judges, on masters. The unhappy "greens," meanwhile, persecuted by their enemies and unprotected by the laws, were forced to resist in self-defence, whilst any magistrate who was just enough to shelter them with his protection had soon reason to repent of his untimely zeal. The Empress had an ancient grudge against the " green" faction from her theatrical days, and she neither forgot nor forgave an insult. From the Court, therefore, they could expect no favour. At last (A.D. 532) an unfortunate accident set the smouldering animosity in a blaze, which laid a great part of the capital in ruins, and cost the lives of hundreds of citizens. It is a scene almost worthy of the great French Revolution—almost as chaotic and bewildering. The Emperor was seated in the Hippodrome celebrating the festival of the Ides of January (13th). But the games were perpetually interrupted by the clamour of the " green" faction, until exasperated almost to madness, the "blues" rose from their seats as one man, and the "greens" fled for their lives. At this moment of frenzy, the mutual hatred of the factions was turned into a common hatred of the government by a passing accident. Two murderers condemned to death, but rescued from fate by the breaking of a rope, were hurried into "sanctuary" by the monks of a neighbouring convent. One of them was "blue," the other "green." The rival factions, united for the moment by a similar indignation, and each anxious to save its man, made common cause, delivered their prisoners, opened the prisons, burnt the Præfect's palace, and did not scruple to attack the troops sent to repress the riot. The fire spread, and reached even the cathedral. Women took a ferocious part in the struggle, showering stones from roof and window. So threatening, indeed, was the state of affairs, that many wealthy families escaped across the Bosporus from the horrors of a five days' street fight, and that even Justinian contemplated flight and abdication. From this fatal step he was saved by the firmness of Theodora, and in hardly a less degree by the military promptitude of a great general, Belisarius. A terrible lesson was given to a fickle population, by a general massacre in the Hippodrome, and by the execution of a score of nobles who had tried to use the opportunity for restoring the family of Anastasius. The Hippodrome itself was closed, to hear no more for several years the watchword of "victory" (νίκα) of the rival factions which gave its name to this riot.

Belisarius compared to Marlborough.—The name of Belisarius recalls us to what in the eyes of his contemporaries was probably the great glory of Justinian's reign, the African and Italian campaigns. For Belisarius as "signally retrieved" the glory of the Empire in the sixth century as Marlborough that of England in the eighteenth. There is, indeed, a strange likeness between the two men, not only of character, but even in their very lives. Each was the devoted husband of an imperious, passionate, and ambitious woman. Each felt the bitterness of disgrace, though Marlborough probably deserved to suffer what Belisarius suffered undeserved. Each triumphed over jealousy and obstructions by the same qualities of calmness, and good sense, and a serene temper. Each was perfectly fearless and unflurried in the face of danger, the very life and soul of the armies which they led. We may say with truth, that each seemed to combine two characters in one person; for in each case he who in the field was calm, clear headed, and more than a match for every foe, was in civil life infirm and pusillanimous, greedy alike of honours and of money, a friend whose fidelity was doubtful. If Marlborough was the greater soldier of the two, Belisarius was the purer character. It could not indeed be said of him, as it was of Marlborough, that he never besieged a fortress which he had not taken, nor fought a battle which he had not won, yet neither could he be accused of having enriched himself by base means, or of having sold State secrets to his sovereign's enemies.

African Campaign of Belisarius—A.D. 533.—Belisarius (Beli-tzar, the White Prince) was probably of Slavonian origin, and born in a little village of Illyria, called "Germania." At an early age he entered on military life in the "Guards" of Justinian. Entrusted with an independent command in Armenia, he was the first to turn the tide of victory against the Persians, and with far inferior numbers to defeat a foe flushed with conquest, and to relieve the province of Syria from invasion (A.D. 529–532). It was a great exploit, significant of powers above the common; and when the African expedition was in preparation (A.D. 533), the name of Belisarius was in all mouths as the fittest leader of so grave an undertaking. Indeed, the African campaign was one of those things which are only justified by success. The Emperor in proposing it met with general opposition. Old men, still living, could remember the shame and the losses of the expedition of Basiliscus (A.D. 468), and feared a repetition of the blunder. Troops, wearied with five campaigns against the Persians, shrank from the thought of a long sea voyage, and of a climate and enemy alike unknown; while ministers of finance calculated with apprehension the heavy expenses of so immense an undertaking, and the dubious possibilities of meeting them. To these various objections Justinian opposed a superior knowledge, or a superior obstinacy, based upon a truer insight into the facts of the case. And his wisdom was proved by success. Yet prior to the event few undertakings could have seemed less likely to succeed, and to succeed with such rapidity and ease.

Position of the Vandals.—When Genseric died in A.D. 477, the Vandals were absolute masters of the splendid province of Africa. They had sacked Rome. They swept the Mediterranean with their fleets. They even threatened Constantinople. There was no barbarian nation that seemed to have so commanding a position, so glorious a future. Yet in the fifty years that elapsed between Genseric and Justinian, their Empire, which still looked as powerful as ever, had become honeycombed by luxury, inaction, and religious and social strife. To the Vandals Carthage became a second Capua. When the strong hand was withdrawn, that had kept up the healthy stir of battle and the excitement of conquest, they relapsed into the vices of semi-civilised life. In religion they were fanatics, and persecuted the orthodox Catholics, thus preparing for their enemies eager allies in the time of need. Lastly, to prevent the strife of brothers so common in the division of an inheritance, Genseric had ordained in his will, that the eldest male member of the royal family for the time being should sit upon the Vandal throne, just as the law of Turkey ordains now. His kinsmen, the English, were wiser in Britain, when they made the English kingship elective, but restricted the election as a rule to a particular royal family. For Genseric's plan failed as wholly as the English plan succeeded. It issued almost of course in jealousies and assassination. Thus Huneric succeeded Genseric in A.D. 476, and steadily set himself at once to prepare for his own son's succeeding him, by destroying all who might stand in his way. And in A.D. 523, when Trasimund died, who had married Amalafrida, the daughter of the great Theodoric, and was succeeded by Hilderic, the eldest member of the family, Amalafrida, unable to bear the prospect of private life, tried to seize the throne; but was defeated, imprisoned, and, after her father's death (A.D. 526), beheaded,—a fate which was shared by many of her countrymen. Hilderic, however, was incompetent. Brought up at the Byzantine court, he was more Greek than Vandal, and shrank from war and the fierce persecuting spirit of his subjects. A friend of Justinian, and tolerant to Catholics, he was no friend of Arian Vandals; and Gelimer, the next heir, easily supplanted him (A.D. 530).

Africa Reduced in Three Months.—No doubt Justinian was well aware of this weakness which political and religious dissension had brought upon the Vandal kingdom, and adroitly used Gelimer's usurpation as a pretext for interference. A force of 10,000 infantry and 5,000 cavalry, of 500 transports and 20,000 seamen, was collected, and set out from Constantinople in June (A.D. 533). By the close of the year the Vandal Empire was at an end, and Africa was once more a province of the Roman Empire for 150 years. It was a curious mixture of races which Belisarius led to the conquest of the once terrible Vandals,—Greeks and Goths, Alani and Parthians, Huns and Syrians. It was a proof of military genius in itself to maintain the discipline and combine the operations of such an ill-assorted host. Three months, however, after leaving the capital, the fleet sighted the coast of Africa, having touched in passing at the coasts of Messenia and Sicily. It is a strange fact, which needs explanation, that it was allowed to reach Africa without attack. Heavy laden transports, and soldiers little used to the sea, would have fallen an easy prey. Why were the Vandals so remiss? Why did not the Ostrogoths help their brothers in distress? The answer is short and ready. The Ostrogoths, indignant at the murder of Amalafrida and her friends, were eager for revenge, and ready therefore to aid, not Gelimer, but Belisarius; while Gelimer had detached his brother with 5000 veteran troops to reduce Sardinia. At the critical moment, therefore, he was without his best troops and without allies, while the friends of Hilderic and the orthodox Catholics were his all but open enemies. No wonder that the struggle was virtually over in three months.

The army landed on September 22 at Caput Vada, on the coast of Byzacium, five days' march to the south of Carthage. A proclamation of Belisarius, that he had come as a " liberator," and the discipline of his troops, won the people's good will, and made the advance safe and easy to within ten miles of Carthage. The capital at this time had no fortifications. A battle in its defence, therefore, was imperative. But Gelimer's army was beaten in detail, and fled in confusion towards Numidia; while Belisarius entered Carthage in triumph the next day, the feast of St Cyprian, its patron saint. It was a marvellous revolution, yet so quietly accomplished, that trade did not

cease for a day, nor was a shop shut.   Meanwhile Gelimer
hurriedly recalled his brother from Sardinia, and prepared
for the decisive struggle.   His numbers were vastly superior,
but they were more than outweighed by the genius of
Belisarius.   The battle was fought on the banks of a
rivulet, twenty miles south-west of Carthage, and was
fiercely contested; but was in the end so decisive, that
Gelimer fled alone from the field, his army was scattered
to the winds, and the camp taken, with all the women,
children, and treasure.   From December to March A.D.
534, Gelimer was an outcast in Numidia, until at last, after
sustaining with a few faithful followers a hard siege in a
mountain fastness, he surrendered at discretion, and being
carried to Carthage, was transported by Belisarius, with
many of his countrymen and with vast treasures, to adorn
the first triumph ever seen in the city of Constantine.
" Vanity of vanities! all is vanity," such is said to have
been his comment on what he had seen.   And indeed it
is the fittest comment on the Vandal history.   Gelimer
was allowed to retire to an estate in Galatia, and numerous Vandals were drafted into the armies of the East.
But the Vandal nation, numbering before the war
600,000 persons, vanishes henceforth from history; and
Africa, like Italy, was ruled by an " Exarch" from
Constantinople.

Pretext for the Invasion of Italy.—Two years
elapsed, and once more the great general of Justinian was
engaged in a struggle, more arduous and not less glorious,
with the Ostrogoths in Italy.   In the ten years which had
elapsed since the death of Theodoric, the same causes had
been at work to undermine the Gothic power which had
undermined the Vandal power in Africa.   As in Africa
so in Italy, Catholics hated Arians and Arians hated
Catholics.   In Italy as in Africa political dissensions

paralysed national strength. Amalasontha, daughter of Theodoric, had been regent for her son Athalaric, whom she loved only too well, and strove to train for his future greatness. But he was dull and self-willed; and as he grew older was easily led into resenting a woman's dictation, and breaking away from her influence, flung himself into debauchery, which speedily killed him. But Amalasontha had enemies besides her son. And when, after his death, she married her cousin Theodatus, but retained in her own hands the substance of the regal power, keeping her husband in the background, he was led by evil counsellors and his own jealous resentment into conspiring against her. This able daughter of a great father, the victim of spite and jealousy, was arrested, imprisoned in an island of the lake of Bolsena (Etruria), and finally strangled in her bath (April 30, 535). Theodatus was king at last; but the insecurity of his position may be realised by reflecting on the crimes which had placed him there, the avarice and cowardice of his character, and the disaffection of his Catholic subjects.

Belisarius Reduces Sicily and South Italy— A.D. 536.—Meanwhile Justinian eagerly caught at this excuse for intervention, this opportunity of reclaiming yet another province for the Empire. His ambassador to Italy loudly protested against the murder of Theodoric's daughter, while he observed with satisfaction the dissensions of the Goths, and doubtless reported to his master the ripeness of the times. Once more Belisarius steered westwards. Hardly had he cast anchor off Catana before he discovered that the whole island of Sicily was like a ripe apple ready to fall into his hands; and this, the first province of the Roman Republic, was reincorporated with the Empire without a blow. A second time Belisarius appeared as " liberator," to set free Romans from the yoke of barbarians, Catholics from the tyranny of Arians. A few brief and fruitless negotiations were followed by the invasion of Italy. Leaving garrisons in Palermo and Syracuse, Belisarius landed at Rhegium, and marching 300 miles along the coast through a well-affected population, besieged and took Naples. From Naples he was invited by the clergy and Senate to occupy Rome,—a matter of no difficulty, as Theodatus had been murdered, and the scattered Gothic forces had retired to Ravenna and the north to concentrate for the final struggle. Belisarius entered Rome on December 10, A.D. 536, and the keys of the city were sent to Justinian.

Siege of Rome by the Ostrogoths—A.D. 537.—But the triumph was short-lived. In the following March Vitiges returned with 150,000 Goths, and crossing the Apennines, appeared before the walls of Rome. The numbers were so unequal, the time for preparation had been so short, that everything seemed lost; but it was at a crisis such as this that the resource and coolness of Belisarius were most marked. Of him it might well be said, that his presence was worth 100,000 men. He had but a few thousand men in the city, and what volunteers he could inspire with his own enthusiasm and courage, to guard fortifications, whose extent was at least twelve miles. The walls themselves in parts were in ruins. Yet Rome held out successfully for more than a year, thanks to the strong arm, clear head, and unfailing calmness of one man, and one man only, who united strategical genius and mastery of detail to dashing and audacious bravery in the field. The Gothic numbers were not sufficient to surround the city, the blockade reaching only from the Vatican to the Prœnestine Gate; and on this side it was that on the nineteenth day of the siege (March 31, A.D. 537) a simultaneous attack was directed on seven points at once. Repeated assaults were met by an obstinate resistance; and only once, near the gate of Prœneste, did the defence waver for a moment. At nightfall the Goths retired, with a loss (it was said) of 30,000 men. Whether this were so or not, it is clear that the result was a heavy blow to the besiegers; for it was the first and last assault attempted, and the siege became little more than an indolent blockade. Nevertheless the superiority of numbers told outside. Porto fell. Entrenched camps were established by the enemy to the north and south of the city. Provisions became scarce; and the frequent sallies, though mostly successful, contributed little beyond honour. And with distress began disaffection within the walls, and with disaffection came treachery. A letter was intercepted, which promised the Gothic king that the Asinarian Gate should be opened to his troops. Nor was this all. The dangerous discontent within the walls was adroitly used by Antonina, Belisarius' wife, to forward the wishes of the Empress. Pope Silverius had thwarted Theodora; and was now accused of treasonable correspondence with the Goths, and degraded; while an unscrupulous and ambitious deacon, Vigilius, was placed upon the Papal throne, who would probably be more compliant.

At last, after urgent demands, reinforcements reached Belisarius from Constantinople of some 7000 men; and negotiations began in consequence, which were the precursors of the raising of the siege. At the same time the general felt himself strong enough to detach 2000 cavalry to operate in Picenum against the Gothic communications with Ravenna, and to seize if possible the many families and large treasures there deposited.

Siege Raised—A.D. 538.—This last blow was decisive; and Vitiges, after one more attempt to surprise and storm the walls, which was vigorously repulsed, with-drew hurriedly across the Tiber and along the Flaminian Road. So great was the demoralisation of the once vast army, that even Ariminum, of which Vitiges formed the siege as he passed northwards, and which was defended only by a low rampart and shallow ditch, held out against him long enough to be relieved by Belisarius in person. The Goths fled in confusion to Ravenna; and all Italy, south of the Po, gave willing allegiance to Justinian.

Fall of Ravenna—A.D. 539.—Italy was virtually regained; and the power of the Ostrogoths would soon have been destroyed, but for the mutual jealousy of the Roman generals. Belisarius was too great to escape envy, too great also to resent it : yet the violence of a Constantine, and the interference or independence of a Narses, paralysed the operations of the Roman army, and gave the Goths time to rally what force they could; while a sudden inroad into North Italy of 100,000 Franks, under Theodebert their king, added to the general confusion. As before, however, so now, Belisarius triumphed over difficulties. Jealousies were smoothed over. Rivals were pacified. Town after town was besieged and taken, which had still been held by the Goths. Finally, Ravenna itself was blockaded. Gradually reduced to extremities, yet lost in admiration of their victor, the Ostrogoths (ignoring Vitiges their king) opened negotiations with Belisarius, and promised to support him, if he would throw Justinian over, and seize the crown of Italy. Belisarius saw his opportunity, and promised to consider the matter. Meanwhile a day and hour was fixed for the surrender of Ravenna: a fleet laden with food was sent in to relieve immediate wants; and at the time fixed the Roman army marched in unresisted, and took possession of the capital, without their general being in any way pledged (December, A.D. 539). It was then too late to oppose what they had themselves invited. Belisarius declined the proffered honour, perhaps had never intended to accept it : Vitiges was sent to Constantinople : the flower of the Gothic warriors was enlisted in the Imperial service; the residue were dismissed to the south provinces; and an Italian colony was planted in Ravenna. The example of the capital was speedily followed by the smaller towns, that still held out, with the exception of Pavia; and thus the whole of Italy was reincorporated with the Empire.

Recall of Belisarius.—It was a wonderful reverse of fortune, which ten years before would have been thought impossible; and yet the great man to whom it was mainly due was pursued by envy and calumny, and was recalled by Justinian from a sphere "no longer (it was said) worthy of his presence." The Gothic spoil was appropriated for the Imperial palace, and Belisarius was denied a second triumph; yet it is satisfactory to know that the hearty admiration of the people made up for the chilling civility and faint praises of Court circles. For indeed it was no common thing which Belisarius had done. It was something to have maintained military discipline, without losing the affection of his soldiers: it was more to have won the respect and admiration of populations among whom he came as conqueror. In an age not distinguished for virtues, either political or social, he was just, liberal, modest, and chaste. He was daring without rashness, prudent without fear; and by the combination of the highest qualities of a general had recovered in little more than six years the provinces of Africa and Italy.

Revolt of the Goths—A.D. 544.—Belisarius was recalled, and sent to the East; and the settlement of

Italy was left to his successors.   But three years' experience of the tender mercies of Greek "governors" was
more than enough; and when Totila (Todilas, "the death-
less") issued from Pavia to reclaim the Gothic kingdom,
town after town from north to south welcomed him as
deliverer.   Once more at the Emperor's command Belisarius turned his face westwards.   But Imperial jealousy
or parsimony refused him the sinews of war: Rome was
twice taken (A.D. 546-549), once under his very eyes;
and once recovered by him, though but for a while (A.D.
547).   For the most part, he was left with the hopeless
task of calculating what he could do, if he had the necessary force; or of collecting forces, when it was too late to
use them.   In A.D. 548 he returned to Constantinople,
leaving Totila master of Italy, and with the mortification
of abandoning what he knew could be so easily recovered.
But although he was jealous of his general, Justinian was
not inclined to acquiesce in the loss of Italy, so lately
recovered.

Narses in Italy—A.D. 552.—A fresh force was raised,
and entrusted first to Germanus, the Emperor's nephew,
and on his death to Narses, the eunuch, who marched
into Italy, defeated Totila in a pitched battle about midway between Rome and Ravenna, in which Totila was
mortally wounded (A.D. 552), and besieged and took
Rome.   One more campaign against Teias, the last king of
the Ostrogoths—one more victory in Campania, and the
work was accomplished.   Italy was for the third time
reunited to the Empire; and Narses was for fifteen years
(A.D. 554-568) Exarch of Ravenna, lieutenant of the
Eastern Empire in Italy.

Conclusion.—Henceforth the Ostrogothic nation dis-
appears from history; and the glory of the name "Goth"
is reserved for the Visigoths.   Twice before had the same

thing happened. Etruscans and Carthaginians vanished from the earth as separate nations, leaving little behind them but a few medals and inscriptions. Only, we must remember, it is the vanishing of a name, and not necessarily of a nation—the bearers of the name being absorbed in the population which they have ceased to rule. This absorption or conquest of the Goths in Italy was to a great degree the work of the Catholic clergy— one of the early steps in that fatal policy of the Papacy, which has always resisted the union of Italy under one native kingdom, whether Gothic, Lombard, Norman, or Piedmontese. And whatever may have been the conspicuous merits of the generals who achieved it, it is the opinion of an Italian authority that greater evil was inflicted upon Italy by the Grecian reconquest, than by any other invasion.[1] It was disastrous in its immediate and more remote consequences. The country was worse, not better governed; and in after years, the irruption of the Lombards, the invasion of the Franks, the usurpation of the Popes, and the separation of Eastern and Western Christendom, are events for which it was in· directly responsible.

[1] Gibbon, Milman's Edition, vol. iv. p. 150, note.

CHAPTER XI

THE EMPIRE IN RELATION TO THE BARBARIANS OF THE EAST—A.D. 450–650.

Subject of the Chapter.—The relations of the Roman Empire of the East to the barbarous nations on its northern, eastern, and south-eastern frontiers, during the two centuries following Attila's death, will be the subject of this chapter. It is a chequered story of frequent disaster, illumined at intervals by heroic deeds. We have names yet more barbarous, barbarians yet more brutal than any hitherto met with; but the knowledge of their origin and fortunes is important, because in some cases they occupied lands which their descendants still possess, and in almost all cases they largely affected the subsequent history of Europe.

Results of the Death of Attila—A.D. 453.—The death of Attila (A.D. 453) was followed by a struggle of several years for mastery between the Aryan and Turanian portions of his Empire. Though the question at issue was too vital to be settled by a single battle, yet the victory of Netad did virtually decide that Europe was to belong to Aryans, by rolling backwards the threatening wave of blank barbarism for a while, and by giving the nobler races time to consolidate their forces, and to assimilate the civilisation of Western Europe, before another struggle was necessary.   But the Turanians did not quietly acquiesce in their defeat.   More than once the Huns attacked the Gepidæ and Ostrogoths, though always without success.   They were compelled to yield to superior strength ; and the sons of Attila—Dengizikh, Hernakh, and Emnedzar—became kings of three separate Hunnish nations, reaching from the Lower Danube to the Carpathians, and from thence to the Don (Tanais). They were sometimes at peace, more often at war with their Roman neighbours to the south.   The death of Dengizikh (about A.D. 470) was the signal of universal confusion among the tribes to the north of the Danube, and of a general rearrangement of their mutual relations.   We have tribes with familiar names occupying new ground, and new tribes with strange names appearing on the scene, and pressing westward and southward.

Dangers on the Frontiers—A.D. 500.—If we take the boundaries of the Eastern Empire about A.D. 500— the Danube, the Euxine, the Caucasus, Armenia, and the Euphrates—there was scarcely a point in this immense frontier which was not threatened by some enemy, and needed constant watching.   And there was not strength enough in the Empire for successful resistance.   Again and again Mœsia, Illyricum, Greece, were overrun by destroying hordes.   More than once Constantinople was threatened, attacked, besieged.   Armenia was a constant battlefield.   And in the south-east Persia, ruled by an ambitious dynasty, was always encroaching on the frontier.

The Middle Danube.—The middle Danube was now a German river.   In Pannonia were Ostrogoths, reaching from Vienna to Belgrade (Singidunum) and Illyricum. On the eastern and northern banks, as far as the Carpathians, lay the Gepidæ and the Lombards.   On the northern banks of the river to the east of Singidunum, and within the territory of the Gepidæ, was a large population of different origin. They were the descendants of the old Roman colonists, who had flocked there 400 years before, after Trajan's conquest of Dacia, and whose children had refused to leave their homes when Aurelian abandoned the province (A.D. 270). These men had endured with sullen persistence the tender mercies of successive barbarians, but clung through them all to their land—the land which their children still occupy. They called themselves Romans; but as in Britain, so in Dacia, the German conquerors called these "men of a strange tongue," Wealh or Welsh. And hence came the double name of their country, Roumania and Wallachia.

Eastern Danube and North Coast of the Euxine.—In what is now the Dobrudscha, near the mouth of the Danube, and from thence as far as the Dnieper (Danapris) was a mixed horde of Huns, the remnant of Attila's host, and of a cognate Finnish race, the Bulgarians (Voulgar). The Empire had good cause during the seventh century to shudder at this name, the synonym for all that was brutal and treacherous. The original home of the people, where indeed the bulk of them were still settled, was the upper waters of the river Etel, called afterwards by their name, the Volga. But, already in the days of the great Theodoric, one of their hordes had been met and defeated by him in the plain of the Dniester (Danaster); and it must have been clear to all who had eyes to see, that there was danger to the Empire in that quarter. The very religion which they professed was of the lowest type. It was that [1] "Shamanism," which still prevails, as the sole religion of thousands in North-Eastern Asia—a religion, or more properly speaking a "terror," inspired by the awful phenomena of

[1] Cf. Kennan's Tent Life in Siberia, cap. 20.

nature, among which they live, and consisting in the pro-
pitiation of the evil spirits supposed to be embodied
therein, the spirits of ice and wind, of volcanoes and
aurora. As in the religion, so in the people, there was
something almost diabolical and less than human. Their
ferocity and treachery were alike unparalleled. And by
their side the Huns, who had been in contact with
Roman civilisation for nearly a century, seemed civilised.

Huns on the Tanais.—Beyond the Dnieper, and
on each side of the Don (Tanais), were settled two hordes
of "white" Huns, called respectively Cutriguri and
Utiguri, in all probability a fusion of Finns and Ugrians
(Igours or Ogors): to the latter of whom, and their
terrible reputation in less barbarous countries, we owe the
familiar "Ogres" of our children's story books.

The Slavonians.—To the north and north-west of
Huns and Bulgarians, between the Dnieper, the Carpathians, and the Baltic, lay a scattered though numerous
population, who were called "Slaves" (Sclavi, Sthloveni,
Σκλάβοι), and were possibly Aryan by origin, certainly
very far removed from Turanians. They were divided
into three tribes—Antes in the south-east, Sloveni in the
centre, and Wends or Venedi on the Baltic. The name
is derived from "Slova," "speech," and is defined as
meaning "those who speak the same language." As a
term of identification, therefore, it was the opposite of
Welsh, or foreigner. Like the Romans of Wallachia, the
Slaves had for generations been subject to nations fiercer
or stronger than themselves; but when the centrifugal
force of disruption after the battle of Netad drove the
Huns to the East, and precipitated the Goths across the
Danube, the Slaves for once were left without a master,
and began to act a part of their own in history. The
Slavonian character was a counterpart of their history.

Less fiery than Germans, less brutal than Huns or Bulgarians, they had the apathetic, lazy, yet hospitable, habits of a serf population, subject to alternations of violent ferocity. Even in war their tactics were not the tactics of freemen. There was no combination or plan of operation. The fighting was individual; and they excelled in ambushes and surprises. Of cleanliness or self-restraint, of modesty or religious feeling, they had only the faintest trace.

Avars, Turks, &c., in Eastern Europe.—Ostrogoths, Lombards, Gepidæ, Slaves, Huns, and Bulgarians—it was a formidable mass, if only in dead weight, against which to defend a long river frontier. But there were other tribes and confederations of tribes in the far north-east and the steppes of Asia beginning to move westwards, whose pressure was already making itself felt, and whose names figure largely in after history—Avars, Hungarians, Turks, and Mongols. Of the first of these more will be said presently. The last three did not affect the history of Europe till some centuries later.

Persia.—The south-eastern frontier was another weak point of the Empire. Here lay the great kingdom of Persia, stretching from the Indus to the Euphrates, from the Caucasus to the Persian Gulf, and conterminous with the Empire from Colchis to the Upper Euphrates. For 1000 years that part of Asia had been the seat of a great Empire. The first Persian monarchy, founded by Cyrus (B.C. 558), and overthrown by Alexander of Macedon (B.C. 330), had given place to a Greek kingdom; which meant, in fact, only the supremacy of Greeks over alien and heterogeneous populations. Against this supremacy the Turanian Parthians successfully revolted under Arsaces (B.C. 255), and gradually established a powerful Empire of their own in its place (B.C. 174). It was these Parthians, with whom the Romans of the later

Republic and early Empire were so often at war, and whom Horace calls indifferently Parthians, Medes, and Persians. But the influence of Greece in the East was not destroyed by the downfall of the Greek kingdom, any more than the influence of Rome in the West was destroyed by the downfall of the Western Empire. Greek ideas, customs, and fashions had spread, and modified even the religion of the upper and learned classes. Zoroastrianism was losing its hold on them. But the mass of the people clung to the belief of their fathers, and shrank from the civilisation of the West as much as Orientals of the present day. A reaction set in; of which Ardshir (Artaxerxes), son of Sassan, cleverly availed himself, and a successful revolt against Parthian domination restored to the Persians their old supremacy (A.D. 226). It was a revolt partly of Aryans against Turanians, partly of conservative feeling against innovations. Greek influence was stamped out, Greek ideas were opposed, whenever and wherever it was possible. The dynasty of the Sassanidæ was in a special sense "*national*," and based its power and popularity on that ground. It was also an ambitious and conquering dynasty, bent on enlarging and extending its boundaries, and hence constantly at war with Rome; from whom, indeed, in A.D. 430 half Armenia had been wrested, and who in the sixth century seemed about to lose Syria and Palestine as well.

Barbarian Irruptions across the Danube—A.D. 500–560.—The pressure southwards from the nations along the Danube was constant and almost irresistible, and the sufferings of the Roman provincials from barbarian inroads so cruel, that it is a wonder the inhabitants of capital and provinces alike did not rise as one man to defend themselves; but the latter were cowed by sad experiences, and the former absorbed in weighing the comparative shades of heresy in a Nestorius and a Eutyches. Meanwhile, however, the danger was pressing. In A.D. 499, a combined horde of Huns, Wends, and Bulgarians crossed the Danube on the ice, crushed a Roman army with the loss of one-fourth of its numbers, and then retired with its booty. In A.D. 517 the invasion was repeated; and in A.D. 530, and in A.D. 533. In A.D. 538, while Belisarius was in Italy, Gothic intrigues precipitated the same people again across the Danube; and we may gather what was implied in such an irruption, if we try to realise the vast numbers of unoffending farmers and citizens involved in a plundering foray, which extended from the Chersonese to the Adriatic, and from the Danube to Corinth, and in which even Asia Minor suffered heavily. In the absence of soldiers, courage, discipline, and patriotism, the Emperors did what they. could. Anastasius carried a stone rampart of fifty miles in length from the Euxine to the Propontis, at a distance of forty miles from the capital, to guard it against a surprise. Justin strengthened the defences of Mœsia. Justinian fortified the great cities on the Danube, and inaugurated the policy of fostering the jealousies and utilising the hostility of tribe against tribe. It would have been well had he been able to repress his own jealousy of his own successful generals—of Germanus, and Narses, and Belisarius. And yet nothing but the courage, skill, and resources of Belisarius saved Justinian and his capital in A.D. 559, when Zabergan led a horde of Bulgarians and Slaves to the south of Mount Hæmus, and almost surprised Constantinople. For this service Belisarius was honoured with a "recall." If few things are sadder than a life of successful energy ending in poverty and failure, the last years of Justinian were sad indeed. The money saved by Anastasius was spent; the Empire was too poor to pay taxes:

the soldiers' pay diminished, and with it the number of soldiers; and the Emperor was afraid to go to war, for the army had dwindled to one-fourth of its numbers, the sinews of war were wanting, and a successful and popular general would have been a dangerous rival.

The Avars—Ψευδάβαρες.—In A.D. 557 an embassy arrived at Constantinople that aroused great curiosity. They were not Huns, so familiar to the capital, for they wore their hair long, and a long double tress or pigtail behind, fastened with ribbon. And yet their dress and language were those of Huns. They called themselves Avars (Ἄβαρες), and offered their arms to the Empire in exchange for money and land, which they demanded with scant courtesy. Justinian temporised. Of land he said nothing (in fact, what land had he to offer?), but they were already on the shores of the Caspian, and money and presents were much at their service, if they would vex and harass the Emperor's restless foes on the Euxine and the Caucasus. It mattered little which conquered. The Empire would gain in having one enemy the less. The Avars obeyed. They fell furiously on Huns and Slaves without distinction, and in five years (A.D. 557–562) had destroyed or subjugated the tribes settled between the Caucasus and the Danube, and far up the valleys of the Dnieper and the Dniester, and founded an Empire of their own. Then came, as might be anticipated, the inevitable claim for " land." A second embassy was sent to Constantinople, reciting the services of the Avars, and requesting to see the lands intended for their use. What Justinian might have felt or said, had he known only what he knew five years before, it is hard to determine. As it was, his eyes had been opened. Shortly before, an embassy had arrived from yet another and a more terrible Eastern people, the Turks, claiming, in the name of the great Khan

(Khakan, Chaganus), the subjects who had fled from his hand, and who had falsely called themselves Avars. He had heard that the Emperor had allied himself with these slaves; where were they? Justinian was confounded, as well he might be, apologised for his strange mistake, and hastened to make an alliance with his new friends, especially with a view to turning their arms against the Persians; while the Avar embassy met with but a cool reception, and, indeed, would have been sent off unheard, had it been safe to do so. The Danube, however, was too near to Constantinople.

True Story of " False Avars."—The true story of these "false Avars" is as curious as any in history. Their real name had been "Ouar-Khouni" (Οὐὰρ καὶ Χουννί), the latter half of which stamps them as Huns; and they were probably a branch of those Ugrians or Ogors who were settled in the fifth and sixth centuries to the north of the Caspian and east of the Volga. They had formed a part of the vast Empire of the genuine Avars, stretching from China to the Volga, and at their downfall had become subjects with them of the great Khan of the Turks. Transplantations of population (as of the Jews to Babylon) were so common in huge Empires, that it is not strange to hear of both Avars and Ouar-Khouni being transported to the far East by their new masters. The Avars were too broken down to dream of escape. Not so the others. Watching their opportunity, the chief horde, numbering 200,000 men, took women and children, cattle and waggons, and essayed to flee, leaving three tribes behind them. Their course was westward, toward their old home. Of the fortunes and sufferings of this mass of human beings in their hurried flight no details are known, save that the terror of their name preceded them (for they were supposed to be the Avars, the old lords of Asia), and that tribe after tribe was trampled under foot, or rudely thrust upon its neighbours as they hurried on. But in one sense history repeats itself. And if we remember that they traversed leagues of wild and difficult country, with an enemy hanging on their rear, we shall realise the greatness of the feat they accomplished, by comparing the famous flight of the Kalmuck Tartars from the tyranny of Catherine II. (A.D. 1771),[2] or the yet more awful retreat of the French from Moscow (A.D. 1813).[3] Thousands must have perished. The mere *speed* of the flight, necessary to ensure safety, must have been an element itself of bitter misery to the women and children. Imagine the sleeplessness, the scanty food, the constant fighting; the rivers to be crossed; the cold to be endured; the old, the sick, the young children, drooping or abandoned. It is little wonder that the vast district which they traversed was thrown into utter confusion by the terrific and unexpected collision—a confusion which became a wild panic when these Huns assumed the fashions of their old masters, and the name of the dreaded "Avars." These were the men who fought Justinian's enemies, who resuscitated Attila's Empire on the Danube, who brought Constantinople to the verge of ruin, and who fell at last only before the sword of Charles the Great (A.D. 791–799).

Avars Attack the Slaves.—Meanwhile these Ouar-Khouni, or false Avars, were on the Danube, and their ambassadors at Constantinople were awaiting Justinian's reply. Their demand was "land." He offered them a corner of Mœsia, between the Gepidæ and the Lombards, whom he had invited from Bohemia to Pannonia. It was the old story over again, playing off one enemy against another.

<hr>

[2] Cf. De Quincy, author's Edition, vol. iv.
[3] Cf. Alison's Hist. Europe, vol. xvi. cap. 73.

But they refused the offer, and being provoked by the
Antes, fell savagely on the Slavonian tribes, one after
another, penetrating to the Baltic, and as far as the Thur-
ingian Forest.   Here, however, they met their match in
the Franks, and returned once more to their old position,
whence they could threaten or cajole the Court of Byzantium.   And either course was now equally easy.   Justinian
and Belisarius were both dead; and Justin II. was no
match for Baian, Chagan of the Avars.   Justin was a
mere pedant, with grand words ever on his lips, but with
no common sense, or force of character, or knowledge of
the world.   As vain of his own powers as he was jealous
of his uncle's glory, he made it his policy to reverse
Justinian's.   Where Justinian had diplomatised, Justin
threatened, though unable to execute his threats; while
the ingratitude and hauteur of Justin lost to the Empire
the conquests of Justinian's generals.   Whether it were
Italians, or Avars, or Persians, he used the language of
Marius to the Teutons, or Trajan to the Parthians, though
he had neither the genius of the latter nor the troops of
the former.   He armed against the Empire all her enemies
at once.   Baian, on the other hand, was a second Attila.
Quick to read other men's minds, and to profit by their
mistakes; ready to fight, yet never making war save for a
purpose; patient to endure even humiliations till he could
strike with a prospect of success; regarding oaths and
treaties as only means to that success; generous, magnificent, luxurious, he outlived three Emperors, and founded
the second Empire of the Huns.   By judicious alliances
and timely wars he aggrandised his subjects at the expense of their neighbours.   He helped the Lombards to
destroy the Gepidæ (A.D. 566), and then occupied their
land.   By alternate force and intrigue he mastered the
valley of the Save.   He fixed his capital on the site of

Attila's, between the Danube and the Theiss, whence he dominated alike Huns, and Slaves, and Bulgarians, and could watch both Franks and Romans. He trespassed on the Empire almost unperceived by a systematic series of small colonies of Slaves or Bulgarians, which he planted surreptitiously to the south of the Danube. The Romans recoiled from the idea of destroying hundreds of unarmed colonists, and so took no notice; but the colonies, once planted, were subjects of Baian, who might, and did, claim the land they occupied. Finally, he brought westward the three tribes of Ouar-Khouni, who had refused to accompany the first fugitives. Baian's career, however, like Attila's, was not unchequered by failure, and before his death the firmness of the Emperor Maurice (A.D. 587–602), and the ability of Priscus, inflicted on the Avars five serious defeats, drove them to the Theiss, and retrieved the honour of Rome.

Persian Encroachments—A.D. 530–615.—All this while, however, when the Avars were threatening the northern frontier, an enemy hardly less formidable was steadily advancing on the south. During the last fifty years Rome and Persia had been constantly at war; and the successful arms of Chosroes I. (or Nushirvan, A.D. 531–579), had reduced Antioch, the capital of Syria, and seemed to threaten even Constantinople. As before in Africa and Italy, and afterwards in Thrace, the genius of Belisarius again averted the pressing danger, and Chosroes withdrew to Mesopotamia (A.D. 541–2). It is needless to follow minutely the details of a varying struggle—the war in the reigns of Justin, Tiberius, and Maurice—the fortunes of Bahram, who defeated both Romans and Turks— the adventures of Chosroes II., the adopted son of Maurice, who was placed on his throne by Roman arms. When Maurice was murdered by an obscure centurion, Phocas

(A.D. 602), Chosroes, to avenge his "father's" death, invaded the Roman dominions. He overran Syria, in vaded Palestine, and took Jerusalem by storm (A.D. 614). Egypt, Alexandria, Cyrene were reduced. A Persian army was seen on the shores of the Bosporus, and Chalcedon taken. It seemed as though between the Avars and the Persians the days of the Eastern Empire were numbered; but it had yet 800 years to live, and in the hour of need the deliverer appeared. Heraclius, son of the Exarch of Africa, had been invited to free, and succeeded in freeing, the Empire from the tyranny of Phocas (A.D. 610). But hardly was he seated on the Imperial throne, before he heard of the fall of Antioch and the rapid progress of the Persian arms. Presently came tidings of heavier loss— of the invasion of Galilee and yet holier places—of the massacre of Christians—of the pillage of the Church of the Resurrection—of the removal of the "true cross" to Persia. This was a cross of wood, which popular belief supposed to have been that on which Christ was crucified, and to have been found by the Empress Helena, mother of Constantine the Great. It was preserved in a case of wrought silver. The emotion and profound grief felt in all Christendom at the loss of this holy relic are to us hardly intelligible. Many Christians even thought Christianity itself doomed.

Heraclius Prepares for War — A.D. 615.—To many others, and Heraclius among them, it acted as a tonic, to rouse them from indolence and luxury. The Emperor swore that he would seek the holy cross even in the depths of Asia. What but a few weeks before would have seemed a Quixotic absurdity, was now caught up as an inspiration from heaven with almost as much fervour as the first Crusade. The ranks of the army soon filled. Bishops and clergy, rulers and people, poured their wealth into the treasury. Churches remained open day and night, and frequent addresses kept up the enthusiasm to a high pitch. It was (for the moment) a genuine "revival" or reawakening of the whole Roman world. The occasion, too, appeared favourable. Italy was quiet, and the Exarchate at peace with its neighbours. Clotaire the Frank was no enemy to Heraclius, and in common with his clergy (being orthodox and not Arian) might be expected to sympathise in so holy a cause.

Treachery of the Avars—A.D. 616.—In one quarter only was there room for fear. The Avars were on the Danube, and the turbulence of the Avars was only equalled by their perfidy. Already, in A.D. 610, they had fallen suddenly on North Italy, and pillaged and harassed those same Lombards whom they had before helped to destroy the Gepidæ. Previous to an absence, therefore, of years from his capital, it was essential for the Emperor to sound their intentions, and, if possible, to secure their neutrality. His ambassadors were welcomed with apparent cordiality, and an interview was arranged between the Chagan and Heraclius. The place was to be Heraclea. At the appointed time the Emperor set out from Selymbria to meet the Khan, decked with Imperial crown and mantle to honour the occasion. The escort was a handful of soldiers; but there was an immense cortége of high officials and of the fashionable world of Constantinople, and the whole country side was there to see. Presently some terrified peasants were seen making their way hurriedly towards Heraclius. They urged him to flee for his life; for armed Avars had been seen in small bodies, and might even now be between him and the capital. Heraclius knew too much to hesitate. He threw off his robes and fled, and but just in time. The Chagan had laid a deep plot. A large mass of men had been told off in small detachments to march on Heraclea by different routes, thus escaping observation; and he hoped by this means to secure his prize. And indeed he only just failed. Heraclius had hardly turned before the Avars burst in upon the defenceless and unarmed crowd. There was a general *sauve qui peut*—officials, peasants, chariot-drivers. The Imperial baggage and robe were seized, but the hoped-for prize had flown. Heraclius was in Constantinople; and when the Avar cavalry arrived there, the gates were shut and the walls manned, and the city was ready for a siege. The promptitude of the Emperor had saved not only himself, but his capital also. And now the question was, What notice should be taken of this piece of treachery? War? But that would interfere with the more important Eastern expedition. And, besides, the Khan was profuse in his apologies for the rudeness and insubordination of his troops, which alone (he said) were in fault. He offered restitution, and added vow to vow as to his own good faith. In fact, if the Persian campaign were to be carried on, what else could Heraclius do but smother his feelings, affect to believe, conclude an alliance, and hope for the best (A.D. 616)?

Heraclius Victorious in Persia—A.D. 622–628.— At last, being at peace with his enemies and all his preparations completed, Heraclius was ready to start (A.D. 622). There is some difference of opinion as to the point of the Persian Empire which he first attacked, and Gibbon accuses of inaccuracy those writers, who nevertheless credit the Emperor with skill enough to attack his enemy at the weakest part. But when we reflect that the Persian armies were posted in Syria and on the Euphrates, and had pushed into Asia Minor, it seems less credible to believe that he landed in Cilicia, where he would have been exposed to a concentrated attack, than that he adopted the more audacious, yet perhaps safer, plan of landing in Colchis and attacking their line of communication. In Colchis he was close to Huns and Turks, possible allies, and certainly enemies of Persia; while the wisdom of his tactics was seen in the fact, that a blow delivered towards the heart of the Empire immediately recalled the Persian armies to its defence. From Colchis he marched into Atropatene, Albania, and Armenia; and in those provinces a series of campaigns was carried on for more than three years, in which Heraclius was mostly successful, and pushed eventually as far south even as Aspadana (Ispahan), if we may believe a doubtful authority. In any case, the effect was the same—an attack on the centre of the Empire at once relieved Asia Minor and Syria of the presence of Persian armies. At this juncture his enemy, taught by his tactics, delivered a counterblow, which nothing but two or three lucky accidents prevented from being fatal to the Eastern Empire. Chosroes opened negotiations with the Chagan of the Avars, inviting him to join in an attack on Constantinople, and offering him the pillage of the city if the attack were successful. Schaharbarz was to be sent with a large Persian force to Chalcedon, and the Avar skiffs and canoes, which they used on the Danube, were to carry them, if requisite, across the Bosporus (A.D. 626). Such a joint attack, in the absence of the Emperor with the flower of his army, might well seem hopeless to resist, unless he returned at once to create a diversion. But he did nothing of the sort. Detaching a portion of his army to make for the Euxine and to reinforce the garrison of the capital, he marched himself with a small division to the shores of the Caspian to invite the alliance of the Khazars, while he left the main body under his brother Theodore's command to compel the presence of a large

Persian army in Adiabene for the protection of Ctesiphon. These Khazars or Acatzires were by origin Huns, and their language similar to the Bulgarian; but having become subject to the Turks they had intermarried, and adopted the Turkish customs and dress and name. To the world at large they were Turks, and formidable in proportion. By the promise of his daughter's hand in marriage to their Khan, Heraclius secured the aid of 40,000 warriors; and gradually forcing the Persians from the field into the fortresses of Armenia and Mesopotamia, he won a great victory in the plain where, 1,200 years before, Nineveh had stood (A.D. 627). This victory enriched his army with all the wealth and plunder of the many palaces that lay along the Tigris, and opened the road to Ctesiphon; while the recovery of 300 Roman standards, and the liberation of numberless captives, might avenge the memories of even Crassus (B.C. 53) and Valerian (A.D. 260). Heraclius was in no position, however, to press his advantage; for his good allies the Khazars abandoned him, when they had filled their hands with booty.

Successful Defence of Constantinople.—Meanwhile Constantinople was hard pressed. The confederate armies of Persians and Avars had converged on the capital from north and south towards the end of June A.D. 626, the latter encumbered with the canoes ($\mu o\nu \acute{o} \xi \upsilon \lambda a$) which they were bringing to ferry their allies over the straits. The first attack was made on the wall on July 31, and lasted for five days, but all to no purpose. The skill and courage of the besieged repelled every assault. Schaharbarz, moreover, was unable to co-operate with his allies; for he had no means of crossing the narrow strip of water between Chrysopolis and the capital, while the Roman fleet kept vigilant watch and intercepted all

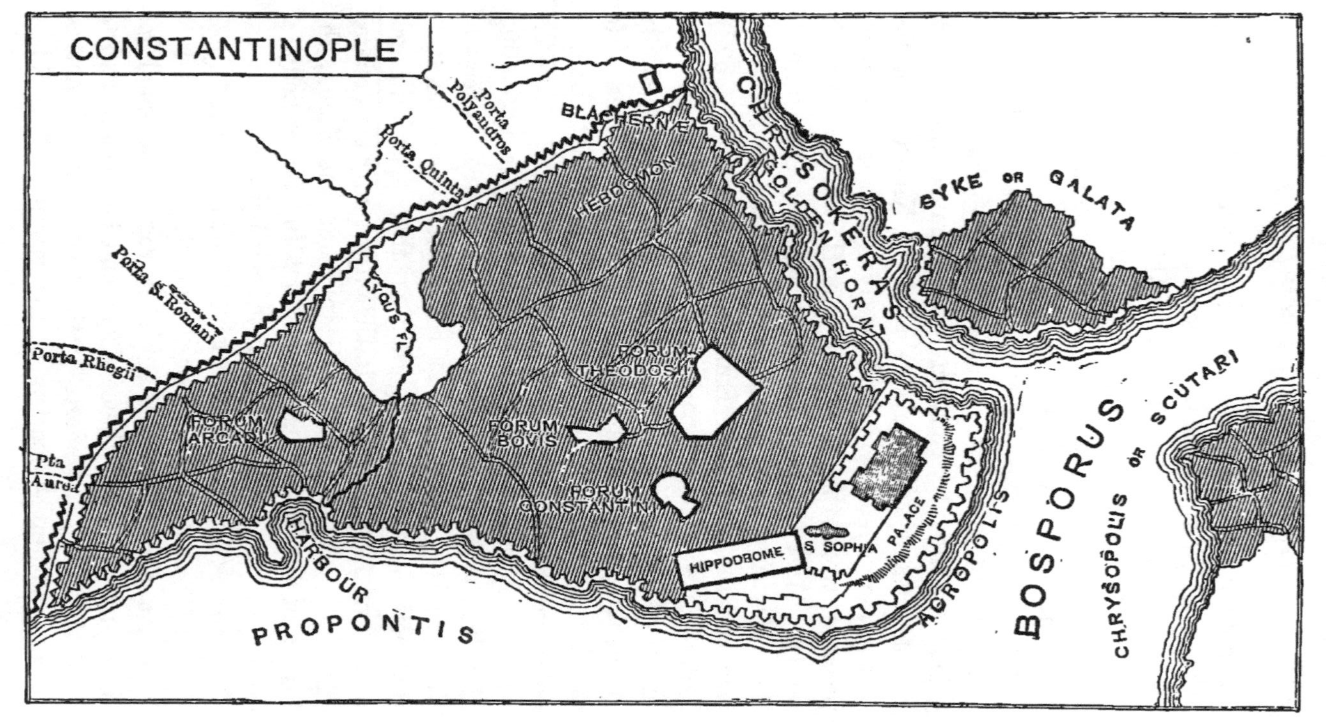

CONSTANTINOPLE
BOSPORUS
CHRYSOPOLIS OR SCUTARI
ACROPOLIS
SYKE OR GALATA
CHRYSOKERAS
GOLDEN HORN
PALACE
S. SOPHIA
HIPPODROME
FORUM THEODOSII
FORUM BOVIS
FORUM CONSTANTINI
BLACHERNE
HEBDOMON
Porta Polyandros
Porta Quinta
LYCUS FL.
FORUM ARCADII
Porta S. Romani
Porta Rhegii
Pta Aurea
HARBOUR
PROPONTIS

attempts of the Avar canoes to cross over. A night surprise even in the Golden Horn was foiled with heavy loss; and at last the Chagan, unable alike to affect a junction with the Persians and to make an impression on the city, reluctantly retired, vowing to return and take vengeance for his repulse.

Effects of the War—A.D. 628–641.—But the Romans had now little cause for fear. Theodore had gained a brilliant victory in Mesopotamia : and by-and-bye there came tidings of the battle of Nineveh; of the restoration of standards and captives, and the yet more precious prize of the "true cross;" of Heraclius' immediate return. And the return was one long scene of triumph, the whole city flocking across the water to Chrysopolis to welcome the victorious Emperor (September 14, 628). Indeed, it was no ordinary exploit which this indolent, luxurious Emperor had achieved, in combating successfully at one and the same time two such powerful foes. He saved the Roman Empire; while the Persian Empire never recovered from the blow, and ere long fell before the new-born enthusiasm of Mohammedanism (A.D. 636–700). Nor did the Avars escape from some disastrous effects of their repulse. The central authority became so weakened, that both Slaves and Bulgarians asserted their independence ; and Heraclius, alive to the opportunity thus offered him, not only allied himself to Samo the Frank, the leader of the Slavonian revolt, but invited a body of Slovenes, who were settled on the northern slopes of the Carpathians, and called themselves "mountaineers" (χρώ-βατοι, Chrobates), to conquer from the Avars, and to occupy a part of Dalmatia. They eagerly accepted his offer, and conquered the country; and being converted to Christianity by the efforts of the then Pope, Honorius, became faithful supporters of the Empire. Nor did he

THE
DIANS
R. Danube
KINGDOM OF
R. Po
OSTROG
Corsica
Sardinia
Rome

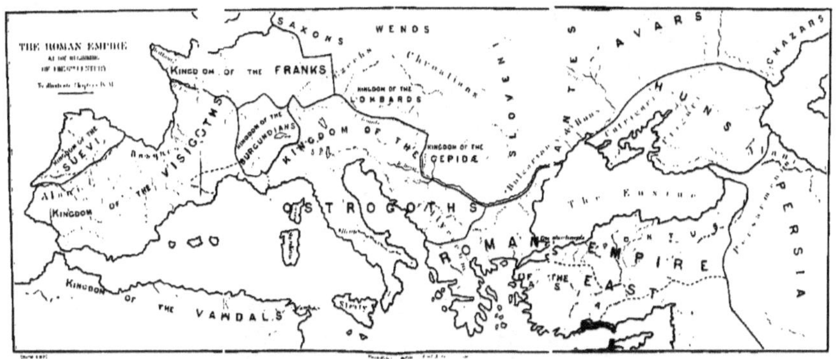

THE ROMAN EMPIRE
AT THE BEGINNING
OF THE 6TH CENTURY
To illustrate Chapters IV-VI
SAXONS
WENDS
KINGDOM OF THE FRANKS
KINGDOM OF THE LOMBARDS
Chroatians
KINGDOM OF THE SUEVI
VISIGOTHS
KINGDOM OF THE BURGUNDIANS
KINGDOM OF THE
KINGDOM OF THE GEPIDÆ
Alans
OSTROGOTHS
SLOVENI
ANTES
AVARS
CHAZARS
HUNS
ROMAN EMPIRE OF THE EAST
The Euxine
PERSIA
PONTUS
KINGDOM OF THE VANDALS
Sicily
KINGDOM
Alans

stop here.   The news of the good fortune of the Chrobats spreading, a body of Wends from the Elbe, who called themselves "Srp" (Σέρβλοι, Sorabi), applied to Heraclius for the same favour, and were settled by him to the south of the Save and Danube, in what are now called Servia and Bosnia.   These, too, became Christians.   This practical defence of the line of the Danube against the Avars was finished after Heraclius' death (A.D. 641) by the settlement of the Bulgarians in the province of Mœsia, to which they gave their own name.   After A.D. 630 the Avars figure no more in the annals of the Eastern Empire. A decaying and disorganised power, they fell in the ninth century before the strong arm of Charles the Great.

CHAPTER XII

MOHAMMED AND MOHAMMEDANISM—
A.D. 622–711.

Mohammedanism — A.D. 622.—The seventh century had seen the Empire saved from ruin by the arms and policy of a single Emperor, the Avars effectually thrust across the Danube, the Persian Empire shattered. It was yet to see a religious revolution, second in importance only to Christianity, and the effects of which are still unexhausted in our own day. In the seventh century there arose in Arabia a religion, which inspired its votaries with such zeal, that in 100 years they had conquered and to a great extent converted or destroyed the Zoroastrians of Persia, the Brahmans and Buddhists of India, the Christians of Africa and Spain. They crossed the Pyrenees. They threatened even Rome. In the end they established their religion in the very heart of Eastern Christendom, at Constantinople (A.D. 1453). Why was all this? How was it, that an obscure country, almost beyond the pale of civilisation—beyond the reach of Greek and Persian and Roman arms—with a frugal, nomadic, and probably decreasing population—divided into petty, hostile tribes —could send forth almost inexhaustible armies, who were inspired with a fanaticism amounting to madness, and blindly obeyed a single leader, at once general, king, and pontiff?

Secondary Causes of Success.—Various secondary causes may, no doubt, be assigned for the rapid conquests of the Mohammedan armies. The prestige of victory is great; one conquest is apt to lead to another: while division and weakness will always end in defeat. Persia was in a state of anarchy. The divisions of Christianity were as fatal as its moral degeneracy. Monasticism, which in one sense was then the salt of religion, was in another its bane; for it robbed religion of the practical and masculine virtues, which alone could make a successful resistance to such fanaticism possible. Rome and her bishop were hardly yet strong enough to take the lead in such a struggle; and neither the Empire nor the Church of the East could unite men, as Mohammedanism united them, in one bond of nationality and religious unity. Hence resistance was half-hearted, partial, and isolated. Nor were the Arabs, like the Vandals or Goths, a nation seeking a new home. They were armies of *men* only, who for the most part put other men to the sword, who seized the women for their own harems, and whose children, at any rate, were Mohammedans. Hence the conquered, stripped of wealth and wives, continually decreased in numbers, and in ability to resist.

But these reasons are not enough in themselves to explain the facts, nor do they at all account for the origin and force of that enthusiasm, which made the Arabs so irresistible. We shall find both the one and the other (if at all) in the conditions of Arab life and history, and in the character of Mohammed himself.

Characteristics of Arabia.—The East, it is said, never changes: and this is specially true of Arabia. An Eastern population, isolated from all the world, and itself split up and divided into small tribes by force of circumstances, will hardly change at all from generation to generation.   Arabia of to-day is in all essentials the counterpart of the Arabia of Mohammed.

Briefly described, the country consists of a central table-land, surrounded by a desert ring of sand to the south, west, and east, and of stones to the north, its entire surface being about four times as large as France, and measuring 1,500 miles in length, by 800 in breadth. Outside the desert again, and fringing the coast, runs a strip of mountain land, varying in height, breadth, and fertility.   The area of country, admitting of cultivation, is estimated at two-thirds; the remaining third being a desert (or ocean) of loose reddish sand, shifting with every capricious breeze that blows, and not seldom piled up in huge ridges or waves, which will at times average 200 feet in height, and to cross which involves toil, suffering, and often death.   The central plateau consists of a series of mountains and mountain slopes of granite and limestone, intersected by sand passes which effectually separate tribe from tribe.   In short, the conditions of life in Arabia are such as to preclude (unless under exceptional circumstances) movement and political activity.

Characteristics of Tribes.—The population of this vast country was probably not more uniform in the seventh century than it is now.   History, language, and character alike testify to as marked a difference between the nomad and the settled population, as between the inhabitants of north and south.   It is a common error to confound Arabs with Bedouins, and to suppose that all Arabs are nomads.   As a matter of fact, the Bedouins or nomad Arabs bear but a small proportion to the settled tribes, forming perhaps a fourth of the whole population, and present a startling contrast in character to the cognate clans of Central and Eastern Arabia.   The latter are pronounced by all travellers to be one of the noblest and most gifted races of the world; Carlyle calls them the "Italians" of the East: the former, identical in blood and tongue, but ignorant, licentious, and savage, are like ill-educated children. They have little or no religion, little or no morality, none of the courtesy of the "noble savage." Nor is the difference·less marked between the settled inhabitants of Northern and Southern Arabia— these inclined to be volatile, ostentatious, and unstable; those serious, reticent, stedfast, and austere. Indeed, 100 years before the era of Mohammed, there was fierce war between the clans of the centre and the south (A.D. 500–520), in which the former established a temporary independence, only to succumb afterwards to the new outbursts of religious enthusiasm from Mecca and Medina. The general conclusion arrived at from these and similar considerations is, that in Arabia, as in Europe, there were two or three waves of population, whose course was from north to south. As Kelts in Europe were encroached upon by Teutons, so in Arabia the original Kahtanic stock was pushed forward by the later Ishmaelitic race, and even across the Red Sea into Abyssinia and Eastern Africa. The latter traced their descent to Ishmael, and so to Abraham. The former to Kahtan (in Hebrew, Joktan), fourth in descent from Shem. Now, whatever may be the value of the genealogies of Genesis, or of popular tradition in such a case, it is certain that the Arabs acknowledge Kahtan as a founder of their race, while at the southern end of the central Highlands a certain marked variation begins from the purest Arabic, which increases to the east and south, as well as a marked variation of customs and character. It is fair to infer a difference of origin in populations whose language and character thus differ.

Political and Religious Confusion—A.D. 600.—
At the beginning of the seventh century Arabia was in a
state of singular confusion, both political and religious.
In the North the Byzantine Empire held an undefined
and dubious sway, while ever and anon its outposts reached
almost to Medina. The extreme eastern and southern
clans were ruled by sovereigns of their own, but in subjection to the Persian Empire; lastly, there was a powerful
and independent confederacy of clans in the central Highlands, ruled by a certain Moseylemah. In the interstices
(so to speak) of these separate powers was a roving element
of predatory Bedouins; while scattered about the Penin-
sula, but especially in the west, were a few small communities of Jews, who were active in making proselytes.
But there were Christian refugees still more active—
refugees from the oppressive orthodoxy of the Empire,
who fought their battles over again in the freer atmosphere
of Arabia, and who also made converts. Indeed, Arab
literature and traditions alike concur in showing that
Christianity was widely spread through Northern Arabia
long before Mohammedanism arose. The bulk of the
population, however, was doubtless pagan—not necessarily
idolatrous, for the Sabæans (like the Magians, who fled
from Persia before the sword of the Greeks) worshipped
the heavenly bodies as symbols of the source of light,
and abstained from the use of images; while, unlike the
Magians, they recognised no priestly caste. The purest
Sabæans were to be found in the east of Arabia; in the
centre and south-west the religion was less refined and
more idolatrous. But whether it were Jew or Christian,
Magian, Sabæan, or idolater, all Arabians agreed in re-
verencing the sacred stone of Mecca, the Caaba—a holy
place associated by tradition with the names of Abraham,
Seth, and Adam. And the temple of the Caaba was the

centre of the commerce as well as of the religion of Arabia; the pilgrims of every creed, the merchants of every nation met in the holy place at Mecca. It was the one bond of union between all Arabians. And of this temple, with its sacred stone and well, the tribe of Koreish, Mohammed's tribe, were guardians.

Primary Causes of Success.—If we now reflect for a moment on the general bearing of what has been said thus far—the comparative isolation, divergence, and disunion of the several Arabian tribes—and then compare it with the spectacle presented by the same tribes 100, or 50, or even 30 years later, the problem to be solved will take a narrower and simpler form. By A.D. 650 the Arabs were masters of Persia, Syria, and Egypt. By the beginning of the eighth century they had advanced to the Pillars of Hercules, and had twice besieged Constantinople. What was the source of this marvellous energy? If the state of Arabia itself was rather adverse than favourable to such an outburst, and the condition of the conquered countries can only be cited as a secondary and concurrent cause, to what can we attribute it but the personal character and ascendency of Mohammed himself in the first instance; and, secondly, to the religious system which he bequeathed to his followers? We have, in short, to weigh the meaning of the life and ideas of a man who succeeded, like Moses, in welding together a disunited people, and, like Buddha (about 600 B.C.), in instituting a new religion for millions of his fellow-men.

Mohammed's Early Years.—Mohammed was born in A.D. 569 or A.D. 570, of the family of Hashem, of the tribe of Koreish. His father and mother both dying while he was a child, he was taken charge of first by his grandfather, and then by his uncle, Abu Thaleb, a just and kind man. This uncle he accompanied in various commercial journeys, especially in A.D. 584 to Syria. It was his first introduction to the great world, and although the tradition may not be false, which speaks of his being instructed in Christian doctrines by the Nestorian monk Sergius at Bosra, it would seem probable that other influences affected him far more deeply. The frequent references, for instance, to " ships " in the Koran seem to point to visits to Syrian sea-ports, and to deep impressions received there. For Mohammed was known as thoughtful and observant from his earliest years; his friends called him " Al Amin," the Faithful. His was a reticent, serious, truthful character; and withal he was pleasant to look upon, with a high broad forehead and oval face, an aquiline nose, keen black eyes, and black and flowing hair and beard. He had a ruddy complexion. Though his manner was ordinarily calm and serious, yet he could laugh genially, and the sweetness of his smile was noted; while if roused to anger he showed the family peculiarity of a curious swelling of the veins on the brow. Though little educated (for it is probable that he could never write), his intellectual powers were far above the common. He had a quick apprehension, keen insight, and vivid imagination; a mind to be deeply impressed by the mingled monotony and "intensity" (so to say) of the physical life around him, the intense sunlight, the brilliant starlight, the interminable desert. Even the man's personal tricks and habits help us to realise him as he was; his mode of wearing the turban with one end hanging down between his shoulders, because (he said) the angels wore it so; his scrupulous cleanliness; his delight in perfumes; his trick of perpetually smoothing his hair when in the presence of women.

Mohammed "called" to be the Prophet of God.—After serving a rich widow of Mecca, Kadijah by name, as steward, she, grateful for faithful services, married him, and they lived happily together for twenty-five years. She was forty, and had already been twice married; Mohammed was only twenty-eight. But his marriage with Kadijah made him one of the most wealthy, as he was already from force of character one of the most influential men in Mecca. This wealth gave him a respite also from the necessities of business, and leisure for that reflection in which he loved to indulge. The first twelve years of his married life were the seed time of the harvest to come. At the age of forty the crisis came in his life. Mohammed had been used, like other Arabians, to pass the holy month of Ramadhan in solitude in the caves of Mount Hira, ten miles north of Mecca. And in A.D. 609, while thus in seclusion, a vision appeared to him (he said) from Heaven in the person of the angel Gabriel. He had been fasting, watching, and praying. In the dead of night he heard a voice, amid an intolerable flood of light, calling to him and bidding him to read what was written on a scroll held in the angel's hand. Enabled by supernatural power to do what before was impossible to him, he read in the scroll the law of God as afterwards revealed in the Koran; while the angel solemnly announced to him that he was to be the "Prophet of God." The fervent belief of Kadijah, to whom he imparted this vision, and the adhesion of her cousin Warkeh, confirmed the wavering mind of Mohammed. But his enemies, and even some of his earlier followers, asserted that the vision was an epileptic fit, to which attacks he was subject; and one of his biographers[1] believes "not that the apparition of Gabriel was alleged to conceal his

---

[1] Dr Weil—cf. Milman Lat. Christianity, book iv. cap. i.

malady, but that the malady itself was the cause of his belief in these apparitions." It may be so. In the absence of definite details, however, one or two points are clear. Mohammed was no impostor. Impostors do not generally begin imposture in the decline of life, or needlessly face personal privations and dangers, or frame religions for half a world. Mohammed believed heartily in his own "call" to be a reformer. As a theory to explain undisputed facts, it seems not impossible that, like Elijah in Israel, or Paul at Athens, his soul was stirred within him by what he saw around. Amidst the fanaticism of the Jew, the hair-splitting word-battles of the Christians, the nature worship of the Sabæans, the idolatry of the Caaba with its 360 images, the root of the matter seemed lost—the one God in and over all. It was no doubt the glory of Mohammedanism (and as we shall see presently its fatal Shibboleth) to insist with even wearisome iteration on the unity of God. That is the doctrine on which Mohammedanism rests, and by virtue of which Mohammed gave to his countrymen unity and a higher life. And to the Arabs Mohammedanism was "as a birth from darkness to light," and the effect which it produced in them comparable only to the effect of Puritanism on the soldiers of Cromwell. There was, indeed, little that was new or strange to the world in the creed, beyond the assertion of the "prophetic" mission of its founder; what was new was the ardour with which it was believed and propagated, and the marvellous results which followed.

Ill Success of Mohammed.—At first, however, Mohammed met with little success. Kadijah his wife, Seid his slave, Ali his cousin, were the first converts. In three years he had only gained thirteen followers; and the pretensions of an unlettered middle-aged man, backed only by a woman and a lad of sixteen, to change a nation's life and beliefs, were greeted with ridicule. But the Prophet persevered. As little by little his eloquence and earnestness gained adherents, so did the bitter hostility of unbelievers, and especially of the Koreish, increase. A price was set on his head. He had to face personal insult, to disguise himself, to take refuge for three years in a castle of his uncle's. At last that uncle's death left him without protectors. His life was in danger from unscrupulous enemies. Success at Mecca seemed impossible.

The Hegira or Flight of Mohammed to Medina —A.D. 622.—He fled (A.D. 622), and from this darkest hour of the Prophet's life Mohammedanism dates its birth. He had already gained a handful of converts at Yathreb, some 200 miles distant, a commercial rival of Mecca, where there was no local hierarchy, and but little local idolatry; and to Yathreb (henceforth called "Medina-al-Nabi," the city of the Prophet) the exiled Prophet fled. But he had much ado to escape. His murder was determined on, but the plot was betrayed to him. His cousin Ali dressed in his robe and lay on his couch, while Mohammed and Abu Bekr stole from Mecca by starlight, and hid in a cave for three days, being fed by the latter's daughter. Finally, they reached Medina in safety, and received welcome and protection. And here the believers rapidly increased in numbers : fugitives fled from Mecca before the persecution of the Koreish, converts were made in Medina, proselytes came in from the desert nomads. Mohammed, in fact, was at the head of a considerable body of men.

First Proclamation of War against Infidels.—At this point it is that we trace the first hint of an appeal to the sword. Far too much has been made of this. If we consider the matter, first of all, how natural

it was that such an idea should present itself to a man
born and bred in the midst of differences, and hostilities
such as have been described ! And, next, we must remember that the sacredness of toleration is a discovery
of quite recent date, and even yet of small estimation.
Christianity is not less, but all the more divine, because
on the whole it has forsworn the sword. Mohammedanism betrays its human origin in taking as a principle the use of persecution. Nor has Christianity been
always true to itself. Charles' Franks and Cromwell's
Puritans acted on the belief of Mohammed's Arabs, that
their own enemies were the enemies of God. Mohammed,
indeed, did not shrink from avowing his position. " I,"
he said, " the last of the prophets, am sent with the
sword. Let those who promulgate my faith enter into
no discussion, but slay all who refuse obedience."

Fall of Mecca—A.D. 630.—There followed battles
with the Jews, who refused Mohammed's overtures;
battles with the infidels of Mecca, until in A.D. 630,
partly by negotiations, partly by surprise, the city fell
into his hands; the idols of the Caaba were destroyed;
Mecca became the capital of Islam, the holy city, the
centre of pilgrimages. And this was not all. As lord of
Mecca, Mohammed gradually gained such influence in
more distant parts of Arabia, that the hereditary feuds
ceased; Arabia assumed the position of a nation among
other nations, and began to have a policy. It was only
natural that the views of the Prophet should expand with
his power; that the political and religious unity of Arabia,
of the East, of the world, should dawn by degrees on
Mohammed's mind. Even the union of Arabia was a
somewhat slow process, and not completed till after the
Prophet's death. The Jews were converted or banished.
Christians were tolerated at first, as being enemies of the

Jews and believers in a true prophet, Christ; but it was not for long. Christians were said or believed to worship three gods, and punished as heretics. " Say not there are three Gods," says the Koran, "God is but one God. Far be it from Him that He should have a son." Central Arabia had to be conquered by slow and bloody fighting, and yielded only to the energy of Khalid, "the sword of God." Eastern Arabia gave a speedier but more transient allegiance, while with the Bedouins of the desert even Mohammed could scarcely do anything. Still the unity of Arabia for the time was so far secured by the energy of Mohammed and the first Caliphs (or successors), that an Arab army could meet Roman soldiers on the field of Muta (A.D. 630), and Arab ambassadors were sent to the Emperor Heraclius and the Persian king. The feeling of strength arising from this unity is well exemplified in a conversation between the ambassador of Omar and the Persian Yezdegerd. " Who are you," said the Persian, " to attack an empire? of all nations of the world the poorest, most disunited, most ignorant?" " What you have said," replied the ambassador, " of our poverty, divisions, and barbarism, *was* true indeed. But now we are a new people. God has raised among us a man, His true Prophet; and Islam, His religion, has enlightened our minds, extinguished our hatreds, and made us a society of brothers." Allowing for the logic of the sword, this reply precisely describes the early effects of Mohammedanism in Arabia.

Death of Mohammed—A.D. 632.—Mohammed did not live long enough to see even the union of Arabia. He had lived a hard life; and the strength of his constitution had been impaired by poison administered to him some years before by a Jewish captive, and when, in A.D. 631, his only son Ibrahim died, it was a mortal blow to.

himself.   One more solemn pilgrimage from Medina to
Mecca he performed, at the head (it was said) of more
than 50,000 pilgrims; but his days were numbered.   A
fever set in; and after great suffering he died (June 8,
632), and was buried in Medina.   So died a great man,
in many respects a good man, one of those whom power
and prosperity corrupt, but not wholly.   He never lost
his simplicity of character, his genuine piety, his unselfishness, difficult as it may be to reconcile such traits
with some points of his creed and character.   Prayer was
his constant practice: "trust in God" his constant motto.
When his favourite wife, Ayesha, once asked him,
whether none entered paradise but through God's mercy,
"None, none, none," he answered, with triple iteration.
"But you, O Prophet, will not you enter except through
His compassion?"   Then Mohammed placed his hand on
his head and replied thrice, with much solemnity,
"Neither shall I enter paradise, unless God cover me
with His mercy."   Whatever were the faults and errors
of this Arab prophet he was a sincere man, whose
religion made both him and his followers better men.

The Doctrines of Mohammedanism.—To speak
of Mohammed apart from Mohammedanism, would leave
the problem before us only half solved.   It was the
doctrine and practice of Islam,[2] which inspired the conquering armies of Saracens, and which, in our own day,
commands the allegiance of 115,000,000 of human beings.

The Unity of God.—"The faith of Islam (as Gibbon
says) is compounded of an eternal truth and a necessary
fiction," that there is only one God, and that Mohammed
is the apostle of God.   The unity of God was a truth of

---

[2] "Islam" is the infinitive mood, "Moslim" the participle of the
causative verb, derived from "salm" = "peace," Islam = to make
peace.

which the world had too much lost sight, not only in Mohammed's misconceptions, but in reality. The "three gods" of the Koran are doubtless a misunderstanding of the Christian Trinity; but the worship of relics, images, and saints certainly obscures true ideas of God. In the Mohammedan profession of faith the unity of God is asserted by raising the forefinger, and exclaiming, "La Ilah illa Allah," "there is no god but God." On the surface these words look like a truism, but they are not. They are the negation of any deity, save one: they are that, and much more. They not only deny all plurality, whether of person or nature, in God, but they imply that this Supreme Being is the only agent or force in the universe, all else (men included) being only instruments, by and through which He works, "as He wills" (a frequent expression in the Koran), communicating nothing to them, receiving nothing from them. Allah is a "jealous God," an omnipotent autocrat, ruling the universe "as He wills." Woe to him who disobeys! Below Him and at His feet lies all creation, from angels to insects, creatures of His breath, all equal in His sight, all created alike only for His will. This is the meaning of the words, stated barely. What the system which is based on such a belief results in, may be seen in the government of the Central Arabia of to-day, where the "reformed Mohammedanism" of the Wahhabees is in full possession.[3] The doctrine inevitably excludes all relations between man and God save those of slavish obedience, excludes therefore all idea of progress and development. Islam is sterile and stationary; and its sacred book, like a "dead man's hand," is stiff and motionless. "The worshipper" (says an Arab proverb) "models himself on what he worships;" and life in Riad,

[3] See Palgrave's Arabia, chapters viii. and ix.

the capital of Central Arabia, and headquarters of Wahhabeeism, is marked by monotonous and chilling reserve on the surface, and beneath by the worst features of religious despotism, jealousy, espionage, and repression.

Angels and Genii.—Mohammedanism includes belief not only in God, but in angels and genii—the former of which are exempt from, while the latter are subject to the frailties of humanity, and both alike created out of fire.

The Koran.—The third article of faith is belief in the Koran (Al-Korân—the Book) as divinely revealed through the Prophet. It was certainly compiled after Mohammed's death, during the Caliphate of Abu Bekr; yet its general integrity is universally acknowledged. It is the Mohammedan code of civil as well as religious law. Mohammedans swear by it, take omens from it, study it. In some mosques it is read through daily.

The Creed. — Mohammedans believe further in 200,000 prophets, of whom six are pre-eminent—Adam, Noah, Abraham, Moses, Jesus, and Mohammed; in the resurrection and final judgment; in a heaven and hell, whose joys and horrors are detailed with singular minuteness; last, and not least, in predestination, so that every event has been predetermined from all eternity, and every man's destiny and hour of death have been irrevocably fixed, a doctrine as potent on the battle-field as it is fatal in the time of peace.

Practical Religion.—There are four articles of religious practice—prayer, alms, fasting, and pilgrimage. Five times a day is prayer enjoined with preliminary ablution, in which the words, posture, and gestures are carefully prescribed, while the eyes are to be turned towards Mecca. Friday is the sacred day of rest, with a sermon in the mosque. Alms must be given by every good Mohammedan to the extent of at least one-tenth of his income.   Fasting is practised for thirty days in each year during the month of Ramadhan, implying abstinence between sunrise and sunset from meat and drink, baths, and all bodily gratifications.   As to pilgrimage, every believer is bound to visit Mecca once in his life, either personally or by proxy.

Was Mohammedanism Original ?—A moment's reflection on the beliefs and practice of Mohammedanism shows that no religion was less original.   Sabæism, Magianism, Judaism, Christianity—Mohammed borrowed from all impartially; while in the four religious "practices" there was nothing new.   The grand central idea of Islam was common to it with Judaism, and a protest against Oriental idolatry on the one hand, and Trinitarian Christianity on the other.   Its angels were Biblical; its genii Eastern.   Even its legends may be traced to the Talmud, or the Apocryphal Gospels.   The one startling novelty in the creed of Islam was the divine mission of Mohammed himself.   " It was this " (says Dean Milman), " forced as a divine revelation into the belief of so large a part of mankind, which was the power of Islam—the principle of its unity, its fanaticism, its propagation, its victories, empire, and duration."   To the question, whether Mohammed deceived himself prior to deceiving others, or was moved by indignation at his people's idolatry, or was filled with a lofty political ambition, or was a single-minded reformer, a preacher of righteousness; or whether rather his character was not a mixed one, made up of these and other conflicting elements—we may best answer in the favourite phrase of Islam, " God knows." Certainly in one point which has been laid to the charge of the prophet, his sanction of polygamy and of slavery, it is well to remember that it had been the established usage of Arabia, and that Mohammed did not enlarge but restricted the privilege. It is well to remember that men who have been born and bred amid particular customs, whether polygamy, or slavery, or suttee, or human sacrifice, are not easily convinced of the wrong of them; and that Mohammed's own indulgence in polygamy may be quite as justly ascribed to his anxiety for male issue to succeed him as to licentiousness. In short, if we judge Mohammed by the standard of the nineteenth Christian century, we shall misjudge him. Compare him with the men of his own day and country—ascribe to him what ambition, fanaticism, violence, inconsistency we will—there will yet remain enough of grand and good to rank him among the genuine " heroes " of the world's history.

Mohammedan Conquests — A.D. 632–711.—Mohammed died on June 8th, 632. The disunion, which would have destroyed his empire almost before its foundation, was happily deferred for a while. Not until three caliphs—Abu Bekr, Omar, and Othman—had cemented union by foreign conquest in Syria, Persia, and Egypt, did the struggle for the caliphate begin between Ali and Moawija. In seven years from the prophet's death Syria was Mohammedan (A.D. 632–9), to remain so for fully 500 years. The Christian opposition was of the feeblest, for Christian virtues in the East were passive rather than active, and a religious war was as yet undreamt of; so far Islam had a distinct advantage. Roman armies were defeated in two pitched battles. Damascus, Emessa, Baalbec, and even Jerusalem were besieged and taken ; its inhabitants were reduced to a subject caste, and the Mosque of Omar was built on the site of the Temple. By the middle of the century the Sassanian dynasty had fallen, and the Persian Empire as far as the Oxus was Mohammedan—a success to be pushed before the end of the century to the very confines of India. Meanwhile, in the opposite direction, Egypt also had succumbed to the arms of Amrou (A.D. 639–641), and the conquest of Africa was gradually though less rapidly effected (A.D. 647–698). The beginning of the eighth century saw the Mohammedans masters of a large part of Spain, invited there (a dubious tradition says) by the Christian Count Julian to avenge the wrongs inflicted on his daughter by Roderic, the Gothic king (A.D. 711). Thus, in less than a century from the Prophet's secret flight to Medina, not only was the Caliph sovereign, but the religion of Mohammed was dominant from the Indus to the Atlantic, in Persia, Arabia, Syria, Egypt, Northern Africa, and part of Spain. Christianity did not indeed die out; but Christian divisions and bickerings paved the way for the triumph of Islam, and not a few Christians found refuge from their perplexities in the simple creed of the divine unity, even at the cost of acknowledging Mohammed; while polygamy at the outset had a constant tendency to increase the relative numbers of the Mohammedan population at the expense of the Christians. Nor was Mohammedanism itself unaffected by the philosophy, the religion, the culture of the Asiatic, Greek, and Roman worlds with which it clashed. Architecture, poetry, science, philosophy, transformed Islam into something very different from the stern and narrow creed of Mohammed; until in the middle of the last century a learned enthusiast of Central Arabia, named Wahhab, undertook the self-imposed task of restoring Islam to its true and original type—a task which has met (if we may believe travellers) with but limited success.

CHAPTER XIII

THE POPES AND THE LOMBARDS IN ITALY—
A.D. 540-740.

Gregory the Great.—The reconquest of Italy to the
Eastern Empire by Belisarius and Narses (A.D. 536-552)
was only the prelude to its final revolt. The causes of
that revolt were as patent, as its effects were deep and
lasting; and it is inseparably connected with the name of
Gregory the Great. Amidst the confusion and panic
consequent on the feebleness of the Imperial rule in Italy
and the ferocity of the Lombards, it was Gregory who
became "the father of the mediæval Papacy," and by
his energy, resolution, and wisdom resuscitated a power
"on which (humanly speaking) hung the life and death
of Christianity"—a power capable of resisting Byzantine
encroachments, of overawing barbarous Franks, of leading
the struggle against Mohammedanism, of reconstituting
(it might be hoped) the liberty and independence of
Italy. Unhappily, that is the last thing of which the
Papacy has ever dreamed.

State of Italy after its Conquest—A.D. 540-590.—
The reconquest of Italy by the Eastern Empire was to a
great extent the work of the Catholic clergy, who disliked
the foreign Goths and hated their Arianism; but it
brought little good to Italy. The country was exhausted

by the drain of money, men, and food during a long war. In Picenum alone 50,000 labourers are said to have died of hunger, and a yet larger number in the south. Acorns became a common article of food. The reviving prosperity which had resulted from Theodoric's policy and the gradual fusion of Goths and Italians was rudely extinguished. A just and vigorous rule was supplanted by feebleness and reckless tyranny. The "Exarch" at Ravenna, as the Imperial governor was styled, was expected to need but little support. The less he asked for, and the more he sent home, the better was the home government pleased. Of "policy," strictly speaking, there was none beyond that of clinging convulsively to the province and its revenues. But of all Italians perhaps the Bishop of Rome suffered the deepest indignity. At Rome now, as for years at Constantinople, the highest ecclesiastical honour became the sport of female intrigues. Pope Sylverius was degraded (A.D. 537), banished, perhaps murdered. Vigilius was appointed by Belisarius at the nomination of Theodora (A.D. 544); Pelagius similarly (A.D. 554) by Justinian. "The period" (says Milman) "between the accession of John III. and that of Gregory I. (A.D. 560–590) is the most barren and obscure in the annals of the Papacy." And meanwhile the Lombards were already in the north of Italy, ready to profit by all this weakness and dissension.

The Lombards.—The Lombards, who in the days of Augustus and Trajan had been settled between the Oder and the Elbe, had been invited by Justinian from the centre of Europe to occupy Pannonia, and to act as a check upon the Gepidæ. For thirty years they had sustained an unequal contest. Its conclusion was a veritable tragedy. Alboin, the Lombard king, had deeply insulted Rosamond, the daughter of Cunimund, King of the

Gepidæ. War broke out, and the Lombards were defeated.   Stung with vexation, Alboin invited the Avars, his terrible neighbours, to help him and take the land of his enemies, promising them in addition a moiety of the spoils and captives.   They gladly acquiesced, and the nation of the Gepidæ was practically destroyed (A.D. 566). Thus the valleys of the Save and Drave fell into Avar hands; while the Lombards, not unwilling perhaps to escape from the presence of friends so powerful, were soon creeping over the Alps, threatening North Italy, and ready to accept any alliance which might offer.   The fame of Alboin attracted numerous followers,—Gepidæ, Bulgarians, Bavarians, Saxons; and an unexpected ally presently appeared upon the scene.   Narses had been Exarch for fifteen years, and had stained the virtues of an otherwise good administration by avarice and exactions. The groans of the province reached the ears of Justin, and Longinus was sent to supersede Narses.   The latter, indignant, withdrew to Naples; and if he did not invite him, at least he gave Alboin clearly to understand that the kingdom of Italy was within his grasp.

Lombard Conquest of Italy — A.D. 567. — The whole country, indeed, from the Alps to Rome fell into his hands almost without a blow.   One city alone, which the Goths had fortified, withstood the Lombards for three years; and Pavia, when taken, became the Lombard capital.   And very terrible (if we may believe Italian witnesses) was this new irruption of barbarians, who burned churches, destroyed cities and castles, farms and monasteries, and left the land a desert.   To many, even to Gregory himself, it seemed a sign of the approaching judgment day.   In the legends of the time, dealing with the virtues of bishops and monks, it is always a Lombard who persecutes; and (as was natural) the general terror passed gradually into a rooted detestation, of which subsequent Popes wisely availed themselves. As regards the Lombards themselves, it is useless to dwell on the confusion which followed the murder of Alboin in A.D. 573, or to write in succession the names of kings who for 200 years were masters of a great part of Italy, and not more than one or two of whom were of any note (A.D. 573–774). There are two things, however, which it will be well to notice briefly in passing,—foreshadowings of customs which were destined to exercise a deep and lasting influence on mediæval Europe. In the Lombard laws, as in those of other Teutons, we begin to observe the marked difference made between the crimes of nobles and of inferior classes—a difference estimated by a different mulct according to the social rank of the injured person (*Wehrgeld*). And not only do we find this practically "feudal" idea existing among Ostrogoths and Lombards, but an actual feudal custom, the very basis of feudalism itself, in force among the Lombards. In the reign of Autharis (A.D. 584–590) the various "dukes" (duces) of Italy engaged to follow him to war, and to furnish troops, as the price of their duchies being made independent and hereditary (subject to forfeiture for felony), and revertible to the Crown only if there were no male heir.

Territorial Limits of the Exarchate.—For 200 years Italy was unequally divided between the Lombards and the Exarchate of Ravenna. The limits of the latter it is most important to remember, as it afterwards became in part the "patrimony of St. Peter." It comprised the modern Romagna, the valleys of Ferrara and Commacchio, and the district lying between Rimini and Ancona, the Adriatic and the Apennines. There were also three subordinate provinces of Venice, Rome, and Naples; and the outlying districts of Calabria, Sicily, Sardinia, and Corsica.

All else of Italy was Lombard. The Pope meanwhile held the anomalous position of being within the exarchate and subject to the Emperor, while semi-independent and with an undefined jurisdiction. It was clear that the relations between the Papacy and Italy on the one hand, and the Eastern Empire on the other, were open to revision, and would be revised as soon as a man of decision and judgment was Pope. Such a man appeared in Gregory the Great.

Gregory I.—Gregory was the son of Gordian and Sylvia, born about A.D. 540. He united every qualification that could gain the respect of Romans. He was the descendant of senators and ecclesiastics, and his family was wealthy. But the wealth no sooner came into his own hands than he devoted it to religious uses,—in alms, and in building and endowing monasteries; one of which, St. Andrew's, on the Cœlian Hill, he entered as a monk, throwing to the winds his dignity as "Prætor," and his worldly prospects. It was 250 years since the great Athanasius had introduced to the West the ascetic monasticism of the East—scarce 100 years since its first great revival by St. Benedict; but there was not now a single country of the West in which monasteries were not plentiful. And Western monasticism was different from Eastern. It was practical, missionary, aggressive. If a man was haunted with a sense of sin or of his own weakness, or of the evil of the world, he retired into a monastery; but it was to perform regular duties, to observe an austere ritual, to maintain severe toil. The three great virtues of the Benedictine rule were silence, humility, and obedience,—poverty had not yet become a necessity; the three occupations of life were worship, reading, and manual labour. Nor was this all. A monastery in the West became a centre and an example to all its neighbourhood of contentment and industry, a place of refuge for the timid and feeble, a support to the poor and old, a means of evangelisation to all. Whatever of poetry was yet left in human life amid the misery and ferocities of the time, gathered round the men and women who flocked into monasteries, and was (so to say) precipitated in the shape of miracle and legend. Gratitude and admiration passed into something not unlike worship. Angels and demons were at every corner. Miracles abounded. Of course a man like Gregory, thoroughly a type of his own age in all except that resolute energy which placed him on a level with the great of all ages, was ascetic from conviction,—equally, of course, his self-devotion and boundless charity became the marvel of his contemporaries, the subject of miracles. They show at Rome a marble table at which he fed daily twelve beggars, among whom on one occasion appeared unbidden a thirteenth,—an angel unawares. Or again, when Rome was devastated by pestilence, and Gregory, with many another good man, was instant with alms and prayers, and in his efforts to alleviate the evil, a legend tells how at the head of a procession, chanting a solemn litany, he was approaching the mausoleum of Hadrian, and saw the angel of death sheath his sword as the procession drew near. Or again, his charity was once tried by an angel in sailor's guise, whose repeated visits drained Gregory's small store, till he had nothing left but a silver cup used by his mother. He gave it, and the angel at once revealed himself. But these stories, though characteristic, are illustrations rather than instances. In his love for children we tread on firmer ground; while his tenderness for slaves, and his noble efforts to soften their hard lot, were no less significant.

Interview of Gregory with English Slaves.— Both traits of his character are well seen in the fine story (*traditione majorum*) told of him by Bæda:[1]—"One day" (says the monk) "Gregory went out with the crowd to the Forum to see the wares of merchants just arrived; and amongst them saw some fair-skinned lads for sale, with beautiful faces and noble heads of hair, presumably therefore of noble birth. He asked from what land they came. 'From Britain,' was the answer. He asked again, 'Were they Christians or pagans?' 'Pagans,' they said. Then heaving a deep sigh, 'Alas!' he cried, 'that the prince of darkness should possess youths of so bright a face, that so graceful a presence should conceal a heart devoid of grace within!' When told that they were Angli (English), 'Well said,' he rejoined, with a play upon the word, 'for they have angelic faces, and such ought to be co-heirs of angels in heaven. And what is the name of the province whence they come?' 'They are Deiri,' was the answer; that is, they were from the 'Dearne-rice,' the land between Tyne and Humber. 'Well called Deiri,' replied Gregory, 'for they have been snatched from wrath (*de irâ eruti*) and called to mercy. And what is their king's name?' 'Aëlli,' they said. 'Alleluia,' he cried; 'the praise of God their Creator must be sung in those parts.'" It is a quaint story, but singularly true to nature.

Gregory prevented from going to England.— Gregory had resolved to go as missionary to Britain, but all Rome resolved that he should not. He had wrung a reluctant consent from Pope Pelagius, and advanced three days' journey along the Flaminian Road. They had stopped to rest at noon, and Gregory was reading, when suddenly a locust leaped upon his book. His quaint playfulness was as ready as his courage. "Rightly is it called locusta," he said; "it seems to say, 'Loco sta.' I see we shall not

---

[1] Bæda, Hist. Eccl., ii. 1.

be able to finish our journey." He had hardly spoken when a hurried messenger recalled him to Rome, where the Pope's life had been endangered by a mob, furious at Gregory's departure. He returned, to enter on public affairs, to conduct an embassy to Constantinople, to be Papal secretary, much against his will to be Pope (A.D. 590). But the plan, which he had vainly tried to carry out as a monk, he saw as Pope successfully carried out by another. The conversion of the English in Britain was begun by St. Augustine.

Sketch of English History—A.D. 410–596.—The Roman province of Britain had been Keltic and Christian, the Britain of Augustine was to a great extent English and Pagan; what had happened in the intervening two centuries?

The independence of the province had been acknowledged by Honorius in A.D. 409, and was maintained with some difficulty till the middle of the century against encroaching Picts and Scots. At last, harassed and plundered, hemmed in between enemies in the north and the sea in the south, the Kelts (so runs the story) begged for help from their Teutonic neighbours across the German Ocean; and those who came to help remained to conquer. In reality, however, Teutons had come to Britain many years before, certainly before the end of the fourth century. Even in the third century the depredations of Saxon pirates on the shores of Gaul and Britain had been such as to compel Diocletian to appoint a special officer for their protection (Comes Littoris Saxonici).[2] It is probable, therefore, that the Teutonic conquest of Britain was rather an immediate consequence of the cessation of Roman protection than the result of invitation. There were doubtless many Teutonic tribes which took part in

[2] Cf. Lappenberg's Anglo-Saxon Kings, vol. i. p. 44.

the invasion; but the three most important were the Jutes, Saxons, and Angles. They were all akin apparently, and came from the district of North-Western Europe, which lies between the Rhine and Denmark.   Of the Saxons we hear first; the Angles were most numerous; and the Jutes least numerous, occupying only Kent, the Isle of Wight, and part of Wessex.   Hence "Saxon" was the name given to the English by the Kelts, while "Englaland" became the name of the country. They were all pagans and robbers.   And though the struggle was long, in the end they drove before them or nearly extirpated the Keltic population, and with it whatever remained of Christianity and of Roman civilisation.   A small proportion they retained as slaves. The Teutonic conquest of Britain, therefore, was different from the Teutonic conquests in other parts of the Roman Empire; for the English did not (like Vandals or Goths or Lombards) simply sit down as a conquering aristocracy amidst a vast surrounding population, in whose mass they were presently lost; neither did they adopt the religion of the vanquished, or their language, or their civilisation.   In Britain a civilised people was swept away by a barbarous, a Christian people by a pagan.   At first (as was natural) there was but little union among the several tribes, and probably not a little strife, until the necessities of self-defence led to "federation," and seven kingdoms (the so-called "Heptarchy") emerged from the obscurity,—Kent, Essex (or East Saxons), Sussex (South Saxons), Wessex (West Saxons), East Anglia, Mercia (men of the "March" or frontier), and Northumberland, which stretched from the Humber to the Firth of Forth.   To give one instance of "federation," the Anglian kingdom of Mercia, in the centre of England, comprised West Saxons north of the Thames, Hwiccas in Gloucester and Worcester, Magesætas in Hereford, Gainas and Lindisfaras in Lincoln. It was not uncommon, moreover, for the king of some one of the kingdoms, by arts or arms, to acquire a certain ill-defined supremacy over the rest, which Bæda terms " Imperium," and the holder of which the Saxon chronicle calls " Bretwalda " (later " Brytenwalda "). Eight kings are mentioned, of six different kingdoms, who gained this predominance, including Ecgberht of Wessex, who not only gained, but retained it, and handed it on to his descendants (A.D. 828). From that time the " imperium " remained with Wessex, which in the sixth and seventh centuries had been mostly held by Northumberland, and in the eighth by Mercia.

St. Augustine—A.D. 597.—It was to these Pagan English that Pope Gregory, unable to go himself, sent Augustine from his own monastery of St. Andrew, with forty followers. They had reached Provence, when they began to hear awful rumours of that " savage, fierce, and unbelieving people, whose language even they did not understand," and sent back Augustine to beg Gregory to excuse them their dangerous task. But the Pope was inflexible, and they were forced to continue their journey. At this time, happily for the missionaries, Æthelberht (who had married Berhte, a Frankish princess, and a Christian) was king of East Kent and Bretwalda, as far as the Humber. When, therefore, they landed with their Frank interpreters in the little isle of Thanet (separated in those days from Kent by a branch of the Stour about one-third of a mile in breadth), they were courteously welcomed by the king, who presently gave them audience, and listened to their message. His answer was no less courteous, declining indeed for himself to abandon abruptly the customs of his forefathers, but allowing them to stay among his people, and to preach as they would. He further assigned them a house in Canterbury. There accordingly they lived, leading a simple apostolic life, and using Queen Berhte's venerable church of St. Martin outside the gates, which dated from Roman times. At first their converts were few; but rapidly increased, when Æthelberht himself was baptised, moved thereto by the sight of their pure lives, and (says Bæda) their many miracles. Shortly the king retired from Canterbury to Regulbium (Reculver), leaving his palace and an adjacent church to Augustine, the second Constantine of a second Sylvester, and here was built "Christ Church," the new cathedral, and very near to it the great monastery of St. Peter and St. Paul, afterwards known by Augustine's own name.

Effects of Christianity in England.—But it was not all peace that the Roman missionaries brought with them. Fierce quarrels arose between the English clergy and the British Christians in Wales on various minor points, in which the latter followed the Eastern, rather than the Latin custom (such as the time for keeping Easter, the mode of tonsure, the marriage of priests, and the like), and preferred to do so; while the former urged the paramount authority of St. Peter and his See. And then there was the constant danger of relapse, and of war between Pagans and Christians, for Latin Christianity was but feebly rooted in England as yet. Æthelberht's reign in Kent and Eadwine's in Northumberland, were in each case followed by a return to paganism. In the latter case, indeed, it was not for long. In a few years Northumbria became once more Christian, at the preaching of the Scottish Aidan, whom King Oswald invited from the monastery of Hii (Iona), and made Bishop of Lindisfarn; and the progress of Christianity, from north to south, would doubtless have been more rapid, but for the obstinate heathenism and warlike genius of Penda the Mercian.   As it was, little was effected for the general Christianisation of England until after his death (A.D. 655).   Then the Christian Oswio overran Mercia and East Anglia, and presently became Bretwalda; and the wave of Christian civilisation, which had flowed from Scotland, and lifted Northumbria to the highest place among English kingdoms, before long touched even the southern kingdoms, and last of all the South Saxons.

Then followed two centuries of brilliant missionary and intellectual activity, especially as contrasted with the heathenism and darkness of Danish times to follow. There was a constant stream of missionaries to the Continent, of pilgrims to Rome.   Learning, poetry, the arts began to flourish.   Bæda, Cædmon, Benedict, Biscop, Aidan, Ceadda, Wilfrith, Aldhelm, Winfrith (St. Boniface) are names which attest the fact.   But not only did Christianity stimulate the intellects of our English forefathers, and bring them into constant and elevating contact with foreigners, especially with Rome; it also mollified the general tone of thought.   Wars of extermination ere long ceased; and the Christian English were content with the political subjection (instead of the extirpation) of the Christian Welsh.   Indeed, it seems hardly too much to say, that the stimulus of Christianity contributed not a little to that general elevation of political ideas, which resulted in the union of England under Ecgberht, first "King of the English" (A.D. 828).

Gregory as Bishop, Pope, and (virtual) King. —But the conversion of England, though to England itself it was the beginning of a new life, and resulted remotely in the conversion[3] of Germany, was but a small

[3] Cf. Milman's Latin Christianity, book iv. cap. 5.

part of the life work of Gregory the Great—to his own
age probably the smallest.   He was Bishop of Rome,
and ruled his diocese with diligence.   He vigilantly
superintended the Church ritual and music, and the dis-
tribution of Papal charities.   He administered the Church
property with equal strictness and justice.   He was also
Pope,[4] "Father of Fathers," and as such exercised supervision over bishops and clergy, not only in Italy, but in
Greece, Gaul, and Spain.   This supremacy was a claim
certainly not yet acknowledged in words, yet continually
acknowledged in deeds—a claim tacitly made, sometimes
resisted, more often allowed.   When the Patriarch of
Constantinople openly assumed the title of "Universal
Bishop," as being bishop of the capital, Gregory protested
vehemently against the assumption of such a title both
to the Emperor and Empress, partly as derogating from
the just rights of St. Peter's See, partly as a mark of
pride.   "No one in the Church" (he writes to the Patriarch
himself), "has yet sacrilegiously dared to usurp the name
of Universal Bishop.   Whoever calls himself Universal
Bishop is Antichrist."   This protest, however, was, in
fact (however much Gregory may have deceived himself),
only a protest against the use by others of a title which
the Bishops of Rome were slowly learning to arrogate to
themselves.   The claim to supremacy, which began in the
fourth century, culminated in Innocent III. (about A.D.
1200), and Gregory was but one link in the long chain of
Popes who, consciously or unconsciously, aimed at despotic
power.   That it was a usurpation grounded in the political
troubles of the times may be true enough ; but none the
less it was a usurpation.   As Patriarch of the West,
Gregory saw the downfall of Arianism in both Gaul and
Spain, and the conversion, as of the English, so of the

<hr>

[4] Cf. Stanley's *Eastern Church*, p. 98.

Lombards through his influence with Queen Theodelinda. But Gregory was not only Bishop and Pope; he was in influence, though not avowedly, a temporal sovereign. And here it must be admitted this position was thrust upon him rather than of his own seeking. The natural defenders of the Imperial city were unable or unwilling to defend her; and the Pope had the best of titles in the love and good-will of his subjects. During his pontificate Gregory found food in Sicily for a famishing people, already decimated by plague, and he encouraged the Romans to stand a siege from Autharis, the Lombard king (A.D. 593). Constantinople was very far away; and to men who had no visible rulers before their eyes, but the fierce Lombard at Pavia, and the wretched Exarch at Ravenna, it is no wonder that Gregory seemed a natural leader, a king with the best of credentials. It is most important, therefore, to remember (as a clue to after history) that Gregory was not only Pope, but that his high character won for him a position as Patriarch of the West not reached by any of his predecessors; and that this and political circumstances combined, gave him the position, though not the name of king.

Gregory II.—A.D. 716.—Gregory the Great died March 10, A.D. 604; and the preponderating influence of the Papacy in the West increased rather than diminished. Rome became increasingly the centre of the faith. Now, however much this may have been due to the feebleness of the Emperors who reigned between Heraclius and Leo III. (A.D. 641–718),—and this was really only one cause among many,—it was certainly not due to the greatness or the character of the Popes. In the century which elapsed between the death of Gregory the Great and the accession of Gregory II. no less than twenty-four Popes filled the Papal Chair, few of whom rose above utter

obscurity (A.D. 604–716).   The high-handed persecution
and miserable death of Martin I. at the hands of Con-
stans II. (A.D. 654) might fairly be matched against the
extraordinary vicissitudes and pitiless cruelties of the
Emperor Justinian II. (A.D. 685–711).   With the accession, however, of Pope Gregory II. (A.D. 716) and of the
Emperor Leo. III. (A.D. 710), we enter on a new phase
of the history of Italy and of Christendom.

Rise of Iconoclasm.—In the eighth century a religious question arose—Iconoclasm—quite different to all
previous religious questions.   It was nothing less than an
attempt on the part of an Emperor to modify the religion
of his subjects, by his own mere fiat—to change the
universal daily worship of the Christian world.   It was
an attempt to proscribe the reverence—or worship—of
images.   At the same time it differed from previous con-
tests, in that it originated with the Emperor himself—
that it was probably suggested to his mind from without
and not from within, by acquaintance perhaps with
Jewish and Mohammedan ideas upon the subject—that
it was a question, not of speculative belief, but of daily
ritual, affecting the inmost and inveterate feelings of
every age and class and sex—that it admitted, therefore,
of no argument, but only of appeals to force—lastly, that
it was a purely *negative* doctrine, a sort of premature
Rationalism.   A small minority in the Empire, headed
by the Emperor, conceived the idea (no matter how or
whence) that it was *wrong* to reverence, much more to
worship, all images or pictures of sacred subjects ; and
having conceived it, they tried to enforce it on the immense
majority of their fellow-Christians, of whose lives the
deepest reverence, and in the case of the great mass, the
actual worship of these images had become an inseparable
part.   The Church indeed in this, as in similar matters, had

shown great practical wisdom, and in order to win the ignorant had adopted from Paganism certain universal, harmless, perhaps beautiful customs, which, however, tended to superstition. Such a custom was the use of altars, flowers, candles, processions, holy water, incense, votive offerings, shrines at cross roads, and the like. Such, too, was the use of images and pictures. But what was symbolism to the educated, a beautiful aid to devotion, had become idolatry in the uneducated, downright worship of the material image—an idolatry which tended to localise, and therefore limit, divine power, and from which the history of 1000 years, and the sharp teaching of a seventy years' captivity, could scarcely wean the Jews. It was in spite of Christianity that such idolatry lingered (and still lingers) in a Christian Church. Nevertheless, the attempt to uproot it by force in the eighth century was an anachronism and a mistake.

Leo III. the Isaurian—A.D. 717–741.—Leo III. became Emperor in A.D. 717. His father had migrated from Asia Minor to Thrace, and the son first saw military service in the guards of Justinian II. Like Tiberius and Justin, and the great Theodosius, the glory won in war raised him to the throne, on which he sat for twenty-four years, and handed down the purple to the third generation. In the second year of his reign he successfully defended the capital for thirteen months against 120,000 Arabs and Persians under Moslemah, the brother of the Caliph, his success being not a little due to the fatal[5] "Greek fire," which for 400 years was the main defence of the Empire. And this defeat of the Saracens by Leo (like the defeat of their brethren at Tours by Charles Martel, in A.D. 732) was one of the greatest events in history ; for had the Saracens in either

---

[5] Cf. Gibbon, Milman's ed. vol. v. cap. 52, p. 182.

case been victorious, it is hard to see how Christian civilisation could have withstood the shock.

Attempts to force Iconoclasm upon Christendom—A.D. 726.—Leo, to us, however, is mainly interesting as the "Iconoclast." He had been nine years on the throne, when he published his first edict against (as yet only) the *worship* of statues and images (A.D. 726). In four or five years (before A.D. 731) a more severe edict followed, commanding their total destruction, and the white-washing of all churches. It is difficult to imagine how a man with even Leo's energy, courage, and prestige, could begin so rash a contest. Riots at once broke out in the capital, in Greece, and the Ægean. In Constantinople an officer was beaten to death by women while defacing an image of the Saviour.

Iconoclastic Controversy in the East—A.D. 726–842.—The monks throughout the Empire openly instigated rebellion. And for once the Bishops of Rome and Constantinople were agreed. The arrival of the Imperial edict in Ravenna (A.D. 728) was the signal for instant insurrection against the Exarch Scholasticus, of which the Lombard Luitprand availed himself to besiege and seize the city, and to overrun the Pentapolis. In vain did the Pope write two letters to the Emperor of mingled defiance and expostulation. In vain did the learned John of Damascus publish three orations in defence of image worship. The Emperor Leo and his son Constantine (A.D. 717–775) were not men to recede lightly from a position deliberately adopted; indeed, it would seem as if they had overawed or convinced a large number of the eastern clergy, for the third Council of Constantinople was attended by 348 bishops, who unanimously condemned the worship of images (A.D. 746). And not only so; Constantine inaugurated, and his subjects apparently abetted him in a cruel persecution of the monks; and had succeeding emperors held the same views and possessed similar resolution, the eighth century might have seen the final destruction of image worship in the East. But in A.D. 780, the Empire fell into the hands of a woman, the Empress Irene, who was at once ambitious and superstitious. Her heart was set upon restoring image worship at any cost; and by persistent intrigue for five years, she succeeded in convoking a council of about 370 ecclesiastics at Nicæa (A.D. 785), who proclaimed the lawfulness of images and pictures as "holy memorials, to be worshipped and kissed," and anathematized all who called images idols. Nor was her heart less set upon retaining power; for in A.D. 797, in order to oust her son Constantine, she had him seized and brutally blinded, so that he almost died. Images were finally re-established as legal in the Eastern Church by the Empress Theodora (A.D. 842).

Attitude of the Popes in the West.—A.D. 726–740.—In the West, meanwhile, matters were progressing at a rapid pace. In A.D. 730, a council was held by Gregory II. at Rome, which renounced communion with the Emperor. The first act of Gregory III. (A.D. 731–741) was to acquaint the Byzantine court with his adherence to his predecessor's views; and his next to decree, by a council at Rome (A.D. 732), that "whoever should overthrow, &c., the images of Christ and the glorious Virgin, of the blessed apostles and saints, was banished from the unity of the Church." The Pope himself set the example of image worship on the grandest scale. In the same year, moreover, the last great effort on the part of the Eastern Empire to reduce Italy and the Pope once again to subjection, ended in utter failure. A large combined fleet and army on its way to Italy was caught in a violent storm in the Adriatic and utterly destroyed. For twenty years more, indeed, the Exarch maintained a precarious position in Ravenna, finally abandoning it for Naples; and the Empire learned to acquiesce in an inevitable loss. But to the Pope this virtual victory over the Empire might well seem to involve a virtual subjection to the hated Lombards— hated even though they were no longer Arians. A new barbarian kingdom seemed on the point of absorbing all Italy. Gregory looked round for help, being cut off in reality (though not in name) from all connection with Constantinople, and found it across the Alps. The alliance, now begun, between the Papacy and the Franks was a "Revolution," fruitful in consequences little foreseen and not yet exhausted, which have affected all subsequent history.

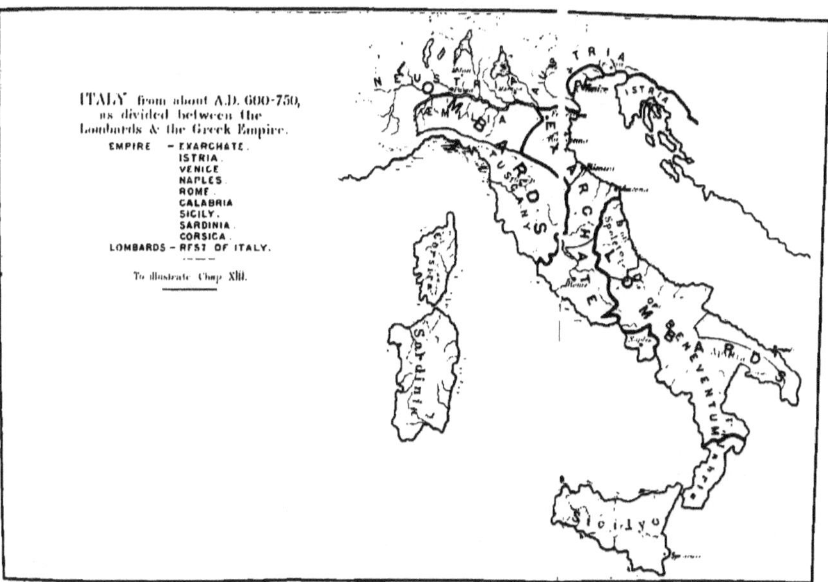

ITALY from about A.D. 600-750,
as divided between the
Lombards & the Greek Empire.
EMPIRE — EXARCHATE.
ISTRIA.
VENICE.
NAPLES.
ROME.
CALABRIA.
SICILY.
SARDINIA.
CORSICA.
LOMBARDS — REST OF ITALY.
To illustrate Chap XIII.
NEUSTRIA
AUSTRIA
AEMILIA
ISTRIA
LOMBARDS
TUSCANY
EXARCHATE
Corsica
Sardinia
Sicily
BENEVENTUM

CHAPTER XIV

THE FRANKS AND THE PAPACY.—A.D. 500-800.

The Franks.—In the middle of the eighth century the Imperial power in Italy was dead, and the Pope and the Lombards were left alone face to face. But the exaggerated, if not entirely unfounded, horror with which the Church regarded the Lombards rendered peace between them impossible; and when Luitprand's conquests threatened Rome and all Italy with subjection, Gregory III., A.D. 731-741 (treading in the footsteps of Gregory II.), appealed for aid to the mighty Frank beyond the Alps, Charles Martel, whose name was in every mouth as the saviour of Europe from the hitherto invincible Mohammedans. A clear understanding of the history of the Franks in Gaul, and of their relations to the Papacy, is an essential introduction to the study of the history of Germany, Italy, and France; and the appeal of Gregory to Charles marks the moment when the dignity and power of "Roman Emperor" was about to pass into quite other hands, and with other prerogatives than heretofore.

Gaul under the Romans.—For 400 years Gaul was a province of the Roman Empire, incorporated with it more entirely, perhaps, than any other province. Its conquest had been thorough in the first instance, and the Roman system had been applied with success. The surface of the country was covered with more than 100 *municipia;* schools were widely established by Augustus and by Claudius; many writers of eminence were born and lived there; wealth abounded. But, below a brilliant surface, there were causes of decay similar to those which were the ruin of Italy. The sentiment of nationality was gradually destroyed when Gaul became only a part of a vast empire, and was not replaced by any feeling of "loyalty," which the Empire indeed was hardly calculated to arouse.[1] When the Emperor Honorius, in the fifth century, tried to galvanise into life the Gallic patriotism by reviving the annual "diet" at Arles, no response whatever was made to the proposal. The Keltic language and religion retreated into Brittany before the Roman tongue and Roman Christianity. The Imperial system, moreover, spoiled the municipal; and its taxation, at once crushing and unfairly assessed, impoverished the farmers and landed proprietors. And the same *latifundia* which had ruined Italy ruined Gaul also, and for similar reasons. But in Gaul, as in Italy, one class of men increased in influence, as all around them decayed. However intolerant or grasping they may have been, the Christian clergy—brave, moral, and educated—stepped into the place of the fading Empire, resisted it when tyrannical, wielded its powers when decrepit, and alone presented a courageous front to wrong, vice, and barbarism.

Invasion of Roman Gaul—A.D. 406.—Such (briefly) was the state of the province, when it was suddenly overwhelmed at the beginning of the fifth century by the long-dreaded inroad of barbarians from beyond the Rhine and the Alps. Vandals, Suevi, Burgundians, Visigoths, Franks, together or successively, swept across or occupied the unhappy province. The two first passed on into Spain and

---

[1] Cf. Guizot's Hist. Civilisation, vol. i. p. 31.

Africa, the others remained to subdue and eventually divide Gaul between them, though but little is known of their mutual relations until the end of the century.

Gaul divided between Visigoths, Burgundians, and Franks.—Speaking generally, by the year A.D. 490 the Visigoths were masters of the country between the Rhone, the Loire, the Atlantic, and the Garonne; the Burgundians of that between the Rhone, the Saone, and the Alps; and the Franks of nearly all the rest (with the exception of the Keltic Armorica or Brittany) as far as the mouth of the Rhine. But the Frank Empire was not only on the west of the river, but comprised a large, though ill-defined tract between the Rhine and the Weser, which touched the Saxons on the north and the Alemanni on the south. Amidst this drifting mass of diverse peoples—of High Dutch and Low Dutch, of Romans, Kelts, and Basques—there was no controlling central power until the time of Chlodwig (Clovis, Ludwig, Lewis, A.D. 486–511).

Chlodwig and the Merwing Dynasty—A.D. 486–752.—By a fortunate marriage with the orthodox Chlothild of Burgundy, which resulted in the conversion of himself and his people, and secured to him the support of the Catholic clergy, and by a series of successful struggles with successive foes, Chlodwig became practical lord of the whole of Gaul and of all Franks between the Weser and Garonne, and virtual founder of the Merwing (Merovingian) rulers in Francia, both Eastern and Western; for Francia comprised two very different populations. On the eastern side of the Scheldt and the Marne (Austrasia) were pure Franks of the old stock, who spoke German and followed German customs; on the western side (Neustria) were Franks, modified by contact with Roman civilisation and more settled life. Among the latter, as was natural, despotic ideas of centralisation became predominant; among the former aristocratical ideas.   Hence followed strong feeling and jealous rivalry; and, indeed, the story of the 180 years which followed the death of Chlodwig (511–687), is the story of a constant struggle for power between Neustria and Austrasia, which was settled in favour of the latter by the battle of Testry.   The reduction, however, by Chlodwig of Burgundy (A.D. 500) and Aquitaine (A.D. 507) was rather an irruption than a conquest, for they were lost almost as soon as won, the Merwing dominion consisting properly of Western Germany and Northern Gaul.   The glory of the family culminated in Dagobert I. (A.D. 628–638), whose influence touched Brittany on one side and the Pyrenees on the other.   Allied with Lombards in Italy and Visigoths in Spain, he sent an embassy to Heraclius at Constantinople, and chastised the aggressions of Slavonians and Bulgarians in Germany, while he chose able men to help him govern.   However, in spite of one or two bright exceptions, the Merwings were mere barbarians compared with the Karlings who followed.   The warlike energy of the nation, indeed, backed by the unhesitating support of the Church, carried their victorious arms over half Europe; but there was the same lack of organisation and discipline in the subjects, of fixed purpose and policy in the kings, which marked the early records of the Northmen in the ninth and tenth centuries.

Rise of the Mayors of the Palace.—Almost all their kings were mere cyphers, surrounded by a number of fierce territorial chieftains, overshadowed more and more by the rising power of the " Major-domûs," who, being at first only the master of the royal household, rose to command the Antrustions [2] (the Principes of Tacitus), and at last to preside over the dukes, counts, and bishops of the great council.   Such powers in the hands of a series of

----

[2] Cf. Tacitus' Germania, caps. vii. and xi. to xiv.

able men (like the family of Pippin) soon obscured those of the merely nominal *cyning* (king), or leader of the people, who was reserved (as Eginhard tells us) for the merely formal duties of kingship. The power of these "mayors" reached its highest pitch in Pippin of Heristal, the Austrasian, and his sons. They secured the supremacy of Austrasia over Neustria, and the reversion of royal power for themselves.

Charles Martel—Battle of Tours—A.D. 732.— Charles, the son of Pippin, indeed gained a glory all his own. He defeated the Saracens at Tours (A.D. 732). The bareness of such a statement ill reflects the true import of such a conflict, or its vast consequences. It was but a century since Mohammed had died; yet half the old Roman Empire was Mohammedan, and from the Oxus to the Pyrenees the Arabs had conquered almost without a check. As yet, moreover, they were at amity among themselves; and the Saracen armies in Spain and Gaul were led by an experienced general, Abderrahman. In A.D. 732 he crossed the Pyrenees with a force of 100,000 men (not for the first time), and met with little serious resistance in the south of Gaul. His African light cavalry (like Hannibal's Numidians) were equally serviceable for battle, for pillage, or for reconnoitring, and carried the terror of the Saracen name as far north as the Loire. Count Eudes in Aquitaine attempted resistance, but was swept away in the torrent. And Charles, meanwhile, the Austrasian Mayor, was busy with a Saxon war far away. But the pressing danger, the panic of Christian Gaul, presently recalled him. The two armies met on the banks of the Loire near Tours, and even Arab historians admit that the defeat of their forces was complete, "a disgraceful overthrow." For one whole day the battle raged with no decisive result, night parting the combatants. It was renewed at the following dawn. But a too long course of unbroken victory had shaken the steadiness and lowered the morale of the Arab armies. In the midst of the struggle a rumour ran, like an electric current, through the Mohammedan lines, that a division of Franks was attacking and spoiling their camp, in which was piled great store of wealth, the plunder of Aquitaine. At once a large body of Arab horsemen rode off to save their booty. To their comrades it looked like flight, and the rest of the army began to waver. It was the critical moment, which comes in every battle, when one army becomes conscious of its moral inferiority to the other as a whole, and, despite the courage and exertions of individuals, is already virtually beaten. In vain did Abderrahman strive to check the confusion. He was pierced by a Frankish spear, and fell, and his fall was the signal for a general flight. We need not admit the preposterous estimates of monkish chroniclers as to the relative losses on either side, in order to perceive that Tours was to Europe a " crowning mercy."

Results of Charles' Victory.—The defeat of the Saracens at Tours, even more than their repulse from Constantinople, meant the salvation of Christendom from an enforced return to the lethargy, sterility, and arrested development which has always marked Mohammedanism. Had the Franks been defeated, there was no power strong enough to arrest the Arab progress ; and what has been said with truth of the victory of Arminius over Varus (A.D. 9), is said with equal truth of the victory of Tours, that it was " one of those signal deliverances which have affected for centuries the happiness of mankind."[3]

Gregory III. Appeals to Charles—A.D. 738.— The fame of Charles "The Hammer" was measured by

---

[3] Arnold's Rom. Commonwealth, ii. p. 317.

the previous panic of Christian Europe. He might seem even the Protector of Christianity itself. It was little wonder that Pope Gregory III., hopeless of aid from any other source, and plundered and insulted by the Lombards, should have sent a letter of piteous entreaty imploring Charles' aid. It seems, indeed, that Gregory deserved his fate; for he had encouraged a Lombard Duke of Spoleto to rebel against King Luitprand, in revenge for which the king wasted the Papal territory, and even probably plundered St. Peter's itself. On the other hand, it is impossible that Gregory should have realised the full importance of his own appeal; for it was nothing less than the first step in a gigantic revolution, from which the Pope was to emerge as a temporal sovereign, and the Frankish king as " Holy Roman Emperor." In Gregory's appeal was involved the very kernel of mediæval history.

The actual offer made by the Pope was perhaps intentionally vague. He sent the very keys of the tomb of St. Peter. He named Charles Patrician and Consul. But were these mere bribes, or actual symbols of an allegiance transferred from the Greek to the Frank? Which they were, it is hard to say; yet two things are clear, that at this stage of the matter neither of the parties was at all alive to the consequences of their new relation; while, on the other hand, indefinite jealousies, claims, and encroachments were possibly involved.

Gregory Succeeded by Pope Zacharias—A.D. 741. —Both Charles and Gregory, however, died in the autumn of A.D. 741; and the new Pope Zacharias (A.D. 741–752) was a different man to Gregory. He combined a majesty and a gentleness truly apostolic, with a far greater insight into character than his predecessors. Where Gregory had quailed before Luitprand, Zacharias led him with threads of silk.　The Lombard was warlike and ambitious; but he was also sincerely religious, with the religion of a superstitious and illiterate barbarian.　Twice did the Pope interfere between Luitprand and his cherished plans of aggrandisement, imploring, threatening, almost forbidding; and twice the Lombard yielded.　It is indeed essential to remark how rapidly the influence of the Church was growing among the new-formed nations, thanks to the intelligence, firmness, and moral purity of the clergy; as well as to note the fact that Church authorities were beginning to use their enormous, though undefined, power for purposes purely secular.　Already kings were abandoning the throne for the monastery, as a purer and happier sphere.　Carloman did so, the son of Charles Martel— a king in all but the name; Rachis, the Lombard, did so; and when Pippin, Carloman's brother, supplanted the Merwing by the Karling dynasty, nothing seemed more natural than that the wretched Chilperic should retire to the peaceful obscurity of a monastery.

Coronation of Pippin.—A.D. 752.—This great revolution was scarcely perceived in passing.　Pippin was elected, as by ancient Frankish custom, by the clash of arms and elevation on a buckler; but the election was sanctioned by the Pope, and Christian bishops were standing round, and the holy oil, the symbol of divine right, was poured on his head by the English Boniface, Archbishop of Mentz (A.D. 752).　It was the first time in history, but not the last, that the Church sanctioned the transfer of a crown; and on this the first occasion her motives were transparently secular, if not selfish.　Sanction on the one side was bartered for protection on the other.

Pippin and Pope Stephen—A.D. 753-55.—And the protection was soon sorely needed.　Luitprand was dead, and Astolph was king of the Lombards, a man of energy little burdened with scruples. He entered the Exarchate and seized Ravenna. He quarrelled with the Pope and advanced on Rome, deaf alike to threats and entreaties. Stephen in despair, for Zacharias was now dead, fled to Gaul and implored, not in vain, the aid of Pippin. But Astolph, aware of the coming storm, persuaded Carloman to leave his convent and claim the Austrasian crown, hoping to sever the alliance between Stephen and his brother. It was a vain attempt, and only ended in the lifelong imprisonment of Carloman, as a monk who had broken his vows. Pippin and Stephen crossed the Alps, and Astolph was shut up in Pavia, and made to swear to restore all Roman territory. But such vows are "writ in water." No sooner were the Alps between the Franks and himself, than Astolph marched once more upon Rome, and demanded the surrender of the Pope. Once, and yet a second time, did Stephen send agonized letters imploring Pippin's instant return. Victory over all barbarian nations was the promised reward, and eternal life. But there was terrible delay. The Frank did not come. And at last, in a paroxysm of terror (it is the only conceivable defence), Stephen sent a letter purporting to have been written by St. Peter himself, adjuring Pippin, in the name of the "Mother of God," to save her beloved Rome from the detested Lombards, and promising again protection and victory in this life, certain salvation in the next. Pippin delayed no more, and recrossed the Alps; while Astolph, forced to throw himself hastily into Pavia, was there besieged and reduced to yield to all demands.

Pippin's "Donation" to the Papacy.—The Exarchate was wrested with impartial violence from Eastern Empire and Lombard king, and bestowed by the sword of the stronger on the Bishop of Rome, who thus became a temporal sovereign, with all a sovereign's prerogatives, taxation, justice, and the like. The "donation" was presently increased by the voluntary surrender of the Duchy of Spoleto, and afterwards confirmed by Charles the Great to Pope Hadrian, and increased to comprise a large part of Italy. On the other hand, Pippin received the title of Patrician of Rome, a name implying powers both vague and extensive. The Lombard Astolph did not long survive this last humiliation, and with his death the weakness inherent in the Lombard kingdom, whose numbers were comparatively few, and whose central government was comparatively feeble owing to the turbulence and independence of the great chieftains, rapidly resulted in its ruin. Desiderius, the last of the Lombard kings (A.D. 757–774), was at intervals, indeed, at peace and amity with the Pope, and an ally of Charles, who married his daughter Hermingard; but the alliance and the amity were alike short-lived, and both Lombards and Italians were absorbed ere long into the " Roman Empire" resuscitated by Charles the Great.

Charles Succeeds Pippin—A.D. 768–774.—Pippin died in A.D. 768, and divided his dominions (according to custom) between his sons Charles and Carloman. Happily for the peace of Francia, the latter died within three years (A.D. 771), and Charles restored or usurped the undivided kingdom of his father. The widow and the sons of Carloman at once took refuge with Desiderius, for Charles had divorced Hermingard only a year after his marriage, to wed the Suabian Hildegard, and Desiderius was eager for revenge. On which side was Pope Hadrian to range himself? His predecessor Stephen had protested against Charles' marriage with Hermingard at all—not, indeed, on the Christian ground that he was married already, but on the un-Christian ground that any alliance between "noble" Frank and "fœtid, leprous" Lombard was abominable, detestable, devilish. And now the claims of righteousness might likewise seem to call for disapproval of the usurping adulterous Charles, and a hearty support of Carloman's sons and their friend Desiderius. But Hadrian was wise in his generation, and steadily declined to commit himself. The Pope's hesitation, and the murder in Rome of one of his own partisans, incensed the Lombard into ravaging Romania (the Romagna), and even advancing on Rome. But Hadrian was neither a coward like Stephen, nor an apostle like Zacharias. He gathered troops, strengthened fortifications, barricaded the Vatican, and sent off hasty appeals to Charles for help; and then fell back on his spiritual weapons, threatening Desiderius with excommunication if he dared to attack him. The Lombard, blind to his danger, refused all negotiations; his son, Adelchis, even defeated a Frank army in the Alps. But it was only deferring the evil day. The Lombards were but a handful in the midst of a native population, who looked on the Pope as their "head," and the Franks as their "deliverers." Charles passed the Alps, and in a moment (as it were) was master of all North Italy, except the cities of Pavia and Verona, in which Desiderius and Adelchis respectively were blockaded (A.D. 774).

Charles Increases the "Donation."—At Easter he went on to Rome, and being there welcomed with such honours as became so orthodox and useful a champion, added to and ratified the donation of land made by his father Pippin. For Pavia had fallen; Desiderius was in a monastery; Adelchis had fled to Constantinople; and the whole territory of the Exarchate, and a part of that of the Lombards, was confirmed as the possession of the

Pope; and however obscure may have been the *conditions* of the Papal tenure, it is no less clear that this donation was the basis and foundation of that "temporal power" which has so deeply affected the character and history of the Roman Church.

Charles Crowned Emperor of the West—A.D. 800.—But even the protection of the great Frank did not save the Popes from troubles. The Archbishop of Ravenna refused submission to Hadrian (A.D. 775), and the Lombards rebelled against him (A.D. 787). Leo III. was set upon during a solemn procession by two nephews and an armed train, beaten, mutilated, half-murdered (A.D. 799). It seemed indeed more than ever necessary to hold fast a powerful protector by strong chains. In the next year Charles crossed the Alps in the late autumn, and Leo, after a solemn trial, was acquitted of certain charges brought against him. And Charles and Leo, Franks and Italians, nobles, clergy, people were assembled at Rome in crowds to celebrate Christmas. All had met together for the solemn service. The Basilica of St. Peter's was crowded. The Pope himself chanted high mass. At its close he advanced from his throne in the centre of the apse, and in the sight of the vast congregation placed on Charles' head, as he knelt in prayer by the altar, the diadem of the Cæsars, while the great church rang with the shout, "Karolo Augusto, a Deo coronato magno et pacifico Imperatori, vita et victoria." In spite of the assertion that Charles disliked the proceeding, and had he known the intentions of the Pontiff would not have entered the church, it is difficult to believe in the spontaneity of the spectacle, or to doubt that it was prearranged between Leo and Charles. But whether prearranged or spontaneous matters little; the fact remains. The current of the world's history was changed.

Results of Coronation.—What, then, was the meaning of this apparently simple act of gratitude? and in what results did it end? It was certainly an act of gratitude (as well as something else) on the part of the Romans, and of Leo their representative, who despised the Greeks and hated the Lombards, and might expect in the future, as they had experienced in the past, the friendship and protection of the Franks. But it was more than this. It was a recognition of the "logic of facts," that the Eastern Empire was a defunct power in Italy, and that the political "centre of gravity" had shifted. For (be it remembered) neither the title nor the office of Emperor was new, nor was the actual power of Charles in any way increased, but only its character changed. And the change was a striking one. Once more the Imperial city gave an Emperor to the West; and that Emperor was neither Roman nor Italian, but German. No longer were charters to be dated or money to be coined in the name of a titular "Roman Emperor" at Constantinople, but of one who was not only patrician, like Pippin and Pippin's father, or king, like Theodoric, but actual Emperor of the West, like Theodosius. Power was *recognised* as being where in reality it *was*. One new factor, however, was introduced into the matter, whose powers were unfortunately indefinite. It was clear to all that the Imperial crown had been bestowed by the hands of the Pope. The question arose in after days, Did he give it as of right; and if so, whence came the right? For the time indeed the question did not even suggest itself, so humble and weak was the Pope, so immeasurably great was the Emperor; but the greatness of the Emperor was personal and commensurate only with his life, while the humility of a Pope detracted nothing from the growing majesty of the Papacy. The prescriptive prerogatives of even an Emperor were relatively weak when men thought of the Pope as God's mouthpiece upon earth; but for the present the two powers were incommensurable; and the idea which arose in Otto's day (A.D. 936–973) of two co-ordinate powers, Emperor and Pope, ruling under God over the temporal and spiritual affairs of men, would in Charles' day have been an anachronism.

It remains to speak shortly of Charles himself—his conquests and character—as of a man who, while he handed down to his successors the dubious advantage of the Imperial title, was himself the first founder of German unity,—a man who was so "great" in every sense, that he took captive (like Attila) the imaginations of the men of his own and succeeding ages, and became the typical hero of mediæval romance.[4]

Conquests of Charles the Great.—The conquests of Charles were the foundation of the great German kingdom. His wars lasted almost without interruption for forty-six years, during which he swept across Europe from the Ebro to the Oder, from Brittany to Hungary,—never meeting, it may be, with any really serious antagonist, yet always needing skill, perseverance, and sleepless energy. Aquitaine he pacified in six months. The Lombards he reduced in less than two years. Against the Avars, by himself or his lieutenants, he waged eight successive campaigns (A.D. 791–9), against the Saxons no less than thirty-two,—the latter a "religious war," and waged with all the tender mercies that distinguish such anomalies. The Frank arms were seen in Slavonia, Brittany, Bavaria, Bohemia, Southern Italy, and Spain. In the last-named country alone, and against the Saracens, he met with little success; Saragossa was besieged

---

[4] See an interesting article on Carlovingian Romance, in the Edinburgh Review for April 1862.

in vain; and as he returned through the Pyrenean passes to more important matters in Gaul, the combined Arabs and Basques fell upon his rear at Roncesvalles and inflicted a loss which romance has magnified into a serious defeat. In fact, the kingdom of Pippin was nearly doubled by the victories of his son. Eginhard enumerates Aquitaine and Gascony—the Pyrenees and Spain to the Ebro—Italy from Aosta to Calabria—Saxonia, "a country" (he says) "twice as large as Francia"—Pannonia, Dacia, Dalmatia, Istria—and lastly, whatever barbarous tribes were to be found between the Rhine, the Danube, the Vistula, and the ocean, as so many additions to the Empire.

His Policy.—Not that all this success was achieved by mere activity. Charles showed the qualities which all great generals show; he improved his war material, his armour, his breed of horses; he out-generalled his enemies by superior tactics, as in his first campaign against the Avars, when he adopted a double base of operations,[5] and anticipated the strategy of Napoleon's famous campaign of Austerlitz (A.D. 1805); he combined self-reliance with reliance on his subordinates; he did not forget policy on the battle-field, but in Italy as in Spain was the champion of vanquished against victors, of oppressed against oppressors. He conciliated the affection of his German subjects by maintaining German institutions. He courted the alliance of neighbouring kings, of the Kings of Scots and the Asturias, of Offa of Mercia, and Ecgberht of Wessex, as well as that of more distant and powerful rulers like the Emperor at Constantinople, or the Caliph at Bagdad. He remained from first to last a staunch friend of the Church, its too liberal benefactor; going far, by the immunities and privileges which he granted, to

---

[5] Cf. Thierry—Histoire d'Attila, vol. ii. p. 156; Alison's Europe, vol. ix. cap. 40.

make claims possible which only his own commanding vigour and wisdom could resist. The untiring energy of his policy and his wars is to be seen no less in his administration. None but energy almost superhuman could have devised or attempted to carry out the gigantic system of " Missi dominii," regulated by a law of A.D. 802. They were a sort of king's messengers deputed to visit every corner of the Empire—to observe, to inquire, to order, to regulate, to punish—organs of a central authority, to whom they sent in an annual report of the wants and condition of every class. And this is only one instance out of many.

Character and Person of Charles.—It sometimes adds life and definiteness to our ideas of a man, if we can picture to ourselves his appearance and personal characteristics; and in Charles' case this is comparatively easy with the minute account left us by Eginhard (or Einhard), his Minister of Public Works. He was every inch a king. Tall and robust, he had a dome-like head, large and piercing eyes, white hair, and an expression full of grace and dignity; and so excellent was his constitution, that until he was seventy he did not know what illness meant. He was passionately devoted to riding, hunting, and swimming; for which latter reason he made Aachen, with its natural warm springs, his favourite home; and bathing parties were one of the common amusements of his court, in which 100 persons or more would take part at a time. He had a quaint humour, and appreciated it in others, as [6] when on a day of storm and rain he made his courtiers, all in furs and silk, accompany him in a sudden hunting frolic; or concocted a scheme with a Jew pedlar for palming off on some bishop an embalmed rat, as an animal till then unknown. So

[6] Cf. Stephen's Lect. Hist. Fr., i. 87.

EUROPE
IN THE TIME OF
CHARLES THE GREAT
To illustrate Chapter XIV.
Saxons
SLAVES
KHAZARS
AVARS
CHARL
AUSTRA
KINGDOM OF ASTURIAS
EMIRATE OF CORDOVA
THE GREAT
BULGA
EASTERN
EMPIRE
Herington, London, Oxford & Cambridge.

intense, in fact, was the mere animal life in Charles, that he seemed to throw all his energy into whatever he was doing, and to do it better than anything else, far better than any one else. His dress and his habits were equally simple. Drunkenness, the bosom sin of his countrymen, was not one of his; while the chastity, however, which distinguished them, was by him more honoured in the breach than the observance. He loved to be read to at meals, especially from St. Augustine, or from those " Barbara et. antiquissima carmina," which were the backbone of the Nibelungenlied.[7] He was a clear and fluent speaker, having perfect command of Latin, and understanding Greek—an eager student of logic and astronomy. His one insuperable difficulty was writing, which no efforts enabled him to master. His generous nature led him to scatter charity broadcast; poor Christians received his alms even so far afield as Syria, Egypt, Carthage. It is hardly needful to add that the Popes were loaded with presents, rich and unnumbered. On the whole, of all the men whom the world has agreed to call " great," it will be hard to find more than one or two, who can equal, much less surpass, Charles the Frank. He was as energetic and undaunted as Frederick of Prussia, as eager a civiliser as Peter of Russia; hardly less successful than Alexander or Napoleon, yet greater than any of them, more generous, more simple, more superior to all his contemporaries. Perhaps one man only in history has been the equal of Charles in energy, courage, wisdom, and success, while morally far superior, and that was the English Aelfred.[8]

General Summary.—We have thus traced the history of 400 years, which have an interest peculiarly their own. Change of some sort is a matter of course in so long a period of every nation's life—change of thought,

[7] Cf. Chapter viii.   [8] Cf. Freeman's Norman Conquest, vol. i. p. 53.

manners, and laws. The Greece of the Achæan League differed from that of Themistocles, as the Rome of Cæsar from that of the Decemvirate, or the England of the nineteenth century from that of the fifteenth; but it was not the same kind of difference as existed between the Rome of Cæsar and the Rome of Theodoric, or of Gregory, or of Charles. It is no longer the same people, living in the same land, whose ideas and customs change as they conquer or are conquered by other nations, or as the balance of wealth and power is transferred from one class of society to another. We are concerned with an " *Empire* "—many nations, not one only—and that an Empire whose population itself was far more deeply modified (if not wholly changed) than the institutions or customs which ruled it. Look at it in the fourth century, and it might seem that a State, so welded together by a far-reaching, all pervading uniformity had nothing to fear from the attacks of barbarians. Look at it in the ninth century, and a hasty glance hardly detects any relics of the old Imperial State. Amid Christians and Mohammedans — between Greeks, Italians, Lombards, Avars, Goths, and Franks—all seems confusion, disunion, strife. But this book will have been written in vain if it has not shown a " continuity of history " even in these confused 400 years. The Imperial Government in the West passed away, it is true, but Imperial ideas survived. Barbarian kings bore sway; but in theory they were lieutenants of the Emperor at Constantinople; till one among them revived what was only in abeyance, the Roman Empire of the West, to drag on a lingering existence even into our own century. As Greece took captive the conquering Roman, so Rome took captive the conquering barbarian, and gave him her language, ideas, laws, and religion. What looked in the fifth century like the ruin of all that was worth preserving, the veritable "end of a world," was, in fact, only a transference of power to those who already possessed its reality. It was a change of form, not of essence; and the men who swayed Europe in the eighth and ninth centuries strove to do so on the principles and in the spirit of the old Empire. Thus, from first to last, it was one idea under varying forms which ruled the minds of men—the idea of one great Roman Empire, which in becoming Christian had become "Holy." "Rome alone (it has been well said) founded an Universal Empire, in which all earlier history loses itself, and out of which all later history grew." [9]

[9] Freeman's General Sketch, cap. i. p. 16.

GENEALOGY OF FAMILY OF THEODOSIUS.

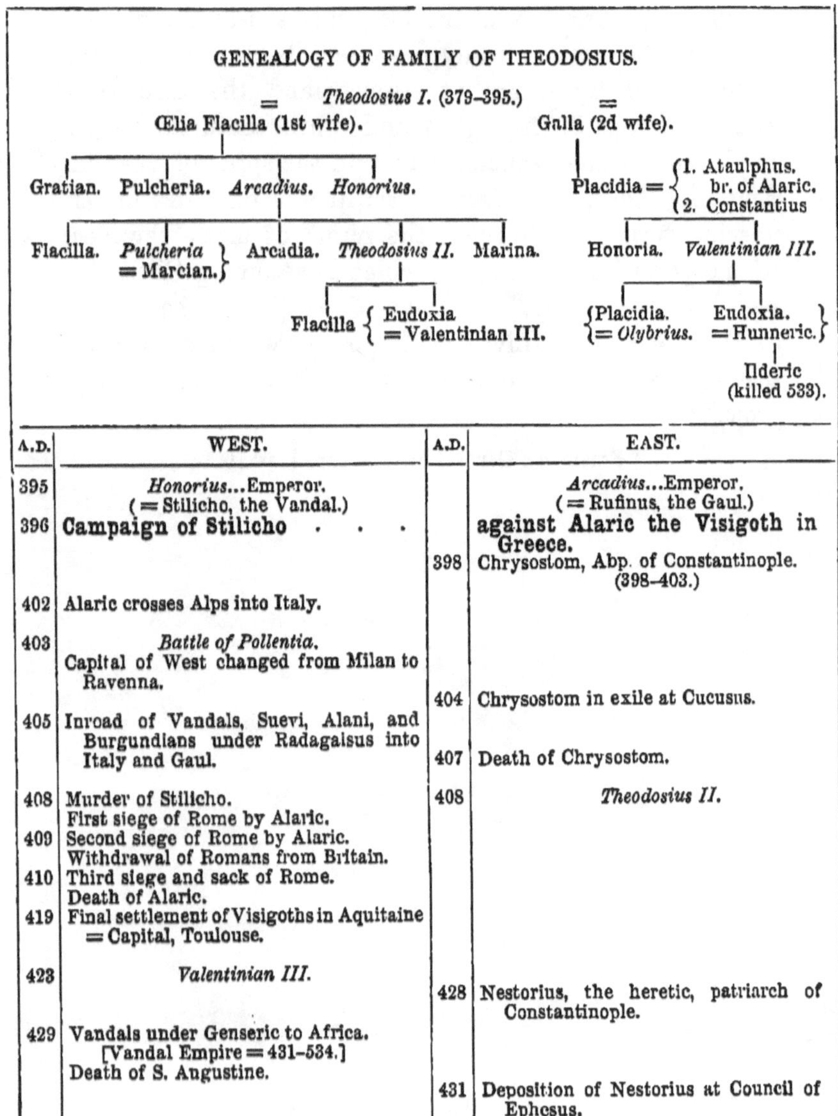

A.D.	WEST.	A.D.	EAST.
395	*Honorius…Emperor.* (= Stilicho, the Vandal.)		*Arcadius…Emperor.* (= Rufinus, the Gaul.)
396	**Campaign of Stilicho** . . .		**against Alaric the Visigoth** in Greece.
		398	Chrysostom, Abp. of Constantinople. (398–403.)
402	Alaric crosses Alps into Italy.		
403	*Battle of Pollentia.* Capital of West changed from Milan to Ravenna.		
		404	Chrysostom in exile at Cucusus.
405	Inroad of Vandals, Suevi, Alani, and Burgundians under Radagaisus into Italy and Gaul.		
		407	Death of Chrysostom.
408	Murder of Stilicho. First siege of Rome by Alaric.	408	*Theodosius II.*
409	Second siege of Rome by Alaric. Withdrawal of Romans from Britain.		
410	Third siege and sack of Rome. Death of Alaric.		
419	Final settlement of Visigoths in Aquitaine = Capital, Toulouse.		
423	*Valentinian III.*		
		428	Nestorius, the heretic, patriarch of Constantinople.
429	Vandals under Genseric to Africa. [Vandal Empire = 431–534.] Death of S. Augustine.		
		431	Deposition of Nestorius at Council of Ephesus.

A.D.	WEST.	A.D.	EAST.
		441–446	Inroads of Huns under Attila into Greece.
449	Conquest of Britain by the English. (449–550.)		
		450	*Pulcheria* (= Marcian).
451	Attila invades Gaul.	451	Council of Chalcedon.
452	*Battle of Chalons.* The Huns invade Italy.		
453	Death of Attila.		
455	*Maximus.* Rome sacked by the Vandals.		
	Avitus [= Ricimer].		
457	*Majorian* [= Ricimer].	457	*Leo I.*
461	*Severus* [= Ricimer].		
467	*Anthemius* [by Leo]. **Joint expedition from Rome**		**and Constantinople under Basi-**
	liscus against Carthage.		
472	*Olybrius.*		
473	*Glycerius.*		
474	*Julius Nepos.*	474	*Leo II.* *Zeno.* The Ostrogoths under Theodoric on the Danube.
475	Romulus Augustulus. *Odoacer.*		
486	Chlodwig the Frank in Gaul, founder of the Merwing Dynasty.		
		491	*Anastasius I.*
493	*Theodoric.*		
	[Ostrogothic Kingdom of Italy.] 493–553.		
		502	Inroad of Persians under Cobades.
		518	*Justin I.* (a Dacian).
526	*Athalaric* { Son of Amalasontha, Theodoric's daughter.		
		527	*Justinian.*
		532	The Nika Riots.
533	**African Campaign**		**of Belisarius.**
534	*Theodatus.*		
535	**Italian Campaign**		**of Belisarius.**
536	*Vitiges.*		
539	**Surrender of Ravenna**		**to Belisarius.**
540	*Theodebald.*	540	Inroad of Persians under Chosroes,
541	*Araric.*	541	Persian Campaign of Belisarius.
	Totila.		
544–552	Totila *v.* { 1. Belisarius. 2. Narses.		
553	*Teias.*		
554	*Narses, Exarch of Ravenna.*		
	[Exarchate of Ravenna lasts from 554 to 752.]	557	Embassy of Avars to Constant, followed by embassy from Turks.
		565	*Justin II.*
		566	The Lombards and Avars unite to destroy the Gepidæ on the Danube.

(Left margin, vertical: *Ostrogoths.*)

A.D.	WEST.	A.D.	EAST.
567	Lombard Invasion of Italy. [Lombard Kingdom = 567–774.]	574 582	*Tiberius II.* *Maurice.*
590	*Pope Gregory the Great.* (590–604.)		
		595	Avar Empire under Baian = successful campaigns of Priscus. 595–602.
596	Mission of Augustine to England.		
		602	*Phocas.*
		610	*Heraclius I.*
		614– 620	Great Persian Invasion = conquest of Holy Land, Syria, Egypt.
			Embassy from Mohammed to Chosroes.
		622	Persian campaigns of Heraclius. (622–628.)
			The Hegira.
		626	Siege of Constantinople by combined Persian and Avar armies.
628	Dagobert I., the greatest of the Merwings in Gaul.		
		632	Death of Mohammed.
		639– 641	Mohammedans conquer Syria and Egypt.
			Constantine III.
		642	*Constans II.*
		668	*Constantine IV.* (Pogonatus).
			Mohammedans besiege Constantinople.
650	Mohammedan Conquest of Africa.	685	*Justinian II.* (banished by)
		694	*Leontius I.* (one of his generals.)
		697	*Tiberius III.*
700		704	Justinian restored.
711– 713	Mohammedan Conquest of Spain.	711	*Philippicus.*
		713	*Anastasius II.*
		715	*Theodosius III.*
		717	*Leo III.* (the Isaurian).
	ICONO-	**CLASM.**	
			Second Mohammedan siege of Constantinople. (717–718 = 13 months.)
730– 732	Council of Rome { Gregory II. *v.* Iconoclasm. { Gregory III.		
732	*Battle of Tours.*	732	Final attempt (and failure) of Eastern Empire to reconquer Italy.
738	Gregory III. appeals to Franks *v.* Lombards.		
		741	*Constantine V.* (Copronymus).
752	Lombards conquer Exarchate.		
	Pope Zacharias sanctions deposition of Chilperic by Pippin = Karlings vice Merwings.	754	Council of Constantinople condemns "all visible symbols of Christ except in Eucharist."
755	Pippin's "Donation" to Pope Stephen = Foundation of Temporal Power.		
771	CHARLES THE GREAT. (771–814.)	775	*Leo IV.*
		780	*Constantine VI.* (Porphyrogenitus).
		797	*Irene.* (797–802.)
800	*Charles crowned by Leo III. in St. Peter's* EMPEROR OF THE WEST.		

www.ingramcontent.com/pod-product-compliance
Lightning Source LLC
Chambersburg PA
CBHW020926120726
47905CB00008B/2399

9 783337 245658